How People Use the Courts

Polish Studies in Culture, Nations and Politics

Edited by Joanna Kurczewska and Yasuko Shibata

Vol. 6

PL ACADEMIC RESEARCH

Jacek Kurczewski and Małgorzata Fuszara

How People Use the Courts

The Disputes and Courts in Poland

PL ACADEMIC RESEARCH

Bibliographic Information published by the Deutsche Nationalbibliothek
The Deutsche Nationalbibliothek lists this publicationin the Deutsche Nationalbibliografie; detailed bibliographic data is available in the internet at http://dnb.d-nb.de.
Library of Congress Cataloging-in-Publication Data
Names: Kurczewski, Jacek, author. | Fuszara, Małgorzata, author.
Title: How people use the courts : the disputes and courts in Poland / Jacek Maria Kurczewski, Małgorzata Fuszara.
Description: Frankfurt am Main : Peter Lang, 2017. | Series: Polish studies in culture, nations and politics ; volume 6
Identifiers: LCCN 2017017253 | ISBN 9783631723715
Subjects: LCSH: Courts--Poland. | Dispute resolution (Law)--Poland. | Conflict management--Poland.
Classification: LCC KKP1582 .K87 2017 | DDC 347.438/01--dc23
LC record available at https://lccn.loc.gov/2017017253

Cover Design: © Olaf Gloeckler, Atelier Platen, Friedberg

This publication was financially supported by the University of Warsaw.

ISSN 2192-1822
ISBN 978-3-631-72371-5 (Print)
E-ISBN 978-3-631-72476-7 (E-Book)
E-ISBN 978-3-631-72477-4 (EPUB)
E-ISBN 978-3-631-72478-1 (MOBI)
DOI 10.3726/b11231

PL Academic Research is an Imprint of Peter Lang GmbH.
Peter Lang – Frankfurt am Main · Bern · Bruxelles · New York · Oxford · Warszawa · Wien

This book is part of an editor's series of PL Academic Research and was peer reviewed prior to publication.

www.peterlang.com

Contents

Preface

This book is not about the law, it is about the law as it is practiced in society. So its focus is not on what lawyers do and courts do but on what ordinary people do when in the court and when considering what to do about a problem, a conflict that emerges in relations with other people and other institutions. To use courts or not, to negotiate on one's own or with mediation of other people or to go the deputy, to the city council or to the court in order to get a satisfactory authoritative settlement. The book starts with introductory theoretical hypotheses that oriented our research done in the mid-2010s in Poland and in some localities abroad in the former communist countries. In fact, this research has been a sequel to the research begun in the 1970s, followed by one done after the democratic legal state had been established in Poland in the early 2000s. The first part of the book deals with how people use courts to defend their personality rights. The second part, based on a series of surveys, raises the question of how various dispute management and, hopefully, dispute settlement patterns are perceived by people, in other words, what is the popular dispute settlement culture as part of the living law of society.

The research as the whole has been financed by the NCN research grant No. DEC-2012/07/B/HS6/02496: *Patterns of Dispute and Dispute Settlement in Popular Legal Culture* and we wish to thank the Polish National Science Centre also for financing the publication of this volume. But we would like to make personal thanks to people who collaborated with us throughout the research and without whom the project would not have been accomplished: Professor Stefka Naoumova from Bulgarian Academy of Sciences and her students from Razgrad, especially Leyman Oluglayeva; Viera Meniok and Svetlana Schudlo, Professors from the I. Franko State Educational University in Drohobych, Andrij Yurkevych in charge of the Drohobych students association „Alter" and Professor Bohdan Sluschchinski, Chair in Sociology, Philosophy and Educational Sciences at State University in Mariupol; Cristina Pop and Cristina Rat from Center for Inter-Ethnic Studies at Babes-Bolyai University in Cluj-Napoca. We wish to thank for help and assistance our friends from the Chair in Sociology and Anthropology of Custom and Law at Institute of Applied Social Sciences, University of Warsaw and Mr Paweł Orzechowski who cooperated as a technical secretary and assistant to the project as well as Małgorzata Mieszkowska, secretary of the Societas/Communitas bi-annual of the IASS. For statistical advice we are helpful to Zbigniew Karpiński and Andrzej Wichrowski from Warsaw. As our long-time friend Mavis Maclean CBE had habitually combed through fragments of our book but she should not be blamed for any remaining errors as we assume our responsibility in full.

Jacek Kurczewski and Małgorzata Fuszara

Part I. Introduction

dispute involves thus the intended "natural" development of interaction and these intentions need to be taken into consideration also when dealing with the typical processes that emerge during disputes. We do not need to assume that in every dispute these processes occurring as a "natural" course of action may be broken. We may, however, assume that in the standard dispute structure the following basic processes occur, or rather begin to occur in the following order.

1. The legal definition of dispute. The terms „legal definition" and „legal interpretation" as are used throughout this paper are intended to cover all the intellectual apprehension of the reality made by actors in the specific categories of rights and duties and their derivatives. This definition and interpretation may be made by professionally trained and acknowledged legal authorities as well as by any average citizen, even by a child if already socialized enough to be able to do so. For a legal sociologist a dispute starts if a conflict —an objective conflict of interests or subjectively perceived one – has been translated by an actor into a specific legal language he thinks in and talks with others. At this stage, the basic problem is whether there will be any dispute at all, and if so, what is its content and in what legal language it has been formulated. The mutual relations of these definitions as made by all the participants to a dispute add an interactional element to this problem, which, however, is not peculiar at this stage, as the multiple perspectives provide for the sociological dimensions of dispute at any stage of its development.

We shall "wander" now through these stages trying to point out some detailed issues the parties confront. These issues may be both interpreted at the more theoretical level and, at the same time, at the level of empirical observation. In doing so, the theoretical problems to be formulated will be also enrooted in the practical problems that the participants in dispute must deal with. It may be added, that the selection of these problems is, to a considerable degree, a representation of the trouble I have encountered myself when trying to understand why and how other people attempt to resolve their own problems through disputes.

One of these problems is related to the very content and justification of the claims made, and, in general, to the processes of legal definition and interpretation that from the first stage onwards permeate any dispute. The degree of precision with which we use terms like rights, duties, etc. is far from the desired one. There is nothing strange in that, as these are some of those words that being thoroughly linked with conflicts of human wishes, interests and aspirations are richly endowed with value-judgements and ideologies that make them full of affective significance. And if such a state of affairs is in the theoretical speculation, it is, by no means, strange that in everyday legal thinking of people the same ambiguities, discrepancies and vagueness may be found too. It would be superficial to hold that everybody has strictly delimited and unambiguously understood concepts of various rural relationships that link themselves and others —fictitious beings included— into subjective legal systems (A. Cicourel 1973). Gaps and vagueness to be encountered in average legal thinking may also be held responsible for the apparent order that governs standard interactions whether of private or public character. The ad hoc interpretation allows in the majority of cases for the intersubjective order to function without crises (J. Kurczewski 1979). Indeed, the attempts at precision may both engender and stem from some clashes of interests and concepts. This makes disputes one of the focal point in the development of the legal order as it both follows from and causes some changes in subjective legal systems in existence.

The development of the legal system through disputes does not need to be a continuous progression towards the ideally precise system. A new situation will always reveal some new gaps and new ambiguities in our law. In general, it seems appropriate to look at legal systems as being in the process of continuous development in which the attainment of a relatively precise and well-defined body of rules appears to be rather a symptom of stagnation of the very social system in question, a stagnation that may be followed either by the resolution of the social system itself (for instance, a dispute-free period that often precedes a divorce) or by the series of radical changes (the elaborated Code of Napoleon was surrounded by major changes and innovations in law challenged by the fastened industrial growth). So in individual, local or national legal systems, legal fictions are necessary to keep the image of the stability of law regardless of the continuous change and re-interpretation.

One of the basic issues that must be settled in this way or another by a potential participant to a dispute concerns the justification of his claims. They may remain self-evident as this would be the case of intuitive legal emotions. The wider the social distance which separates an actor from his opponent or the third parties, the greater the risk that such a legal intuition will not be corresponding to the views held by these other participants. The more experienced a person is with disputes in general and with particular procedures, the more open he or she becomes to the possibility of fault in interpretation of dispute, that is to define their claims in a way which will not be justified by others. We may reasonably expect that such experience increases a chance that rights and duties, claims and obligations will be justified positively, such as the invocation of common practice or written legal rule, and the experience with official procedures such as court will increase the use of official positive justification. Possibly, the social distance increases a tendency for passivization and officialization of legal interpretation too. Another thing is our ability to make a legal definition of our and other people's problems. Resignation from a dispute may result either from the fear of consequent processes or a boastful lack of interest, that is from the legal imbecility in this respect. As legal psychology remains awfully undeveloped, there is little to be developed here on this subject, except for some apparent trivialities. Disputes are cyclic processes, the last stages influence the first ones, and, thus, dispute experience will make someone more trained in such a method of reasoning. In developed societies some people get professional training in this and later on they are paid for this skill and receive the exclusive privilege to be called „lawyers". This skill they claim to possess may be, however, irrelevant for some types of disputes that people have. That official jurisprudence will be of no or almost no use in case of disputes emerging among the parties to an officially illegal transaction. Finally, it has been often observed that the development of legal reasoning skills may be controlled by more powerful persons, groups, and organizations through various means (W. Felstiner 1975).

2. Entrance into a dispute. Once a legal definition of a matter in dispute and the related claims have been formulated one may enter into a dispute or leave it. The old raised issue of avoidance clearly belongs to this stage (J.Kurczewski, K. Frieske 1978). The first actor who instead of avoidance enters into a dispute, in fact, opens it. This is why it is important to observe the order in .which the entrances are made, as some decisive effects for the whole further development of dispute are thus possible. Next actors just join a dispute, some of them cannot avoid it, and some others must even intervene. At this point the real character of the developmental stages becomes clear as the first definition must precede the first entrance, that is the opening of a dispute, while for some next participants the legal interpretation of dispute may arise once they have been involved in a matter.

Dispute seems to be a painful experience to those involved. It creates stress in mutual relations. People will try to forget about this experience as soon as possible. They will try to invent a better justification for their participation in a dispute if there are worse ones or none available. Disputes will therefore be justified on some ethical grounds even if there is no apparent ethical motive that guides participants. Moreover, there is a strong tendency to avoid disputes and to end them as soon as possible. The responsibility for dispute and all the blame for it is put on other parties. Any dispute triggers a tendency to settle it.

Let us assume temporarily the truth of the above statements. The obvious "Why?" may be answered in terms of the social motives. We are taught and we teach others that a dispute is something abnormal to be avoided in the long term. All this belongs to a set of assumptions concerning a normal social interaction that gives us a feeling of security in the company of other human beings. Furthermore, this is related to some more general premises of social order. We are taught and we teach others to follow some rules of a social intercourse so that this order could not be endangered by mutual hostility and at the same time we forgive and we are forgiven for a fairly large number of "mistakes" and other faults ensuing from following these rules. In this way the psychological enrootment of human being in a social situation is made. Some positive reinforcement for the compliance with social order is offered, and negative sanctions are visible in some cases of failure. And all this is linked to the sediments of previous experiences that have developed in our personality a disposition to act in a certain way.

Still, disputes are a common event in a social interaction. They are both practical problems to social order and to an individual that is enrooted in it. Were the irenic motives so important for people, how would it be possible to dispute at all? Introducing a positive reference by persons is probably of great influence here as well as the need to defend one's own image. The importance of the endangered interests is another type of factors that tend to influence a decision to enter into a dispute. There are also pro-social motives that may be involved when someone starts a dispute in order to make a precedent either of an action itself or of a settlement he hopes to achieve. Various positive and negative, egocentric and pro-social motives may render the entrance into a dispute psychologically possible. Thus, we cannot expect to find some of these motives predominant for disputes in general, although some peculiar combinations of motives may be related to the specific types of disputes or the specific types of participants. Still, it seems worthwhile to make a distinction between two types of motivational orientation that may play a role here.

The first one, when the effects of a settlement are considered, for instance, a value of the land tract to be adjudicated by a court together with the subjective probability of winning the case, and the second one, when the preponderance is given to the immediate effects such as a display of one's determination or respect paid to the local customs. There is nothing in the first type that makes it more rational. The longer it takes to obtain the effects of one's action, the higher the chance that the estimated probabilities of success will change, as the utilities may also change, thus making the whole action perceived as ridiculous. However, the distinction seems important in another aspect. Being oriented to immediate rewards motivates more when it comes to entering into a dispute rather than in the case of meeting all initial claims. It is more probable then to expect a compromise in the future than in the second type of cases in which the claims-orientation prevails.

Another important distinction is whether an opponent himself is important or just the issue at stake. In the first case, even full satisfaction of one's claims may be not be enough for him to withdraw from a dispute as he may, for instance, wish the other party to .be humiliated, while in the second case such motives may not play any significant role in the moves taken by someone who just wants this or another settlement. This is also of importance for the next decisions as some procedures that will lead eventually to the fulfillment of the formulated claims (a civil trial, for instance) may be of less appeal to someone who is interested more in, say, final humiliation of an opponent (then, for instance, a criminal trial serves this motive better). Intervention into a dispute made by the third parties, including various official agencies, may also be studied in relation to these distinctions, when we observe that a police action may be primarily a personality-oriented action aimed at the immediate effects of pacification, while a court aims at the settlement of dispute in terms of final allocation of assets according to some official standards. Inadequacy of these motives and orientations assumed by the whole set of participants to a dispute produce one of the most acute adjustment problems that will affect all the subsequent stages.

The decisions to enter into a dispute are to be contrasted with avoidance. An actor avoids it, firstly, if he thinks that there is an incompatibility of claims, and secondly, when he decides not to undertake any action that would make the fulfillment of claims he supports possible. As an example of hypotheses related to the avoidance-entrance opposition there may be formulated one which is linked to the previous comments on dispute as pathology of social order. As a state of ordered social interactions does not need to be (and some would even say that never is) equally rewarding for participants, dispute avoidance may be expected on part of those more interested. These "interests", however, are to be understood widely as human wishes of a material as well as ideological character, and the "social order" in a more specific way than it often happens in the sociological literature. An old, poor widow has as much interest vested in the quiet perseverance of her relations with neighbours, or shop assistants and clerks as a manager in relations with his supervisors and subordinates in a factory he manages. Thus, for instance, disputes in "in-groups" will be relatively less often open, even if conflicts happen more often, while disputes with "strangers" with whom one interacts sporadically, will result in conflicts more frequently (T. Eckhoff 1966).

3. Choice of an action. Here the choice is between the various procedures that may lead — according to the knowledge and experience of participants — to the fulfillment of respective claims. Contrary to some views, thus, we will not treat avoidance as a procedure, while avoidance of some particular type of an action may be

seen as a choice of procedure. Procedures understood as types of actions leading to the fulfillment of one's own claims are a familiar subject for both sociology and anthropology of law that deal with it in terms of the variety of procedures that are at the disposal of potential participants to a dispute and in terms of a variety of motives that underlie practical choices made. Procedural interactions that usually constitute the main object of the study are, however, incomprehensible if earlier problems and solutions have not been taken into consideration.

There is one more issue that should be raised at this point. An analytical distinction may be made between the agonistic and the irenic actions and procedures. While the former may be described as attempting to bring about a fulfillment of a claim that is incompatible with someone else's claims, the latter are, in fact, intended to reduce this incompatibility of claims. The areas of agonistic and irenic procedures cross-cut each other and it is my contention that each of them has its own theoretical as well as practical problems. For some purposes it may be wise to divide the whole domain discussed here into the theory of disputes and theory of the dispute settlement and it is at this stage that having been intermingled so far, they start their separate lives. The third important issue that consequently arises during dispute participation is the choice of a procedure for action, and as for the next participants the choice of a procedure for counter-action. It is a classical question for both sociology and anthropology of law whether the institutionalized or uninstitutionalized (or informal, as it is more often said) way of action will be chosen. Two basic approaches may be illustrated by means of a typology of those actions including mediation, adjudication and administration as developed by T. Eckhoff or by the more quantitative approach as advocated by R. Abel, when he makes use of the concept of the „degree of institutionalization." Less theoretical approach is taken by numerous studies in which the concrete forms of the institutionalized dispute settlement and management are discussed, such as courts, conciliatory bodies, arbitration tribunals, etc. (J. Kurczewski 1982).

As far as I am concerned, for years I have been using a taxonomy that was based upon the cross-section of two dimensions: (a) whether the entrance of a third party depends on the will of a disputant(s) or not: (b) whether the settlement made by the third party is binding depending on the will of a disputant(s) or not. In this way four basic procedures as mediation, arbitration, mandatory conciliation and authoritative settlement may be distinguished. All the above-mentioned approaches, including the ones presented by T. Eckhoff and R. Abel are more abstract and the various institutional choices are described in general terms. This means neither that these studies, which take into account the distinctions elaborated by the local (official) legal .systems, can be enriched with the theoretical interpretation, nor that the abstract definitions of the procedural alternatives must necessarily lead to some deeper theorizing, as it happens with a theoretical definition of adjudication which is used only for the purpose of identifying civil procedures based on which the statistical data is collected in the sociographic way.

I think that the main risk involved in the choice of procedures is not that of efficiency in dealing with claims. In the preceding paragraph we have tried to point out that only some disputes do really focus on the ultimate fulfillment of claims worked out by participants. For all disputes, however, regardless of the motives and orientations behind them, an important question is the degree of control the participants may enjoy over further developments. If a neighbour sues another one in court, it may well happen that he will be cross-questioned, eventually he may even be punished for perjury. In the socialist system the risk of this kind is even more evident as courts are obliged to actively seek the objective truth for themselves, but even in the adversary procedures all these things could happen. Courts or the police may take a dispute into their own hands, and even in the case of a voluntary conciliation some loss of control occurs. In this way the familiar dimensions of power enter our picture. The various procedures vary, amongst other things, in the degree of power and control that various types of participants have over the further development of dispute processes. From the viewpoint of a private „opener" various interventions ex officio, for instance, a police patrol which tries to pacify a quarrelling couple, are at one end of this dimension, and bilateral fights, bargains and negotiations, as this quarrel in itself, are at the opposite one. Would it be safe to assume that on average people prefer situations that, at least seemingly, are under their own control, and I see no reason to reject such an assumption as it may be predicted then that with the first procedural move the choice of bilateral action will occur. The less control, the less probability of choice until the more controllable procedures have been used. Thus, after the opportunities of a bilateral action have been used, the next choice will involve predominantly mediation, and later on, arbitration, or mandatory conciliation, with the authoritative settlement as the last choice.

Some further qualifications seem at place, though. In claims-oriented disputes the subjective probability of winning a case through each of the available procedures will be important. If one feels this probability is almost equal in the case of the authoritative settlement, as it is in the case of mediation, then everything will correspond accordingly to our previous predictions, but it will be contrary to them, if the subjective probabilities are inversed, at least because further developments are controlled as to the predictability of those. So why are these conflicting predictions introduced at all? My answer to this is that, first, we may expect the overall tendency to choose the procedures that give more control, while at the same time different procedures will be selected as appropriate in a given case. This is not without the practical effects as the same people may advocate an informal conciliation to others, and at the same time, choose innocently the authoritative adjudication for themselves. Secondly, the whole issue may now be formulated theoretically as to why people choose such ways of actions over which they have less power and control and, thus, the practical problem of choosing a court assumes a bit more general interpretation. If we take into consideration personality-oriented disputes, our answer will be different. This procedure will be selected to allow for more power and control over the opponent. So, if I have more power over him than he has over me, then I will select bilateral contacts or mediation, whereas if in a worse position I will allow other persons to enter the case – already having little control I relatively lose little in contrast to my opponent. In a family quarrel it may be beneficial for a wife to call the police in and in this way the power relations are restructured even if the most efficient way of settling the matter of dispute could be the mediation of the relatives.

Thus, it seems justified to formulate a hypothesis that in disputes involving opponents with unequal power, underdogs will choose a loss of control in favour of the third parties, either in order to put the opponent under the alien control in personality-oriented disputes or in order to increase the chances of winning one's own case in claims-oriented disputes. We may expect, therefore, that, e.g. in labour disputes individual workers will prefer courts and a manager will opt for direct negotiation or mediation; on the other hand, organized workers will prefer bilateral action or mediation and an individual manager will then prefer a court. In these processes the subjective status of congruence also seems to play its role. A well-known idea in the social psychology is that incongruence of components in one's social status results in the insecurity of such a status because others tend to react to an individual as if he or she had a lower status than the real one as perceived by the individual in question. The perceived status of incongruence will make an actor intimidated by bilateral procedures, mainly for fear of underestimating his status, which in turn will lead to the expectation of a compromise that is too far-reaching. The procedures that involve the authoritative settlement, and especially, the procedures in which settlement depends upon the external standards and not on the wishes of participants will therefore be more appealing for such individuals or groups (J. Kurczewski 1982).

4. Choice of solution. If we accept the usage of the word "settlement" as in the expression "they settled their dispute by a fight" then there is nothing to prevent us from including the various types of forced (negative) settlements here. A settle-

ment may be enforced by a third party to the point of even open dissatisfaction of the original opponents or may as well be imposed by one of the opponents upon the second one who must subdue himself, for instance, for political or financial reasons. Practically, the indicators of the final settlement serve the culturally and interpersonally understandable sings of acceptance of what may be termed as an exit from a dispute. Solutions are planned when the legal interpretation and definition of the issue in dispute are worked out but achieving a solution requires, first of all, the previous stages to be completed. Even in the case of resignation of one of the opponents, the choice of a solution is a social event involving a decision of all participants.

As the preceding paragraphs concerned more or less directly the last two stages of the standard structure of dispute development, we feel free to mention here only one issue specific for each of these two stages as an illustration. As disputes centre around the incompatibility of claims, any outcome of the dispute processes that eliminates this incompatibility is a solution or a settlement. It seems safer to deal here with settlements as an agreement aimed at the elimination of incompatibility of claims and an end put to actions oriented towards the fulfillment of mutually incompatible claims, even if these agreements have been imposed on a participant(s) by coercion and one or all interested opponents are left unsatisfied. Individual choices as to a solution can be made from the very beginning, but the social settlement, as defined above, is effected not in every dispute that has been opened.

As the previous deliberations may seem overpsychologized for the reader's taste, it would be of interest to locate the irenic processes in a wider social perspective. These processes may be dealt with in terms of the social regulation, and the three following most general types may be distinguished (J. Kurczewski, K. Frieske 1978):

Autonomy of an individual	**others influence Ego's decisions**	**others do not influence Ego's decisions**
Ego decides himself	A. CONTRACT	B. EGO'S POWER
Ego does not decide	C. EGO'S SUBMISSION	D. CONVENTION

These four cells may be reduced to the three basic cases that will be called respectively authoritative (B and C), conventional (D) and consensual (A) —as this type of contract is considered — a regulation. For our two quarreling neighbours settlements negotiated directly or through mediators will evidently belong to a consensual dispute regulation, while a .settlement imposed on them by the police or by court is an example of the authoritative one. It could happen, however, that another neighbour will remind the two in dispute that there is an old rule (local "custom" or national "law") that says exactly what their respective duties and rights are as to the matter. If this suffices, we may feel inclined to call it a conventional regulation.

Now, an interesting question may be posed whether there is a homology between the regulative processes that operate at the level of disputes and the type of regulation that is prevalent at the scale of a wider social system in which a dispute takes place. Some evidence may be quoted in favour of the hypothesis of homology. Authoritatively regulated societies will tend to maintain the same approach in the official agencies that deal with disputes. The development of cognitio extraordinaria in the Roman Empire with growing absolutization of power, administrative character of court's actions throughout the Chinese history or an active role of the judiciary and public prosecution, and a doctrinal rejection of adversary civil procedure in the socialist legal doctrine may serve as corroboration. A series of examples could be cited also in order to prove this point as to the conventional and consensual regulation. *Legis actiones* clearly represent a conventional type of the procedure that is historically linked to the most traditional stage of Roman society until it gave place to more consensual procedures that allowed for more autonomy on part of participants as economic liberalism during the capitalist industrialization of Europe has been correlated with relaxation of various aspects of contracts and civil procedure. The conventionality of the basic procedures of dispute settlement in the traditional pre-state societies (given the label of "customs") is also easy to be documented, even if it does not need to be linked with the restrictive formalism. On the other hand, all these societies make way for unofficial procedures and settlements, either *de facto* or *de iure.* Thus, the hypothetical homology is limited to the levels of the official structure of society and its wider occurrence may be doubted, although it should still be subject to an investigation, this time with reference to the relation between the basic mechanisms and premises of official legal systems in force and the legal psychology and culture of people.

4. Re-definition of dispute. Be it this or another solution, even involuntary accepted, the final stage in our model standard and "natural" structure of disputes involves the processes of re-definition and re-interpretation of the whole experience. The result of these processes is decisive for a further conduct of participants. They may come back to mutual interactions as before the start of a dispute or they may decide to continue it by repeating or by changing their claims and proce-

dures. The enforcement of a solution depends heavily on the effects of this stage. The whole experience will add to the already accumulated legal psychology of participants as well as observers, and.— to approach the more classical issues of the sociology of law — it may be included in the institutionalized law as when, for instance, a precedent is made or a change in the written legal texts is made as an effect.

The issue we have chosen to briefly elaborate on in relation to the last distinguished stage, that is the re-definition and re-interpretation of disputes, is the one that may appear only at this stage, at least once. The problem is how to memorize the dispute experience and it is also one of the most important problems for a researcher who intends to study disputes, while, at the same time, it is also an acute problem for a participant, for whom such an experience may be traumatic one. Simple self-observations allow for a conclusion that nobody is able to remember all the disputes in which he has taken part. Since some types of them are common and obvious element of the everyday life, the categorization of them as disputes involves not only a decision as to the subjective rights and duties but also as to the hierarchy of importance. It is quite probable that in a given society people differ not so much as to the content of their subjective legal systems but as to the importance they attach to various abuses of their own and of other people's (and individual persons') rights. To label a dispute as "the dispute", to interpret the past experience in terms of rightful claims endangered and fulfilled even if these claims have been formulated in full, a sincere feeling of being bound which gives rise to the respective actions, may be a result of complex intellectual and emotional processes influenced by situational and cultural factors.

All this may be stated as the problem faced by any of participants to a dispute: will I remember this as a dispute and on what conditions? Some purely psychological questions may be involved here, for example, whether something like Zeigarnik's effect is working here and whether the disputes in which I lost my case or didn't fulfill my legal expectations in their totality will be remembered better. More reasonable suspicion, on grounds of common observation, points to the fact that that we all remember more difficult cases better, and these include difficult as well as important cases, in many aspects, whether with a satisfactory solution or with a negative one or resulting in no solution at all. But apart from this, one thing is certain that these re-interpretations will differ among participants.

As it has already been mentioned, there is a need to justify an entrance into a dispute on moral grounds. One of the effects of such justifications is that usually an opponent is defined as responsible for a dispute, even if he is not defined as "guilty" of a specific action that has led to a given dispute. Even if a voluntary conciliation is achieved among the parties, it is most often observed that at least one of them still needs the other opponent to be defined as "guilty" or "responsible" and to perform some symbolic act of humiliation which the other rejects or expects from the first one. The meaning of such an act and such a conciliatory agreement is differently memorized by the participants, as it ensues from my research experience. What for the first neighbour is just a sign of approval of conciliation, for the second one can be the punishment for his actions performed before the dispute or for his refusal to accept a compromise settlement offered at the beginning, even if no such compromise was then acceptable to any of them. In this way, not only the phenomenon of dispute as such but also its content and the structure of roles played in it by the participants will undergo selective re-interpretation that helps to keep one person's good image, at least for him and for a legal sociologist, and to fulfill those claims that have been practically left unfulfilled once a settlement ended the whole affair. These different interpretations may very soon give impetus to a renewed dispute if an occasion allows both ex-participants to learn what the other thinks of the past. First formulated in Kurczewski(1979).

All these complexities should not stop us from the study of disputes, although we need to remember that if a well-to-do and well-educated person tells us that in the past he had no dispute with an arrogant waiter, it may have resulted from the same hierarchy of values that makes some sociologists of law unwilling to investigate everyday disputes.

For a sociologist law seems to have two basic and strictly related tasks: dispute-resolution and securing general acceptance of legal norms. This is not so evident for common people, who recognize the functioning of official law usually through contact with the rank-and-file agents of public order, and the detailed regulations which, with growing specificity, regulate social life. Studies conducted in 1977/8 in Warsaw provided an occasion for deciding how important dispute resolution, as a function of the legal system, seemed to be to public opinion. The majority (57 per cent) when asked what, according to them, were <<the goals the law should serve above all>>, selected from our four possible answers the reply: <<law secures order and discipline in the state>>; while <<the law is the instrument of dispute- and conflict-settlement among the people>> was placed second (21 per cent), before the answers: <<law makes change and development in our society possible>> (11 per cent), and <<law makes the fulfilment of the personal needs and interests of the people possible>> (8 per cent).

Withdrawal, bilateral negotiations, and the introduction of extra-judicial institutions into a dispute are the three basic patterns of reaction, and are found frequently in the milieux under study. The degree of <<urbanization>> of a milieu—in other words, the degree to which local bonds exist—was unrelated to the frequency of these patterns. Vengeance, passing information to the authorities, or brutal self-help appeared only sporadically in the interviews, but one cannot doubt that these occur often in private conflicts. Our data may, therefore, give us more information about the desired hierarchy of acceptable patterns of dispute-settlement and the ranking of the patterns followed in practice. It is evident that with regards to the latter the importance of official procedures increases.

The main objective of the research presented in this book is to test the hypothesis that a sudden change in a political and economic regime does not result in the change of patterns of dispute and dispute development. Polish society provides the unique chance of checking this hypothesis as since 1960s the empirical sociological investigations related to attitudes towards law have been systematically conducted starting with Podgórecki's study of Prestige of Law (1965). In 1970s the investigations concerning the disputing practices started and resulted in the accumulation of data concerning general patterns of disputing (Kurczewski, Frieske 1978) and declared patterns of disputing in several types of conflicts as experienced in the average population (Kurczewski 1982). This early research confirmed Leon Petrażycki's theory that disputes brought before a court reflect only a small fraction ("a tip of the iceberg") of everyday conflicts that are settled in an unofficial way. The second outcome was that apart from the preference for an unofficial way of dispute settlement, people prefer the conciliatory and compromise settlements. Under communist rule it might have been interpreted as resulting from the distrust towards the repressive and restrictive state and the courts as their agencies. The project implemented in the late 1990s led to a conclusion that despite the opening of public space and the reintroduction of the market economy the basic patterns of disputing have not changed in Polish society as represented by three Polish local communities – two small towns and one metropolitan district. But this could have not been treated as convincing because a counterargument could have been brought stating that a short period of time from regime change could prevent the concomitant cultural patterns from changing. Now, twenty two years after Poland became a democratic and capitalist society such an argument could not hold any longer. Therefore, the time is ripe to test more fully the effect of regime change. However, the uniqueness of data collected in the 1970s results in the inherent difficulty in testing the main hypothesis as there is no other similar case to consider. In contrast to Germany, Poland was not divided into two different jurisdictions. Unlike East Germany Poland was open to sociological research (despite the preventive political censorship). It necessitates the complex web of comparative research. The Polish data need to be compared with the data from other ex-Communist countries. If Polish contemporary data differ from those of other post-communist countries and similar to the data from Communist era, the central hypothesis seems supported, nevertheless, this might lead towards the explanation in terms of national peculiarity. Our claim is that some elements of popular legal culture are transmitted across generations under the common historical circumstances like the lack of political independence in the modernization period 1792–1918 and consequently are similar to the political Polish nation as emerged afterwards. Such a claim necessitates a comparison with Polish communities living outside the Polish state as well as with non-Polish minorities living within its post-1945 borders. When Podgórecki (1966) introduced the three-levels of operation of law, the civil law as mostly ruling conflict management was to be interpreted as (a) used differently under different political and economic regimes; (b) within the confines of sub-cultures being versions of the national (state) culture and (c) according to the individual (personality-related) characteristics of actors. This is a starting point for the recent project that will touch upon all the three levels of operation of civil law regulating the interaction. As for the (a) level the Hypothesis 1 claims that the sudden transformation of Communist party dictatorship and the socialist state economy into parliamentary democracy and the capitalist market economy would have led to change in dispute and disputing patterns. Kurczewski and Fuszara (2004) attempted the first test of this hypothesis using their own data from 1970s and 1990s. In literature there is no other study of effects of regime change on the patterns of disputes and disputes management. Poland in 1989 ceased to be ruled by one party controlling the society politically and not allowing for free elections, and it became the standard parliamentary democracy. This was accompanied by the change in the position of judiciary made independent of political control of the party in rule. Hypothetically this should have led to the growing trust in court justice and increased popularity of official and authoritative dispute management provided by courts and other official agencies. Simultaneously, the more evolutionary process occurred when restoring the capitalist market economy, which meant sudden widening of market relations and private property. This should have led to the development of civil law mechanisms, the use of court and the increase in frequency of disputes related to property and economic interests. The first check of this hypothesis made about 10 years after the regime transformation led to surprising effects. Contrary to our expectations, the economic transformation was not accompanied by an increase in conflicts over property, or conflicts at work, or the ones related to consumers or other commercial matters. The political transformation, similarly, was not accompanied by the change in the incidence of conflicts with the administration. When these results were presented at international conferences one of the arguments introduced was that the amount of time passed was too short and that new political and economic relations have not settled down for long enough to afford the concomitant change in people's perception of the situation. Despite customary political turmoil exaggerated by the events-oriented media, the democratic regime has in the meantime consolidated. The same refers to economy still judged as successful by international bodies. In 2009 the share of private ownership in gross value added reached 77,1% (latest figure available). This is why, more than twenty years after the transformation, it is important to test the hypothesis again with the attention focused on the young generations who up to 40+ years of age have lived under the new regime and to compare its declared and actual practices with those of the elderly. It does not mean, though, that the changes have not been recorded. According to our earlier research (Kurczewski and Fuszara 2004) the sense of one's private rights was strengthened but this was accompanied by the increasing privatization of disputes. Why? Is it because people prefer to negotiate their own deal with the other party or because they distrust courts and official settlements in general? A second observation: privatization does not apply to disputes with official institutions. Here the average reference to court or another official agency in cases involving town, hospital and police has increased from 55.3% to 63.3% of the answers, whereas withdrawal has fallen from 26.3% down to 8% of answers on average. People are more willing to use courts and other agencies against perceived abuses on part of public agencies, in addition, they have dramatically increased their sense of their rights against those agencies. Yet, another interesting change suggested by these figures is that radically more often today people are willing to keep their domestic disputes within the confines of their homes.

H2. Apart from the regime change hypothesis, the important second hypothesis which is to be settled with the help of comparative research is in contrast to the one claiming that there is a stable national pattern. In fact, Fuszara (1989) remarked that the sub-Carpathian region characterized by the highest incidence of interpersonal disputes concerning one's own honor and dignity is already described by historians as the region full of conflicts in the 16th century and the same village names appear in the old court books as in the 20th century. On the other hand, this cannot apply on the large scale due to the extinction of some populations (Holocaust) and the resettlement of others during and after World War II. One could hold, however, that the patterns of disputing persist through the participation in the same national culture where the school lectures, local and national history and church teaching tend to focus on certain models of conduct in conflict situations. That would locate the operation of civil law at the level of (b) Podgórecki's model.

Polish society holds the ideal settlement of a dispute to be a voluntarily accepted compromise satisfying both parties at the expense of full satisfaction of the claims and the official law. Such an irenic ideal was traditionally attributed to the Oriental, and more specifically to the Japanese legal culture ever since T. Kawashimas writings (Kawashima 1963, Murayama 2011)). Perhaps, in fact, it is universal when framed in objective terms; the question is to what degree it is felt applicable to one's own case when it actually happens. However, due to the lack of comparative studies, we still do not know if that is the result of the collectivism officially imposed during 45 years of Communist rule in Poland. Contrary to such an explanation one may point to the increase in the acceptance of such an ideal in the metropolitan sample. The transition coincided with the growing distrust in law and courts as the best methods of dispute settlement. There are various ways to explain such a result. One which seems consistent with the other findings reported here is that the growth of Warsaw reflects the growth in the privatization of disputes. Niels Christie wrote a famous essay on Theft of Conflicts (Christie 1977). He might not like this idea, but it seems that capitalist democracy allowed Poles to think about reappropriation of conflicts. After all, the liberal notion of the limited state extends to the idea of a limited and last resort state justice. Even though the way of asking this question differs, it seems obvious that today the share of answers pointing to the social position of parties (money and personal connections) has dramatically increased. If this is seen as the perceived inequality of chances, one should also point to the fact that the share of answers pointing to the merits of a case as the condition of success in court has remained practically unchanged over time. The tempting explanation would refer to the hidden suspicion of political bias of the so-called socialist justice as opposed to the social-economic bias openly attributed to justice in democratic Poland.

The transformation was made under the rule of law and the scope of judicial power was rapidly extended covering also the new areas that were created by transformation such as privatization, etc. The resulting judicialization of life created new opportunities for disputing before a court that had not existed prior to 1989. But this is not disputing between physical persons which is as privatized as possible. Disputing relates to legal persons that may and should be sued in order to defend ones' rights and interests or to expand those. Privatization of private disputes goes hand in hand with judicialisation of disputes with legal persons. The court serves a totally new and pivotal role in the private market economy. All litigations have changed their meaning from interpersonal disputes that engage a person into business transactions that need to be processed by the court in a non-antagonistic or quasi-antagonistic way. The distinction into disputes and non-disputes has lost its meaning; courts are not for settling disputes but for managing business transactions. Poland over the span of a few years has thus undergone the process of gradual change that normally may take a hundred years. Blankenburg (1991) holds the culturalistic explanation that its proponents ascribe mentalistic states to differences in the legal culture while these differences may be explained with the help of institutional arrangements that differ from country to country. As an illustration he compared litigation rates in general and in some specific types of problems in the Netherlands and in the Rhineland-Westfalia country of German Federal Republic. He claimed that the differences could not be attributed to differences between neighboring people so closely similar to each other but to the differences in formal procedures between these two countries. However, his argument is doubtful as he did not provide data on the patterns declared by Dutch and German people. It follows from the literature that in order to check the Hypothesis Two one needs to have two ways of comparison – the patterns of disputing compared between people of different national culture but within the same institutional arrangement and between people of the same national culture but with different institutional arrangement. This is difficult to do so at the national-state level as overall in Europe (except for United Kingdom) the institutional arrangement of law and justice were deliberately unified in the previous decades if not in the previous centuries, in Poland in 1930s. The "national" is then equal to the national state legacy.

H3. Polish nation-state today comprises the populations that lived throughout the 19th century under Prussian, then German, Russian (after the abolition of the Polish legal autonomy in Russian Kingdom of Poland in 1864 that ended the continuity of the Polish native legal system) and Austrian political order, including the law and administration of justice. The regional differences in political practices are nevertheless still attributed to the past partition (Bartkowski 2003). Since the 19th century is commonly treated as the formative period of modern nation-states it could be claimed that this was when and where the modern Polish legal culture had been formed before it was moulded into Polish national state of democratic turned into semi-authoritarian, turned into totalitarian then again turned into democratic propensities. According to this hypothesis the difference in the 19th century legal state cultures has produced the differences in the popular legal culture as opposed to the unified professional lawyers' legal culture.

H 4. Minority status tends to lower the interest in approaching official agencies as the means of dispute management for (a) the lack of trust in state agencies as being in hands of dominant group and (b) willingness to close conflicts within one's own group in show of its integrity and solidarity. This leads further into the socio-psychological variables representing the (c) level of operation of law in Podgórecki's model.

H5. The Hypothesis Four introduces two issues that were studied otherwise separately while they need to be considered in the common context, that is of a social status of (potential) litigants and inter-ethnic conflicts. The first of them was already suggested in the pre-1989 study pointing to a divergence in status between the parties at an individual level (Kurczewski 1982) but may be re-stated in more general terms referring to Donald Black's theory of law (1976). In Black's terms the use of the official agencies of dispute management, especially the court is equivalent to the increase in the amount of law in the interpersonal or inter-group relations. The status divergence is important as top-dogs will more likely use the official law against underdogs than inversely. One may also expect that there is less "law" (Black sticks to the narrow definition of law as threatening with the use of force and juxtaposes it to the conciliatory style of social control) amongst the equals than between people of different status. The observation that the use of court is more likely to appear amongst the better educated ones (Kurczewski 1982, Kurczewski and Fuszara 2004) confirmed in the English study (Genn 1993) could be subsumed under this statement in tandem with the well-established practice of multiple players (users of court), that is corporations, etc. to sue individuals, by definition more likely multiple players than inversely.

H6. An individual multiple player is commonly stereotyped as a "querulant" and a pathological type. Fuszara (2004) identified the complex character of such persons pointing to the social usefulness of such actors who first test the law working out the locally relevant "precedent" for its use or abuse; second, often serve as direct advisors, and para-legals assisting lower educated people in their attempts to get a just settlement of their problem.

H7. On the other hand, the ethnic antagonism is explainable in terms of mutual perception of a relative status position. The current research into inter-group antagonism and reconciliation (Kurczewski 2014;Kurczewski and Herman 2012) has led to the conviction that the demand of the party that feels wronged to humiliate the opponent by acknowledging by the latter the wrongs done and making the apology is a significant way to lower the opponent's status as against the wronged party. This mechanism was independently observed by Fuszara (1989) when pursuing the issue of rationality of the private accusation actions in the case of insult or injured sense of dignity of individual.

Małgorzata Fuszara, Jacek Kurczewski

Chapter II. Courts and conflicts in public opinion research

The old concept used in the sociology of law in the 1960s was that of "knowledge and opinion about law" (KOL) or "legal consciousness". As the concept of "legal culture" came into use in the 1980s, the concept of "popular" or "folk legal culture" appeared. In short, it refers to the concepts that people have of the law, administration of justice but also to what they consider as their or others' rights and duties. The last formulation brings us closer to Petrażycki's concepts of "intuitive law" and "unofficial law". In the original theory of legal emotions, these two cross-cut each other. The follower of Petrażycki, Adam Podgórecki reformulated these concepts in order to bring them close to the "living law" as described by Eugen Ehrlich. In his "Sociological theory of law" (Podgorecki 1991) unofficial law is based upon the intuition of people. Three types of legal phenomena classified by Petrażycki as "positive and non-state law", "unwritten and state law" (e.g. of equity) and "unwritten and non-state law" are all the intuitive law based upon the interdependent attitudes of claiming and demanding. Certainly, the opposition: the official – the unofficial is a projection of the power structure in society. The unofficial law is the law of those not holding the power that authorizes the legitimate decisions on what the law is and administering justice within the frame of a politically organized society. It does not need to be in contrast to the official law, in fact, it may support it. This would even create an ideal situation in society. But as we know even in procedurally democratic societies this is only partially the case. The official law is a complex of mutually binding rights and obligations recognized as valid by the ruling power. There are always differences, bones of contention, resistance and struggle concerning what is recognized as the proper law. American society was procedurally democratic when the movement for equal civil rights emerged and led to the legal emancipation of black citizens. Secondly, the "unofficial law" is not necessarily intuitive, in fact, as Petrażycki observed, it may be based upon positive normative reference. Moreover, the unofficial law may be based upon the "official law" but may be interpreted differently as it was in the case of the American Constitution and civil rights.

Opinion on Courts

The empirical question that the sociologists of law must ask is whether in a given society the popular concept of law is dominated by the official legal culture by which we understand the concept of law as present within the ruling domain of law and justice. This, amongst others, is shaped by the direct contact with the official administration of law but also by indirect communication through politics and media. To illustrate the point we shall start with the question posed in our national 2014 survey[1]: Which of the following factors are decisive in winning the case before a court? By allowing the respondents to make ad libitum choice of any of those seven factors listed and to add any others, we introduced a bit of entropy into the findings. It was evidently difficult for the respondents not to make use of the freedom they received during the lengthy interview as they were usually offered a limited choice of answers so the results seem inconclusive at surface:

Table 1. The Factors Decisive in Winning the Case In a Court in Polish 2014 National Survey on Dispute Settlement Patterns (N = 1060) In %

Factor	Primary Importance	Secondary importance	2+3	Unimportant	Difficult to say	Total
Merits of the case	41	33	74	18	7	100
Who is the judge	66		64	11	6	100
Defence lawyers	65	24	90	6	5	100
Witnesses	59	31	90	6	4	100
Personal ties	50	26	76	16	8	100
Bribes	30	24	80	26	19	100
Luck	26	31	57	36	7	100
Other	5	9	14	46	40	100

1 The all-Polish survey of 1059 people was carried out during the period of time between 22.04–4.05 2014 by the professional part-time staff of Centre for Research of Social Opinion (CBOS) being in Poland the only public polling agency functioning as the public foundation. Survey was funded by the NCN research grant No. DEC-2012/07/B/HS6/02496: „Dispute and dispute settlement patterns as element of popular legal culture" and the questionnaire (see Appendix B at the end of book) was prepared by J. Kurczewski and M. Fuszara. The standard method used by the CBOS was the CAPI supported individual face-to-face interviews with respondents randomly taken from the all- Polish address database

This question allowed for the stereotypes of administration of justice to be revealed by the public. At first glance it is obvious that the picture is ambivalent and needs more thorough study. The stereotypes may be far from reality but they may determine the overall attitudes towards justice and decisions whether to use them or not. Instead of judging these judgments as false or true we need to delve on them in the detail.

First, one must remember that this time we allowed for the free choice of the answers not limiting the choice to the most important ones or ranking the order of importance. That would be a necessary move forward in the future study of the subject. Having the limited space we made a decision in favor of such a format of questions that enabled the respondents the expression of unpleasant views of justice as much as possible. One may wonder now what the patterns of choosing the factors are – are positive and negative judgments given by the same people or is there a division of public opinion into adherents to „dark" and adherents to „clear" vision of what is going in the administration of justice. This is why we need to start with studying the correlations between the choice of particular factors of success.

All correlations in the matrix were positive and statistically significant at $p< 0.05$ level. This raises doubt as to the depth of the judgments involved. The next question is – despite the overall correlation – whether there are any groupings of factors, for instance, along the main components. K-M-O test equal 762 and Bartlett's test value 1073.567 ($df = 28$, $p =.000$) allow us to make such an analysis.

Using standard VARIMAX procedure of rotation with Kaiser's correction we arrived at two components that together account for ca. 46% of the total variance (Component 1 26,516%, Component 2 – (20,098%) in the data set.

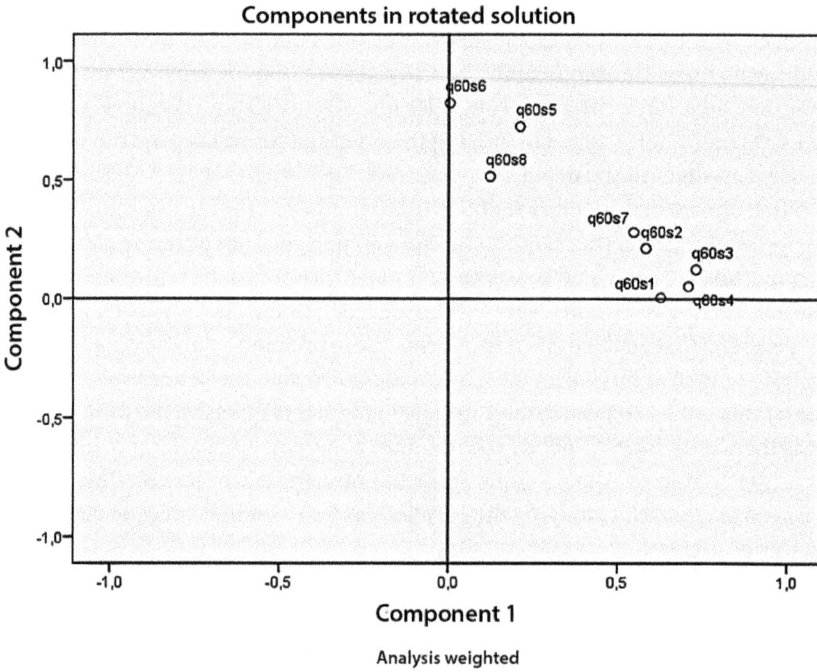

Table 2. Matrix of Rotated Components [a]

a

	Component	
	1	2
Defence lawyers	,729	,123
Witnesses	,707	,052
Merits of the case	,626	,005
Who is the judge	,582	,212
Luck	,546	,280
Bribes	,004	,823
Personal ties	,211	,725
Other	,123	,514

Main Components Analysis, rotation – Varimax with Kaiser's normalization. Rotation in 3 iterations

Quite evidently the two rotated components reflect the division into positive and negative evaluation – Component One has the highest loadings on the choice of defence lawyers, witnesses and a person of the judge but also on the merits of a case and good luck. This is also quite a realistic view as the merits of a case are not separated from sheer luck and professionalism of lawyers. The second component is certainly that of the Dark Side of Justice, such as corruption – bribes and personal ties – and some other unlisted factors that are highly decisive.

As for the Clear Image of Court Success the linear regression analysis led to a conclusion that age (elder) and education (higher) are significant (positive) predictors; secondly, as for the Dark Side of Justice Component gender (female) and age (elder) emerged as statistically significant predictors.

Opposite in contents but mutually independent both scales predict significantly (negatively) court and other institutional settlement indices, demonstrating the ambivalent popular image of justice, while a position on the Clear Side of Justice scale predicts also significantly (positively) the position on Withdrawal index and the Dark Side of Justice scale predicts also significantly (negatively) the private pursuit index and (positively) the Compromise index.

Logistic regression analysis of dichotomized success variables (1 – important, 2 – unimportant or DK) pointed to several socio-demographic variables as significant predictors differing from factor to factor:

The merits of a case as an important factor of success in court were predicted by social habitat (B = .572), who is the judge – by age (B = .596), living conditions relative self-assessment (B = .961) and social habitat (B = -.425), legal defence – by age (B = .307), witnesses – by education (B = .432) and living conditions relative self-assessment (B = .300), the personal ties and contacts – by living conditions relative self-assessment (B = . 449), bribes – by age (B = -.021) and luck – by employment (B = .492), while other factors were not predicted significantly by any of the socio-demographic predictors. Naturally, we were also interested here in the potential role of the past court experience and knowledge of an unjust verdict as predictors. Adding those two to the particular models resulted in two valuable findings: first, in none of the success factor choices the personal court experience of a respondent played a statistically significant role and, secondly, in almost all cases the knowledge about an unjust verdict was one of the significant predictors.

Conflicts in public opinion research

In the same public opinion survey we asked about some types of conflicts and methods applied to resolve them. Three out of ten conflicts listed in the survey questionnaire were inspired by cases that are often lodged in court under the private complaints procedure and sometimes also submitted to civil courts as a way to protect personality rights. Therefore, we asked questions concerning involvement in conflicts related to damage to reputation, infringement of personal inviolability and conflicts between neighbours.

Table 3. Over the past three years, have you been involved in a conflict or a dispute related to…? (percentages):

Conflict type	Involved	Not involved	Not sure, refusal, missing answer
Damage to reputation	13.6	86.3	0.1
Infringement of personal inviolability	3.4	96.4	0.2
Neighbour conflict	6.5	93.4	0.1

It turns out that Poles are not involved in conflicts very often, and the most common type of conflict is the one that involves damage to reputation. It is worth noting that the latter was mentioned more often by the respondents than all other types of conflicts asked in the survey. Given the sample size, it is interesting to note that as many as 144 respondents told us about damage to their reputation and their statements became an additional source of insights about this type of contemporary conflicts. The respondents were asked about the course of a dispute, i.e. who inflicted damage and how the case ended and, most notably, whether or not the matter was taken to court. Those who did opt for the court route were asked about their opinion on the final solution. People who did not go to court were asked why they had decided against this way of defending their personality rights.

Persons who inflicted damage to the respondents' reputation were usually described as 'a friend/a colleague'. In total, as many as one third of those surveyed (34%, or 49 cases) could use this label, even though ten of them are clearly different because the persons involved were in a dependency relation connected with a job position or a role (current or former supervisor, teacher, student). There were also numerous cases of damage to reputation inflicted by neighbours: 32 opponents (22%) were described in this way. Last but not least, some opponents were family members: 19 respondents used this phrase to describe their adversaries. If we added former family members and former partners (5), the frequency of such conflicts between family members would increase considerably, reaching 17% (24 people). Only slightly fewer people did not know the offender or did not know the source of rumours about them (20 people). Some respondents refused to answer the question about the person inflicting damage (6). Other answers included: home improvement team, store customers, a driver, 'a high-ranking person', a rival or business competitors.[2]

When asked a closed question about the feelings that this situation aroused, the respondents most commonly mentioned indifference (68 people, or 47%), with aversion being mentioned almost equally frequently (64 people, or 46%). However, if we add aversion to the very negative feelings mentioned as 'other', we will find that such feelings prevailed. Among 'other' feelings, the respondents mentioned hatred (7 cases), disgust (6), anger (8), resentment (2), contempt (1) and revulsion (1). It is also worth noting that 8 people (5%) experienced shame and guilt in the situation concerned. The survey does not allow us to say anything about the causes of such feelings but perhaps those were private complaint disputes where parties commonly violated each other's personality rights.[3]

There is no doubt that many of the respondents described damage to their reputation, however, they reacted indifferently to the event. This is probably the reason why only 11 people turned to court. Three of them would also take the matter to court in a similar situation, 7 opted for 'it depends', making litigation dependent on the possibility to reach an agreement with the other party, the level of stress experienced or continued damage to reputation.

The reasons why the respondents chose not to bring the case to court proved to be very interesting. The cases that draw attention are those where the respondents reconciled with the other party without involving the court (e.g. 'we immediately clarified the matter on the spot and he apologised to me', 'an amicable settlement', 'we reached an agreement', 'we clarified it to each other' – 16 cases in total). Another socially important reason for not taking the matter to court was the aversion to courts and procedures (12 people). This aversion was sometimes expressed in a mild form, e.g. 'I avoid courts', 'I don't like courts', 'I hate being hauled to court'. Sometimes, however, opinions were more critical, e.g. 'I don't believe courts' 'or 'courts are unjust'. It is optimistic that the most critical opinions were uttered only by three people, who sometimes added: 'especially because I've got a criminal record'. Nevertheless, we should also take note of the respondents' doubts as to the impartiality of institutions other than courts, namely the prosecutor's office, mentioned by two respondents ('he's got an uncle in the prosecutor's office').

2 The number of adversaries in a conflict exceeds the number of participants since some respondents talked about more than one adversary, i.e. 'a neighbour and his relatives'.

3 The number exceeds 144 because some respondents mentioned more than one feeling, e.g. anger and revulsion.

Sometimes the respondents did not opt for the court route as they believed they had small chances of winning ('I'm one person against so many people, I wouldn't manage to win the case', 'I didn't have any evidence') or thought that even a win would not bring the expected result ('a positive verdict in this case wouldn't bring me satisfaction, his apology wouldn't help me anyway', 'because this person has financial burdens, I wouldn't gain anything'). Therefore, in those cases a court verdict could not bring a satisfactory settlement of the conflict.

The commonly expressed feeling of indifference is in line with the fact that most people felt the matter was too trivial to be taken to court. This was directly stated by 31 people, but we could add another ten cases if we look at the statements about 'relative invalidity' of the matter in contrast with other aspects, such as the legal costs ('this involves high costs and the outcome is disproportionate', 'the costs were higher than the value of the dispute', 'it would be a waste of time and money', 'I won't spend my money on silly things' etc.), or the stress involved ('it's stressful', 'it would be a waste of effort').

Very few cases which are worth mentioning here include the fear of revenge, lack of evidence, the awareness that both parties infringed on each other's interests or an unknown perpetrator.

Unfortunately, many answers are difficult to classify into any category, for example 'I didn't want to', 'I don't need to' or a rhetorical question 'What for?', which is difficult to interpret. Occasional statements suggest that answers such as 'I didn't want to' were given, among others, by people who had been accused or offended by their family members ('these are family disputes which can't be resolved by human courts, only by the judgment of God', 'I didn't want to make my daughter more upset', etc.).

Because of their small number, cases involving an infringement of personal inviolability are more difficult to analyse. Only 36 people in the entire sample were involved in such conflicts (3.4%). The largest subgroup consists of ten cases where the respondents were harassed and hit by an intoxicated person in a public place, e.g. at a bus stop, in the street, in a parking lot, at a disco or a pub. In addition, three respondents were hit by sport fans or football hooligans. In three cases, women talked about taunts, scrambles or sexual violence. Other respondents spoke of being hit by family members or a former partner (ex-husband, former cohabiting partner). They also mentioned beating during neighbour disputes, a dispute on grounds of nationality in England' and during a dispute about money. What is of particular interest is the case involving assault, threats and warnings: 'I had to be a witness in a murder case, I knew too much.'

Much more commonly than other conflicts, violations of bodily integrity involved a stranger: this happened in more than half of all the cases (19). In three cases those were sport fans or football hooligans. The second most numerous group (7 cases) was quite different: the perpetrator was a close person, e.g. a family member, husband, ex-husband or former cohabiting partner. Moreover, two people mentioned neighbours, friends and the police. One case involved a driving instructor who was, in fact, trying to sexually assault a learner.

Violations of bodily integrity were reported less commonly than damage to reputation, but if they did happen, the majority of victims reported very negative feelings, such as aversion (17 people, or 48%), anxiety (10 people, or 27%), hatred (2 persons), fear and revulsion (2 persons), or sadness and malaise (2 persons). Indifference in the case of a violation of bodily integrity is twice as rare as in the case of damage to reputation. Only ten people (28%) declared this reaction. In comparison with damage to reputation, the respondents were relatively more likely to take the matter to court (6). And when asked to explain why they had not turned to court, the respondents mentioned the involvement of other institutions, e.g. the police (7 cases). The police responded in a variety of ways: some victims reported that the perpetrators had been punished with a fine (2 cases), others had the opposite experience and spoke about virtually no response from the police despite of them being called to the site ('the police intervened but let them walk out'). In the case of conflict related to a violation of bodily integrity, the conflict fairly often became institutionalised whereas the personal conciliation between the parties was rare. Reconciliation was mentioned only in two cases, which meant that there was no reason to approach any institution. One respondent mentioned his reluctance to courts ('the court is an institution I'd rather steer clear of'). One of the respondents clearly emphasised his regret about not taking the matter to court.

Victims suffering a violation of bodily integrity were more likely than others to claim they would now take the case to court (14 people) yet those who would not opt for this course of action were still more numerous (18 cases).

Neighbourhood disputes are more common than violations of bodily integrity. There were a total of 69 such cases and, obviously, the opponents were neighbours, sometimes referred to as 'alcoholics' or 'drug addicts'. A neighbour is sometimes also a family member (an aunt, the wife's cousin), or, in a handful of cases, an institution, e.g. the management of a condominium unit, a person running a business or employees of a nearby business. The dominant feeling towards the conflict is indifference (36 persons or 51%) or aversion (30 persons or 43%). This should be supplemented with cases where other negative emotions were experienced, such as occasionally declared fear, revulsion or anger (2), annoyance (3) or irritation. When combined, negative feelings would outweigh indifference.

Neighbour conflicts include a large share of 'urban cases' related to loud music, night life, loud conversations and other noises from adjacent dwellings, outside the building or on the staircase. Nearly a half of the respondents involved in neighbour disputes talked about these reasons (30 persons, or 43%). Other 'urban' neighbour conflict related to staircase cleaning, a shared basement or laundry room, a flooded flat, division of costs of an intercom facility or redecoration, or violations of collectively agreed rules and order ('the neighbour doesn't comply with the rules of the condo'). Another type of neighbourhood issues is much more 'rural' in character: those disputes relate to boundaries of land plots, driving through a common road, or a refusal to consent to the extension of a house. Of course, the 'rural nature' of such cases is just a conventional label: such conflicts traditionally prevailed in the countryside but currently they are more likely to occur also in urban or suburban areas with detached houses. Similarly, traditionally 'urban' disputes currently take place also in multi-family houses in the countryside, although in the past they happened almost exclusively in cities and towns. In total, there were 13 cases (19%) related to boundaries between properties or the use of common property.

Cases of this kind were rarely taken to court: this happened only in four situations. A few more respondents (7) said they would have referred the matter to court today.

In six cases, the respondents resorted to another institution for help, primarily the police, city guards or housing administration. In total, the conflict was institutionalised in 11 cases (16%).

Neighbourhood disputes were much more likely than others to end with an agreement. As many as 11 participants to such disputes (16%) declared that they had reached an agreement with their adversary. Sometimes they did it 'for the sake of peace', which reflects the importance attached to peaceful coexistence with neighbours, even when the respondents believe the other party is wrong. The number of cases ending with an amicable settlement should be expanded by further six cases where the malicious actions stopped, sometimes as a result of reproach, though it was also occasionally associated with other decisions: a person moving home or going away.

In 14 cases where conflicts were never reported outside, the respondents stated that the matter had been too trivial, had not involved enough harm, the risk had not been high or the matter was 'relatively unimportant' (i.e. 'a waste of time and money' or 'it would be a waste of effort'), which indicates that other values were regarded as more important than the defence in court. In four cases, the respondents mentioned either reluctance to courts or the fact that the court would probably not have met their expectations ('I don't like courts', 'convoluted judicial procedures', 'the solution sought by the condo wouldn't have been found', 'I'm afraid nothing would have come out of this because of minor social danger'). In the case of neighbour disputes, a separate group of people were afraid of making the conflict more intense if taken to court ('I didn't want to get into a conflict with the neighbours', 'I don't like publicity', 'taking the court route would make me an enemy to my family').

Regardless of their involvement or non-involvement in any type of dispute, all the respondents were asked whether they would turn to court if various types of conflicts occurred. The frequencies of positive answers are clearly correlated with the type of conflict and defended values.

Table 4. If this kind of event happened, would you take the matter to court? (in %)

Conflict type	Yes	No	It depends	Not sure, refusal, no answer	Missing data
Damage to reputation	7.7	54.7	20.3	3.7	13.6
Infringement of personal inviolability	37.5	33.5	20.8	4.8	3.4
Neighbour conflict	10.6	66.5	12.6	3.8	6.5

Hence, as respondents' answers suggest, Poles are much more likely to go to court when the matter involves an infringement of personal inviolability. This was the most common answer of all. Also, the respondents were least commonly certain that they would not opt for the court route in such a case.

Few people were willing to go to court in cases involving other types of conflicts. What draws attention is the fact that in all the cases a large share of the respondents replied 'it depends' while specifying the conditions that would determine their decision. The main factor is the gravity of the case and the degree of infringement, or, in the respondents' words: 'what the scale of damage would be', 'if this was really insulting', 'depending on the intensity', 'the degree of aggressiveness', the scale of these problems', 'it would have to be something serious'. In case of damage to reputation, they also talked about the subject-matter of the insult: 'what the accusations would concern', 'the nature of those insults'. For many respondents, it was also important who the infringing person would be. Another significant factor concerned repeatability, i.e. whether or not the infringements were single cases or a repeated, persistent action ('depending on the persistence of events', 'if this were a single case, I'd give it up but I'd intervene if this thing was repeated'). Another thing taken into account is the outcome of such an infringement, especially in the case of damage to reputation: it was important for many respondents to know whether accusations or insults would have any unpleasant consequences: 'if I experienced any other consequences of this, if this were detrimental to myself and my family', 'if it undermined my reputation'. Finally, a group of respondents would make their decision dependent on the possibility of out-of-court settlement: they said they would not go to court if the infringer apologised and an amicable settlement could be found ('only if I couldn't solve it amicably', 'I'd first try to resolve the matter on my own', 'if we couldn't reach an agreement with the other party', 'if there couldn't be a compromise, we'd go to court'). This possibility was mentioned particularly frequently in response to the question about willingness to take a neighbour dispute to court.

We should also emphasise that the lack of willingness to refer the matter to court does not mean that there was no response or that the case was not reported to another institution. Some respondents claim that they would report a violation of personality rights mainly to the police, to the housing administration or the prosecutor's office: in other words, they are ready to approach an institution but not necessarily a court. This may stem not only from the respondents' reluctance to going to court but, above all, from the belief that other institutions would be more appropriate in a particular case, e.g. the police would be called in in the case of noisy neighbours.

We have discussed respondents' declarations. But what about the defence of the aforementioned interests in the light of conflicts that *are* actually taken to courts? This question can be answered only once we have analysed court cases.

Part II. In the Court

Małgorzata Fuszara

Chapter III. Hate crimes

In Poland, hate crimes represent a peculiar category. On the one hand, they are considered as particularly dangerous and are punished more severely than crimes not motivated by hatred but, on the other hand, unlike in many other European Union countries, more severe punishment is based on selected motives, which can be generally described as related to nationality and religion. Crimes driven by hatred on other grounds, for instance disability, sex, age or sexual orientation, do not belong to this category and may only be prosecuted under legal provisions protecting dignity or honour or, if other interests are violated, on the basis of legislation protecting physical integrity. It is worth adding that people in Poland can seek protection of their interests in those latter cases only via private prosecution (criminal law) or in a civil lawsuit (protection of personal interests).

Therefore, pursuant to the Polish Criminal Code (PCC), punishable crimes are those driven by hatred on grounds of nationality, ethnicity, race, religious beliefs or lack of religious beliefs, and involving either the use of violence or an unlawful threat (Article 119 of the PCC),[4] inciting hatred on those grounds (Article 256 PCC),[5] insulting a group or an individual on these grounds, or violating their physical integrity (Article 257 PCC).[6] Such cases represent over 88% of all hate crimes recorded by public prosecutors' offices. Reports referring to crimes committed for racial, anti-Semitic or xenophobic motives also comprise some

4 Article 119 § 1. Whoever uses violence or an unlawful threat towards a group of population or an individual because of their national, ethnic, racial, political or religious affiliation or because of their lack of religious beliefs shall be subject to imprisonment from 3 months to 5 years.

5 Article 256 § 1. Whoever publicly promotes a fascist or other totalitarian system or incites hatred based on national, ethnic, racial, religious differences or due to lack of religious beliefs shall be subject to a fine, community sentence or imprisonment for up to 2 years. § 2. The same penalty shall be applied to those who, with the purpose of distribution, produce, record or import, acquire, store, possess, present, carry or send printed matter, a recording or another object containing the content specified in § 1 or a carrier of fascist, communist or other totalitarian symbols.

6 Article 257. Whoever publicly insults a group of population or a particular person because of their national, ethnic, racial or religious affiliation or because of their lack of religious beliefs or who, for such reasons, violates the physical integrity of another person shall be punished by imprisonment of up to 3 years.

crimes classified under other articles of the Polish Criminal Code, especially those against freedom of conscience and religion, some cases of damage to property or participation in fights and beatings, especially when co-occurring with other crimes driven by racial, ethnic, national or religious hatred.

Prosecution and adjudication in such cases is complicated, for a number of reasons. For a long time, many such cases were discontinued in Poland by prosecutors' offices at the preliminary stage of proceedings. Above all, such cases were considered be neither very important nor highly dangerous. In many cases, complete proceedings were not conducted and the social threat of the deed was recognised as negligible, or the criminality of certain behaviours or symbols was directly negated. The simplest example is a case when the fascist nature of the swastika was challenged. The situation had remained unchanged until the Prosecutor General's guidelines were issued on 26 February 2014[7] and prosecutors started pressing charges in a larger number of such cases. The Guidelines directly stated that public incitement to hatred on grounds of national, ethnic, racial or religious differences or lack of religious beliefs (Article 257 PCC) occurs in cases where a text is placed 'in the public domain and, in particular, on the Internet or in a public place'. This applies not only to verbal texts but also to graphic signs or symbols. They do not have to be targeted at a specific person or a group of people, and it does not matter for the crime whether the person or the group concerned actually belongs to the insulted social group or not. The need to prepare insightful and universally understandable justifications of court decisions in such cases was highlighted. One important section of the Guidelines refers to the organisation of proceedings in hatred-driven cases, indicating their special nature, great importance and the need for prosecutors to specialise in handling such cases. The Guidelines obligate regional prosecutors to appoint district prosecutors' offices to handle hate-related cases. In turn, the latter offices should appoint prosecutors to deal with such proceedings. Any litigation related to a hate crime was described in the Guidelines as a case of great importance in the meaning of relevant legislation (para. 81 of the Minister of Justice's Ordinance of 24 March 2010), which means that the superior prosecutor must be notified whenever preparatory proceedings are instigated. Prosecution authorities have been charged with the task to monitor such cases on a regular basis and to present semi-annual reports on 'examining the accuracy of criminal proceedings conducted in this category of cases.'

7 Prosecutor's General Guidelines of 26 February 2014 on conducting proceedings in hate crimes, PG VII G 021/54/13.

Once the Guidelines were issued, the number of proceedings rose very clearly. This is reflected primarily in statistics: in 2013, prosecutors' offices conducted 835 proceedings, 719 of which were new, whereas in 2014 there were as many as 1365 proceedings, 1062 of which were new. In comparison with 2012, the number of such cases saw a threefold growth. An even greater increase in the number of proceedings can be noticed if we compare these data to previous years. Regretfully, the significant increase in the number of proceedings was not accompanied by a comparably high increase in the number of indictments brought to courts because many proceedings were discontinued, mostly due to a failure to identify the perpetrators.

Table 1. Proceedings in racist, anti-Semitic and xenophobic hate crimes, conducted by prosecutors' offices

Year	Number of proceedings	Of which: new proceedings	Charges brought	Number of people against whom charges were brought
2006	60	48	–	–
2007	62	41	25 (40%)	50
2008	123	98	33 (27%)	58
2009	166	124	30 (18%)	54
2010	182	146	39 (21%)	64
2011	323	272	56 (17%)	85
2012	473	362	121 (26%)	235
2013	835	719	157 (18%)	284
2014	1365	1062	259 (19%)	389
2015	1548	1169	331 (21%)	468
H1 of 2016	863	566	224 (26%)	–

Author's own summary based on National Prosecutors' Office reports

Therefore, an increased number of such proceedings is accompanied by a higher number of cases where charges have been brought against specific individuals. There has also been an increase in the number of people against whom charges are brought. Regretfully, there has been also a visible decline in the percentage of cases where charges have been brought against the accused (from 40% in 2007 to 19% in 2014), even though the rate of this decline recently slowed down, with charges being brought in 26% of cases in 2016. There has also been an increase in the number of cases discontinued due to the failure to identify the perpetrators: in 2010 they represented 23% of completed cases, with as many as 42% in 2013, slightly fewer, i.e. 36%, in 2014 and 32% in 2015. This is presumably related to how those crimes were committed: many of them were committed using the Internet. For instance, in 2014 as many as 46% of crimes were committed using the Internet, with over 50% in H1 of 2016, and the identification of perpetrators often turned out to be too difficult. In 2014, the victims of hate crimes mostly included Jews and Muslims, black people and the Roma.[8] In 2015 and in H1 of 2016 the share of Muslims as victims went noticeably up,[9] with a threefold increase in the first half of 2016. When speaking of particularly disturbing phenomena, the National Prosecutors' Office mentioned the recent rise (H1 of 2016) of the number of crimes under Article 119 PCC, i.e. involving physical violence on the racist, religious or xenophobic grounds, a rise in the number of acquittals, and an increase in the number of cases discontinued due to minor social harm. These developments expressly show that the rising number of aggressive attacks is accompanied by a mitigated response from institutions against the perpetrators which, consequently, translates into a weaker protection of the victims of racist and xenophobic assaults. Moreover, the National Prosecutors' Office points out to the disturbing rise of the number of proceedings resulting from aggressive behaviour during demonstrations, rallies and meetings, and it proposes enhanced police protection during such events. Therefore, we can say that recently we have witnessed a surge of assaults taking more aggressive forms, with fewer insulting wall inscriptions or purely verbal attacks, and a greater number of public demonstrations with assaults driven by racism, xenophobia or religious hatred. Moreover, attacks increasingly take the form of aggressive acts, not just words.

A discussion on whether Poland has indeed seen an increase in hate crimes has visibly divided the ruling party and the opposition forces. The opposition blames the government for not taking any measures despite the intensification of this phenomenon: '*In recent months, there have been really many hate crimes against people with a different skin colour and people with different political views but, contrary to previous years, none of those acts has been condemned by politicians currently at power in Poland. None of those acts has met with a reaction*

8 Extract from a report on cases of crimes motivated by racism and xenophobia, dealt with in the organisational units of prosecutors' offices in 2014.

9 Extract from a report on cases of crimes motivated by racism, anti-Semitism or xenophobia, dealt with in the organisational units of prosecutors' offices in the 1st half of 2016.

from the Polish authorities where we could say that the authorities has tried to revile such events (...) It is hard to understand (...) why the Police have stopped using the 2010 manual on hate crimes.'[10] On the other hand, the government claims that hate crimes represent an insignificant fraction of all criminal acts in Poland. '*We are talking about crimes which can be counted in hundreds. If we compare this with hundreds of thousands of all crimes committed, we will see that there are no grounds to claim that those crimes represent some high number and a dominant phenomenon in public life. Such claims are unfounded. It is also unfounded to claim that the number of such crimes has been on the rise, and we can see it from the data (...). Indeed, the figure rose in 2014 versus 2013 but it has now stabilised at a roughly comparable level. Let me reiterate that 2016 has not seen an increase until today.'*[11] Representatives of the ruling party add that Poland is exceptionally safe and hate crimes are far less widespread here than in the West.[12]

Complaints about violations of rights of national and ethnic minorities have also been filed with the Polish Ombudsman. According to the Ombudsman's office, there were 133 such violations in 2013–2015, involving, among others, racist incidents, assaults and vandalism. In 2015, the Ombudsman approached the Prosecutor General for information on the effectiveness of measures aimed to combat hate crimes. The Prosecutor General replied that it was a priority in the prosecutors' activities and also pointed out to the training of prosecutors specialising in combating hate crimes.

In 2015, the Government Plenipotentiary for Equal Treatment also approached the Prosecutor General about hate speech, asking about the anti-immigrant poster campaign and the initiative to collect data about Muslims living in Poland (incl. their place of residence and work), conducted by the Polish Defence League.

Regardless of whether we agree with the opposition forces that the number of hate crimes in Poland has been on the rise, or if we side with the ruling party

---

10 Marek Wójcik, Civic Platform party, meeting of the Parliamentary Committee for Administration and Home Affairs, 4 October 2016.

11 Jarosław Zieliński, Secretary of State at the Ministry of Interior and Administration (Law and Justice party). Meeting of the Parliamentary Committee for Administration and Home Affairs, 4 October 2016.

12 Andrzej Melak, Member of Parliament, Law and Justice party: '*the situation in Poland today is very good*'. Edward Siarka, Member of Parliament, Law and Justice party: '*Europe has many more drastic examples than our local Polish ground.*' Meeting of the Parliamentary Committee for Administration and Home Affairs, 4 October 2016.

and say that this number has shrunk but the perpetrator detection rate has gone up,[13] new crimes of this kind are regularly reported. One example is related to the most recent[14] typical case described by the poviat police station in the town of Zgierz, which reported detaining five men in connection with a video clip posted in a social media portal, inciting to national and ethnic hatred. In the recorded video, the main performer was accompanied by '*other young people holding axes, machetes and items resembling firearms. Some of them appeared with covered faces.*' The police portal reported on the detainment of the prime suspect: '*The man tried to make an attack with a crowbar and an axe but the rapid anti-terrorist action effectively prevented him from doing it. During the search of his flat and car, the police seized pneumatic weapon, a gas revolver, hunting and gas ammunition, blank gun ammunition, white weapons such as machetes, sabres and swords, as well as two laptops and a central processing unit. In addition, the police also found 64 grams of marijuana. The man has already heard charges of incitement to national hatred and drug possession, carrying a penalty of up to three years of imprisonment.*'

Courts examine various cases resulting from hate crimes, involving either physical aggression or hate speech, and often combining those two forms of attack. Let us begin our discussion with physical assaults. We will use the portal of decisions delivered by common courts (*Portal Orzeczeń Sądów Powszechnych*) in Poland as the basis for our analysis. In November 2016, the portal contained data on five cases where the perpetrators were accused of committing a crime under Article 119 PCC. All were examined by the Regional Court in Białystok and all followed a very similar course of action: intoxicated men, usually acting in a group, were picking on people of different nationalities with different physique and skin colour, insulting them and using physical violence: '*Having noticed a black man, K.S. with the other men started hurling insults at him, commenting on his skin colour.*' In another case the perpetrator '*publicly insulted R.W. because of his race and then used violence on grounds of his racial identity, hurt his body by hitting the man with his left fist in the area of the left eye, and, as a result, the victim suffered bodily harm in the form of an injury to the conjunctiva and external angle of the*

---

13 'In the first half of 2016 the detection rate for these types of crimes was higher than in the respective period of 2015. It was 26% versus 21% in the first half of 2015. One cannot talk of an overall increase in detection rate since it stood at 40% in 2007.' Extract from a report on cases of crimes motivated by racism, anti-Semitism or xenophobia, dealt with in the organisational units of prosecutors' offices in the 1st half of 2016, p. 12.

14 '*Rapując nawoływali do nienawiści*' (They incited hatred while rapping), news dated 12 November 2016, at http://www.zgierz.policja.gov.pl

left eye as well as a concussion of the retina of the left eye, leading to a disturbance in the function of that part of the body for a period exceeding seven days.' In the same case, the perpetrator's associate '*acting jointly and in concert with another identified person, applied violence against individuals of the Chechen nationality.*' In another case '*when the foreigners approached them and walked past, among them there were women dressed in traditional national outfits, i.e. headscarves, with Z. L. additionally wearing a long dress, D.P. (1) and P.M. (1) made negative comments about their appearance and origin (…). Both delivered blows (…) with their hands, on the torso and on his head, which he protected by hiding his head in his forearms. The man was also repeatedly kicked.*'

All the assaults occurred in public places: in a pizza shop, in the street, on a bus or at a bus stop. The victims, who were defending themselves against the assault, were pulled out of a bus, the perpetrators followed them along the street and attacked them in the stairwell, often in front of other people's eyes. In none of the cases the courts had any doubt that the assault was motivated by the nationality or ethnicity of people selected as victims: '*The case file and the behaviour of the accused K.S., reflected in the description of the deed ascribed to him, clearly indicate that he used violence against the victim on the grounds of the victim's racial identity.*' In another case, the court stated: '*The depositions (…) leave no doubt that the entire event was motivated by his nationality and that of his friend's.*' The perpetrators in all the cases were sentenced, most of them to imprisonment, suspended for a specific period. The case files indicate that the perpetrators sometimes seek reconciliation with the victims, even offering financial compensation for the damage. Following such efforts, some victims testify in a way that belittles the perpetrators' guilt. One example can be taken from a rationale behind a conviction, where the court stated that '*the (victim's – MF) statement was influenced by the fact of his reconciling with them, or perhaps by receiving pecuniary gratification as compensation. Not wanting to be disloyal to people he made peace with, and from whom he accepted money, the victim decided to help (the accused – MF) by belittling his guilt.*' The counsels for the defence endeavoured to reach a settlement and the victim stated that '*it wasn't them, it was just vodka.*'

While recent reports indicate that more hate crime cases involve physical assault nowadays, the largest number of such crimes consist in hate speech.[15] This is a special, debatable category and, as such, deserving separate attention.

---

15 The aforementioned report by the National Prosecutors' Office covering hate crimes in the first half of 2016 states that 39% of proceedings were conducted in cases under Article 256 PCC and 34% under Article 257 PCC.

Hate speech and related dilemmas

It is stressed in literature that hate speech has three characteristics. '*First, it is directed against a specified or easily identifiable individual or, more commonly, a group of individuals based on arbitrary and normatively irrelevant feature. (…) Second, hate speech stigmatizes the target group by implicitly or explicitly ascribing to it qualities widely regarded as highly undesirable. (…) Third, because of its negative qualities, the target group is viewed as an undesirable presence and a legitimate objects of hostility*' (B. Parekh, pp. 40–41). A definition of hate speech was proposed by the Council of Europe in its Recommendation No. R 97 (20):[16] '*The term "hate speech" shall be understood as covering all forms of expression which spread, incite, promote or justify racial hatred, xenophobia, anti-Semitism or other forms of hatred based on intolerance, including: intolerance expressed by aggressive nationalism and ethnocentrism, discrimination and hostility against minorities, migrants and people of immigrant origin.*'

The ban on such statements stems primarily from the concern that lack of reaction may aggravate aggression against a group and entail other attacks on its members, including physical assaults. Psychological research also indicates that members of minorities exposed to hate speech are more likely than others to commit suicide (B. Mullen, J. Smyth 2004). These are certainly the most serious concerns about the potential consequences of hate speech but those cases, or at least some of them, also help to defend the honour of the group and its members before the court. Analogies between hate speech and defamation are most clearly stressed in the context of the USA, where freedom of speech is usually seen as a value so strongly protected by the Constitution that no regulations prohibiting hate speech can be introduced. However, there are some important exceptions, referring to the analogy between hate speech, insult and defamation. One example is the case of Beaucharnais v. Illinois, where the Supreme Court stated that '*hate speech (…) amounted to group defamation, and reasoning that such defamation was in all relevant respects analogous to individual defamation, which had traditionally been excluded from free-speech protection*' (Rosenfeld 2012, p. 253). The problem is even more relevant since current migration is often accompanied by a growing dislike towards 'aliens' and a surge of hate speech, observed in many countries, including Poland, Germany or the United Kingdom (in the latter case, it followed

16 Recommendation No. R (97) 20 of the Committee of Ministers to member states on "hate speech", Adopted by the Committee of Ministers on 30 October 1997 at the 607th meeting of the Ministers' Deputies).

the Brexit decision and the hate-filled, anti-immigrant discourse disseminated, among others, by politicians before the British referendum).

When we think of penalising hate speech, we are faced with a dilemma: how can we strike a balance between two values and their protection, i.e. dignity and protection of various groups against humiliation or incitement to crimes on the one hand, and freedom of speech and the freedom of expressing one's views on the other hand. The USA is most commonly cited as a country which focuses not on curbing hate speech but, instead, on assuring freedom of speech and creating a 'free market of ideas'. It is stressed in literature that the protection of this value had four phases. The first one was connected with the fight for independence of Britain. The main purpose at that time was to protect the citizens against the government which the independence fighters wanted to combat. The second stage occurred after democracy had been established, and when freedom of speech was seen as an important way to protect citizens against the 'tyranny of the majority'. In other words, it was supposed to guarantee unrestricted expression for people promoting unpopular ideas and to protect them against the 'anger of the majority'. The third phase fell in mid-20th century, when it was popular to believe that the majority shared the same values and opinions and, consequently, the focus shifted from speakers to listeners, and freedom of speech was supposed to guarantee the 'opening of the mind' for the latter. And, finally, the fourth phase took place in 1980s when the official discourse was being attacked by alternative movements, the feminist movement, and minority movements. The discourse which had been previously considered universal and shared by nearly everyone began to be criticised as oppressive, predominantly masculine, reflecting the position of 'middle-class white males'. While the third phase entailed a ban on hate speech, the subsequent phase opened the path to curbing hate speech (Rosenfeld 2012).

The attitude towards hate speech is completely different not only in Europe but also in Canada, despite its proximity to the USA, which authors link to its different concept of multiculturalism. In the United States, multiculturalism is based on the idea of a 'melting pot' where cultures mix and blend, whereas Canada professes the idea of an 'ethnic mosaic', where groups co-exist, demanding mutual respect and recognition (Rosenfeld 2012). The Canadian Constitution protects freedom of speech as well as the equality and rights of minorities, which means that freedom of speech does not permit hateful utterances targeted at various groups. Such utterances are penalised in the Criminal Code.[17] The emphasis is put not only on

17 319c.c. (1) Everyone who, by communicating statements in any public place, incites hatred against any identifiable group where such incitement is likely to lead to a breach

the freedom of the speaker but also on the freedom of those who listen to such messages. It is stressed that in the long run hateful statements give rise to prejudice and aggravate the situation of the group targeted by such public statements. As the Supreme Court of Canada stated in Saskatchewan (Human Rights Commission) v. Whatcott of 2013,[18] justifying the protection against hate speech: '*The objective for which the limit is imposed, namely tackling causes of discriminatory activity to reduce the harmful effects and social costs of discrimination, is pressing and substantial. Hate speech is an effort to marginalize individuals based on their membership in a group. Using expression that exposes the group to hatred, hate speech seeks to delegitimize group members in the eyes of the majority, reducing their social standing and acceptance within society. Hate speech, therefore, rises beyond causing distress to individual group members. It can have a societal impact. Hate speech lays the groundwork for later, broad attacks on vulnerable groups that can range from discrimination, to ostracism, segregation, deportation, violence and, in the most extreme cases, to genocide. Hate speech also impacts on a protected group's ability to respond to the substantive ideas under debate, thereby placing a serious barrier to their full participation in our democracy.*'

European countries penalise hate speech but do so to a different extent and in a variety of ways. The United Kingdom has a long story of such penalisation: it had regulations against hate speech already in the 17th century, especially hate speech targeted at the queen but also at various groups of citizens. There are known 18th century cases against authors of anti-Jewish pamphlets inspiring physical assaults of Jews (Rosenfeld 2012). More recently, in 1936, such bans were included in the Public Order Act in the section entitled '*Prohibition of offensive conduct conducive to breaches of the peace*' and they were described as guarding peace: '*Any person who in any public place or at any public meeting uses threatening, abusive or insulting words or behaviour with intent to provoke a breach of the peace or whereby a breach of the peace is likely to be occasioned, shall be guilty of an offence*' (Public Order Act 1936, section 5). Authors link the introduction of this regulation to the growing anti-democratic, totalitarian and fascist sentiments, and, as a result, the

---

of the peace is guilty of (a) an indictable offence and is liable to imprisonment for a term not exceeding two years; or (b) an offence punishable on summary conviction. (2) Everyone who, by communicating statements, other than in private conversation, wilfully promotes hatred against any identifiable group is guilty of (a) an indictable offence and is liable to imprisonment for a term not exceeding two years; or (b) an offence punishable on summary conviction.

18 A case of 2013, SCC 11, (2013), 1 S.C.R 467 http://scc-csc.lexum.com/scc-csc/scc-csc/en/item/12876/index.do, accessed on 3 November 2016.

aforementioned penalisation comprised any deeds and words that could provoke violence, no matter whether violent consequences occurred or not. Similar provisions can be found in the Public Order Act 1986 in its section 4.[19] In subsequent years, the scope of protection against hate speech was extended twice: in 2006, hatred against persons on religious grounds was penalised (Racial and Religious Hatred Act 2006), whereas hatred on grounds of sexual orientation was penalised in 2008 (Criminal Justice and Immigration Act 2008).

In Germany, the hate speech legislation is very extensive,[20] and the German approach to this issue is based on two assumptions: constitutional protection of dignity, honour and personality[21] and the experience of the Second World War and the Third Reich. As stressed in literature: *'Freedom of opinion as guaranteed by Article 5(1) GG finds its limits according to Article 5(2) GG in general legislation, general youth protection provisions, and the law of personal honour. Additionally, constitutional limits inherent in the Basic Law may also restrict the freedom of opinion'* (Developments Legal Limits of a Permissible Criticism of Religion, Christian

---

19 (1) A person is guilty of an offence if he -(a) uses towards another person threatening, abusive or insulting words or behaviour, or (b) distributes or displays to another person any writing, sign or other visible representation which is threatening, abusive or insulting, within the hearing or sight of a person likely to be caused harassment, alarm or distress thereby.

20 The key provision relating to this issue is contained in Section 130 of the Criminal Code entitled 'Incitement to hatred': "(1) Whosoever, in a manner capable of disturbing the public peace 1. incites hatred against a national, racial, religious group or a group defined by their ethnic origins, against segments of the population or individuals because of their belonging to one of the aforementioned groups or segments of the population or calls for violent or arbitrary measures against them; or 2. assaults the human dignity of others by insulting, maliciously maligning an aforementioned group, segments of the population or individuals because of their belonging to one of the aforementioned groups or segments of the population, or defaming segments of the population, shall be liable to imprisonment from three months to five years" and 166: "Whosoever publicly or through dissemination of written materials (section 11(3)) defames the religion or ideology of others in a manner that is capable of disturbing the public peace, shall be liable to imprisonment not exceeding three years or a fine." (Translation of the German Criminal Code provided by Prof. Dr. Michael Bohlander).

21 [Freedom] of opinion by no means always takes precedence over protection of personality.
(…) Rather, where an expression of opinion must be viewed as a formal criminal insult or vilification, protection of personality routinely comes before freedom of expression (BVerfGE 66, 116 [151]; 82, 272 [281, 283 ff.]) After: Winfried Brugger: The Treatment of Hate Speech in German Constitutional Law (Part 1), p. 9.

Hillgruber, German Law Journal, Vol. 17, No. 2, p. 268). Authors emphasise that German lawyers agree that legal constraints and the state intervention into the freedom of communication must exist not because of the artistic or substantive value of the statements or because of the moral judgements over their content but, instead: '*the state can and must intervene if the expression of opinion, the press product, or the artwork is either actually harmful to third party rights or the public good, or if there is a reasonable probability of such harm*' (*ibidem* 268).

The dilemmas associated with the primacy of freedom of speech or protection against hate speech are experienced not only by lawmakers and courts but also by citizens. Research conducted in Poland indicates that, generally speaking, people who either distance themselves from the penalisation of hate speech or directly oppose the idea tend to refer to two types of justifications. The first type is based on concerns about censorship and the need to retain people's right to express their views freely in a democratic society. In this case, freedom of expression is valued more highly than the protection of group or individuals who may become offended, hurt or wrongly accused through someone's statements. In Poland, such arguments are given by people from older age groups who oppose the penalisation of hate speech. In younger groups, the rejection of the idea to penalise hate crimes has a different source: it is opposed mostly by people with right-wing views and a hierarchical vision of the world, who believe that some individuals and groups occupy a higher position than others in the social hierarchy (Bilewicz, Marchlewska, Soral, Winiewski 2014).

In the vast majority of EU countries the law penalises hate speech targeted at various groups and individuals. More precisely, Belgium, Denmark, Estonia, France,[22] Ireland, Lithuania, the Netherlands, Portugal, Romania, Spain, Sweden and the United Kingdom penalise hate speech and hate crimes on a variety of

---

22 The relevant regulations can be found in Loi du 29 juillet 1881 sur la liberté de la presse, modified in this respect in 2004: Ceux qui, par l'un des moyens énoncés à l'article 23, auront provoqué à la discrimination, à la haine ou à la violence à l'égard d'une personne ou d'un groupe de personnes à raison de leur origine ou de leur appartenance ou de leur non-appartenance à une ethnie, une nation, une race ou une religion déterminée, seront punis d'un an d'emprisonnement et de 45 000 euros d'amende ou de l'une de ces deux peines seulement. Seront punis des peines prévues à l'alinéa précédent ceux qui, par ces mêmes moyens, auront provoqué à la haine ou à la violence à l'égard d'une personne ou d'un groupe de personnes à raison de leur sexe, de leur orientation sexuelle ou de leur handicap ou auront provoqué, à l'égard des mêmes personnes, aux discriminations prévues par les articles 225-2 et 432-7 du code pénal. (Version consolidée au 12 août 2010).

grounds: membership in a nation or a religion but also sexual orientation or gender. Moreover, many countries (Belgium, Denmark, Finland, France, Lithuania, the Netherlands, Portugal, Romania, Spain, Sweden and the UK) consider prejudice on these grounds as an aggravating circumstance when a crime is committed. In other countries, such as Germany or Hungary, hate crimes on certain grounds, such as sexual orientation or gender identity, do not represent a separate category but they have been singled out in case law (the Fundamental Rights Agency). Poland is among the few exceptions in the European Union as a country which, as I mentioned earlier, penalises hate crimes (including hate speech) only on grounds of race, ethnicity, nationality, religion or absence of religious beliefs.

Before moving on to examples of Polish cases related to the protection against intergroup hatred, let us take a look at how such cases are adjudicated at the European level, by the European Court of Human Rights. The ECHR must often adjudicate[23] on dilemmas arising from the fact that, on the one hand, it guards the freedom of expression guaranteed by the Convention for the Protection of Human Rights and Fundamental Freedoms and, on the other, it considers forms of expression reflecting racism, anti-Semitism, xenophobia, discrimination of minorities or migrants to be insulting and in breach of the Convention. The ECHR considers whether the applicants' statements have constituted hate speech and, as such, negated the core values of the Convention since its Article 17 prohibits the abuse of rights.

Generally speaking, one can say that complaints about violations of the freedom of expression lodged with the Court give rise to two dilemmas: one is related to the admissibility of a complaint lodged by a person who was accused and finally sentenced for spreading hate speech in his/her country. The other dilemma which emerges once the complaint has been recognised as admissible is to establish whether the state intervention has been, in that particular case, reasonably justified by the need to protect the reputation and rights of others in a democratic society.

The ECHR repeatedly refused to admit applications to defend freedom of expression when they were lodged by a person whose statements, in the Court's view, constituted hate speech against a group (religious, national or ethnic). A refusal to admit an application meant that the applicant's attack at a religious, national or ethnic group was seen by the Court as obvious and, as such, in breach

---

23 https://static1.squarespace.com/static/56330ad3e4b0733dcc0c8495/t/56bacf5307eaa040332cbbf0/1455083348748, accessed on 3 July 2016.

of the values guaranteed by the Convention, such as tolerance, non-discrimination or peace. For instance, the Court decided on the inadmissibility of an application lodged by an author of clearly anti-Semitic articles (Pavel Ivanov v. Russia, application No. 35222/04) and an application submitted by a British national sentenced for incitement to hostility against a religious group when he hung a window poster with the burning Twin Towers in New York reading 'Islam out of Britain – Protect the British People'. In both cases the Court decided that the messages were incompatible with the values proclaimed and guaranteed by the Convention (tolerance, social peace, non-discrimination) and, for this reason, it decided that the applicants who had authored such statements or slogans cannot benefit from the protection of the freedom of expression afforded by Article 10 of the Convention. A similar decision was adopted in the case of Garaudy v. France, when the author of a book entitled 'The Founding Myths of Modern Israel' wanted to file an application. Garaudy was sentenced in his country for incitement of racial hatred, defamation of the Jewish community and disputing the existence of crimes against humanity. He himself believed that the right to the freedom of expression allowed him to make the statements and opinions included in the book, which is why he submitted an application to the Court in order to defend that right. Also in this case the Court stated that the application was inadmissible because the applicant's deeds were obviously incompatible with the underlying values of the Convention. In all those cases the ECHR considered the applications inadmissible and did not examine them further.

However, the Court admitted a whole range of cases involving the dilemma connected with recognising the author's right to the freedom of expression versus recognising the priority of the protection against hate speech. The examples of those cases demonstrate that the Court carefully weighs its choice between the freedom of expression and the protection against hate speech. For instance, the Court considered that the Swedish authorities did not violate freedom of expression when they convicted some citizens for the distribution of insulting leaflets in a secondary school. Those leaflets contained insults against homosexuals and referred to homosexuality as a 'deviant sexual inclination', describing homosexual persons as having a morally destructive impact and being responsible for spreading of HIV and AIDS. A similar decision was issued in the case of Sürek v. Turkey, where the owner of a weekly magazine published letters condemning the authorities' actions against Kurds. In this case, despite the defence's attempts to demonstrate that the opinions were not those of the owner but of the authors of the letters to editor, the Court ruled that the publication of the letters was particularly dangerous, as they put it, for a bloody revenge against people identified by their full name, which could have stirred up hatred and provoke violence against them. For this reason, the Court decided that the owner of the weekly was responsible for the content of the letters as he had disseminated them, contributing to the intensification of the conflict. In consequence, the Court ruled that the Turkish authorities who sentenced the owner did not interfere with his right to the freedom of expression (Article 10 of the Convention).

The Polish portal of decisions delivered by common courts shows only two cases of sentences delivered under Article 256 and 257 of the Polish Criminal Code, i.e. hate speech. Those were complex cases, involving a number of accused persons. The first one was tried in the city of Białystok where the following slogans were shouted in a group of about 30 men during a demonstration: *'No apology for J.', 'All Poland only white' and 'It's Poland here, not Israel'*. A similar case in the same city involved chanting the following slogans during a public gathering: *' Poland for Poles. We'll do them and if not, Hitlerjugend will be back and will do it.'* The accused defended themselves by invoking the right to the freedom of expression and stated that their utterances were not intended to incite hatred or to insult anyone. The slogans *'No apology for J.'*, *'God. Honour. Homeland.'* or *'Great National Poland'* were uttered only to express their own views: *'There is freedom of speech in Poland and everyone should have the right to express their views (…) I chanted the slogan 'No apology for J.' because I believe that Poles should not apologise for that, I'm interested in history and I've read a lot about the murder in Jedwabne, I know it was Germans who did it, they forced Polish people to use violence against Jews (…) So I think that nobody should apologise for Jedwabne, in their own name or in the name of Poland and Poles.'* (file card 588). A similar line of defence was adopted by the defence counsel who wrote an appeal against the conviction and stated: *'In the interpretation of people not involved in the events of 4 September 2011, the phrases 'No apology for J.', 'All Poland only white' and 'This is Poland, not Israel' do not contain phrases so crude that they could shape specific attitudes among the audience, namely hatred motivated by national, racial or religious differences; independent respondents stated that there were no clear grounds to consider those expressions as a token of insult against a group of people on grounds of their nationality, race or religion.'* The court issued judgements of conviction in the case.

The second case is much more complex. A few men were accused of taking part in an organised criminal group, *'an organisation with a covert structure and membership, which invoked the totalitarian methods of Nazism, pursued a policy of hatred on racial, ethnic and national grounds and on grounds of different political views and belonging to the so-called sexual minorities and other minorities.'* The group engaged in various activities which led to the accusations of hate crimes:

its members produced and disseminated materials praising '*a totalitarian system and inciting hatred on racial, ethnic, and religious grounds,*' they distributed leaflets insulting Muslims and organised concerts during which similar messages were spread. Members of the group took part in neo-Nazi concerts and some of them publicly incited others to national hatred and publicly insulted groups on grounds of their ethnicity, religion and race. Also in this case the court delivered judgements of conviction.

However, those two cases do not exhaust the list of court cases involving hate speech. The database returns more results from a query using the phrase 'hate speech' (*mowa nienawiści*). Those are cases where courts expressly invoked the concept of hate speech when justifying their decisions. There were a total of 11 such hits,[24] but the actual number of cases is smaller since a single case is sometimes found under two symbols: first examined by the district court and then by the appellate court. It is worth noting that nearly all those cases relate to mass media content (TV, radio, Internet), considered as insulting by the audience. Those cases were usually widely discussed in the press and online, which means they are easy to identify, despite the far-reaching anonymization of rationales. Not all cases were prosecuted under the Criminal Code. As many as four cases were lodged by broadcasters punished by the President of the National Broadcasting Council under Article 18 of the Act on Radio and Television Broadcasting.[25] In some cases, the court agreed with the broadcasters, e.g. in two lawsuits concerning the same satirical programme, where the authors were accused of ridiculing priests and paedophilia, and ridiculing the holy relics (the pope's blood) and the assets of the T.R.'s foundation. The broadcaster emphasised that the programme was purely satirical and largely focused on socially harmful phenomena, notably paedophilia, and the party who filed a complaint at the National Broadcasting Council formulated the accusations in a way suggesting that any criticism of priests was unjustified. The court, justifying its decision in a very diligent and

24 The search for 'hate speech' returns 13 results but two are not relevant (accessed 10 April 2016).

25 The first two paragraphs of Article 18 of the law are most relevant for this discussion. They read as follows: '18.1. Programmes or other broadcasts may not promote illegal activities, activities going against the Polish raison d'etat, beliefs and attitudes contrary to morals and social interest; in particular, they may not contain incitement to hatred or discrimination on grounds of race, disability, gender, religion or nationality. 2. Programmes or other broadcasts shall respect the religious beliefs of the audience, especially the Christian system of values.' (Act of 29 December 1992, Dz.U. – Polish Official Journal of 2011, No. 43, item 226, as amended).

extensive manner, released the broadcaster from punishment, stressing the satirical nature of the programme and, in fact, noted the absence of offensive content despite the presence of highly critical content. Nevertheless, in the court's view, this was compatible with freedom of speech, the right to criticism and the satirical formula of the programme. A completely different judgment was delivered in another case, even though the broadcaster argued that the show had a satirical profile. In the rationale of the judgment, dismissing the motion to waive the penalty imposed by the President of the National Broadcasting Union, the court wrote: '*The content of the message was exceptionally insulting for people of the Ukrainian nationality and for women in general. People of the Ukrainian nationality were depicted as ones who are hired by Polish citizens and who accept humiliation when providing work. The humiliation had two core aspects. Firstly, the objectifying aspect, where people of the Ukrainian nationality were treated like objects (...), and it was highlighted that such a behaviour should be approved (...). Secondly, the sexual aspect, suggesting that Ukrainian women accept sexual abuse for fear of losing employment (...). The said utterance has yet another dimension. It shows that a woman's beauty is a criterion for sexual abuse and that such behaviour can be generally acceptable.*' Further on, the court stated: '*The content of the message violated important interests protected by law (human dignity), it was discriminatory (discrimination on grounds of nationality and gender) and could be classified as the so-called hate speech.*'

While the aforementioned cases entailed hate speech targeted at a group, the remaining ones concerned specific individuals, who were insulted, offended or accused in press materials, online or in other mass media. For instance, the court ordered that the Archdiocese and the editor-in-chief of the said journal should publish an apology to a woman who lodged a complaint with the European Court of Human Rights against Poland after she was denied the right to have a legal abortion. The judgment contained detailed wording of the apology: '*The Archdiocese (...) and M.G., as the editor-in-chief of the (...) weekly apologise to Ms. A.T. for unlawfully likening Ms. A.T. with Nazi war criminals responsible for the Holocaust of the Jews in the A. camp and for the martyrdom of Jews in ghettos. The Archdiocese (...) as the publisher and M.G. as the editor-in-chief of the (...) weekly regret the fact that they caused pain and hurt Ms. A. T. through the unlawful infringement of personal interests of Ms. A.T. and by using hate speech.*'

Another case where the court did not accede to the demand for an apology concerned statements contained in a book-length interview with an activist of the Polish in Latin America. The activist was described as an anti-Semite and the interview stated that the Institute of National Remembrance in Poland considered bringing a lawsuit against him for blackmailing Jews and demanding money from them during the war. The court considered those statements to be true and written about a public person in socially justified interest and, therefore, it did not find any grounds to order an apology. The only element that was not fully justified in the court's opinion was the phrase 'a shady individual'. However, this did not provide the grounds for an apology, either. A different decision was issued in the case of a politician who pronounced certain words about another politician. As a result, the former was ordered to publish the following apology: *'I apologise to Mr. J.K. for an unlawful breach of his personal interests during an interview published on page (...) on 14 September 2010. I declare that my statement about Mr. J.K.'s psychopathic tendencies is untrue and the likening with Hitler and Stalin is unjustified. I apologise for harming the reputation and personal dignity of Mr. J. K.'* Another similar case must be viewed as typical slander of a public person: he was accused of firing his/her subordinate and engaging in non-entirely-transparent financial business involving his/her relatives. The slanderer was ordered by court to apologise.

Therefore, the nationality theme features prominently in hate speech-related cases. This is not surprising since the structure of the relevant provision of the Polish Criminal Code clearly narrows down the range of cases that can be prosecuted as hate speech under Articles 256 and 257 PCC. Notably, even if a case involves other charges (an attempt to enforce one's right to abortion, criticism of a political opponent), insults contain references to the Holocaust, Nazism and Stalinism.

The cases discussed above have a few distinctive characteristics. Their vast majority involve dissemination of insulting content via the mass media. The remaining cases relate to the use of hate speech during public gatherings. Two types of cases can be distinguished here: attacks on a group (whether national or religious) or on an individual. Perpetrators associate groups with attributes which are usually part of the unfavourable stereotype of that group, and, consequently, its members may feel insulted and degraded because of the negative attributes or behaviours attributed to them. '*Forcing powerful labels and stigmas upon others constitutes degrading treatment that denies individual self-definition or social 'visibility' and can, therefore, impinge upon, distort or even revoke one's sense of self. While the law deems human dignity inviolable, in reality it is fragile and precarious, in need of protection and defence*' (Making hate crime ...: 2012, p. 21). The research has shown that stigmatisation may even lead to the adoption of a negative stereotype by members of a given group (Czykwin 2002). Such attacks are harmful for the group identity and individual identities of the group members. There is no doubt, therefore, that defence against negative labelling is a defence of the dignity of the group as a whole and of all its members individually.

Attacks on specific individuals usually affect public persons (politicians) or those whose case was widely publicised by the media (when a woman was denied her lawful right to abortion in Poland).

Similar conclusions may be drawn from the analysis of the court cases conducted in 2011–2012 by 'Open Republic – Association Against Anti-Semitism and Xenophobia'. This was not an easy endeavour because, as written in the introduction, '*analysis of court files was a serious challenge because (…) 90 courts out of 100 which we approached replied that no cases under Articles 119, 256 and 257 of the Criminal Code had taken place.*' The Association managed to find a total of 24 cases. However, even when a judgment of conviction was issued, the courts did not always give an answer as to the subject-matter of the case. Hate speech against national or ethnic groups was most common during public gatherings, especially during football matches and concerts. It took the form of shouts at listeners, song lyrics or song titles (e.g. 'Out with Jews'). As regards the online or published media, most cases involved an attack on groups or specific individuals of a different nationality or skin colour: Jews, Turks, Belarusians, Chechens, Gypsies, as well as dark-skinned citizens of other countries, including a Nigerian and a Frenchman.

As mentioned earlier, when someone's honour, virtue or reputation is attacked on grounds other than hatred driven by nationality, ethnicity, religion or lack of religious beliefs, matters are taken to court either as a civil case (protection of personal interests) or as a private complaint filed at a criminal division of a court. Those cases will be discussed in the subsequent chapters of this publication.

Małgorzata Fuszara

Chapter IV. Honour and reputation in civil courts

In Poland, personality rights can be defended via two procedures: as a private complaint filed with criminal departments of courts, and under protection of personality rights at civil departments of courts. Each of these methods of defence follows a separate procedure. Moreover, the access to court varies, depending on the competence of courts in such matters. Private complaints are heard by district courts at the first instance (there were 317[26] of them in Poland in 2015) whereas cases involving the protection of personality rights fall within the competence of circuit courts (45[27] of such cases in the same period). These data already indicate that the access to court under each of those procedures varies: district courts are geographically much closer to citizens, also in the case of people living in small towns, whereas circuit courts are much more accessible for citizens living in major cities where both district and circuit courts have their seats. On the other hand, people living in locations which are not in the vicinity of major cities have a more difficult access to the civil procedure at circuit courts.

Personality rights have not been defined by the lawmakers. The Polish Civil Code mentions only a partial catalogue of protected personality rights,[28] among them health, freedom, honour, freedom of conscience, surname, pseudonym, image, secrecy of correspondence, inviolability of the home, and creative work. This catalogue is not finite, and the authors stress that new personality rights emerge in practice as societies change, and they are considered to be protected

---

26 *Mały Rocznik Statystyczny* [Concise Statistical Yearbook], GUS Warsaw 2016, p. 82. Ordinance of the Minister of Justice of 7 October 2014 determining the seats and areas of competence for appellate courts, circuit courts and district courts (Dz.U. – Polish Official Journal of 2014, item 1047, as amended).

27 Ordinance of the Minister of Justice of 7 October 2014 determining the seats and areas of competence for appellate courts, circuit courts and district courts (Dz.U. – Polish Official Journal of 2014, item 1047, as amended).

28 Article 23 of the Polish Civil Code: A person's personality rights, in particular health, liberty, honour, freedom of conscience, name or pseudonym, image, secrecy of correspondence, inviolability of the home, scientific or artistic work, inventions and improvements shall be protected by civil law regardless of the protection provided for in other regulations.

even though they are not mentioned among the examples listed in the Civil Code. According to the case law and doctrine, such rights also include, for instance, the closest relatives' right to bury and commemorate their deceased, the right to privacy and intimacy, the right to gender, to peaceful use of one's home (Nazaruk 2014). The Supreme Court also ruled that the disclosure of the salary or wages of an employee without the employee's consent may also represent a violation of their personality rights.[29] Personality rights include not only the rights to which natural persons are entitled to but also the ones vested in legal persons, including, e.g., the symbol of a legal person: '*The symbol of a legal person is a carrier of its identity in external perception and, much like the name or the brand, constitutes a personality right which is protected under Article 24 in connection with Article 43 of the Civil Code.*[30] Personality rights are intangible, which does not mean that their violation may not have tangible consequences. Those rights are held by a specific person, they are inalienable and non-transferable to heirs – even when protecting the memory of a deceased person, it is assumed that such protection is granted to the deceased person's immediate family members as a separate right, and the deceased person's right to good reputation is not transferred to the heirs (Nazaruk 2014).

Moreover, personality rights are absolute in their nature, which means that they are valid vis- à-vis everyone, both natural and legal persons.[31]

In line with the current case law, it is assumed that both the assessment of whether a specific right is a personality right, and whether or not it has been violated, must be made objectively in every single case. It is worth noting that another view can also be found in the doctrine, whereby a violation of a personality right should be defined subjectively, since the feelings of the person who demands legal protection are decisive here.[32] Currently, it is commonly acknowledged that this assessment must be objectivised, and the person responsible for the violation may not be exposed to another individual's excessive sensitivity or unpredictable and subjective assessments made by the complainant. The Supreme Court took a position on this matter a number of times, in various years, for instance in 1969: '*when it comes to the dignity/honour of a person, it is the objective assessment of specific circumstances rather than the subjective feeling of the person concerned*

29 A resolution adopted by seven judges (I PZP 28/93) on 16 July 1993.

30 Judgment of the Supreme Court of 7 March 2003, I CKN 100/01, LexPolonica No. 375443, after: Nazaruk 2014.

31 S. Dmowski, S. Rudznicki 2011, P. Nazaruk 2014.

32 S. Grzybowski 1957.

that determines whether a violation of a personality right has taken place at all.'[33] A similar passage can be found in a much later judgment issued by the Supreme Court in 2009: '*The assessment of a defaming nature of a statement may not be based on the sensitivity of the individual concerned, who may feel hurt, but, instead, it must be based on an objective criterion which takes into account the reactions of an average reasonable person.*'[34] This line of ruling was adopted by the Supreme Court, and common courts have been issuing their judgments in a similar vein.

A person whose personality rights are threatened by someone's action has a number of claims. Above all, they may demand that the violation of their rights be ceased. Secondly, they may demand that the effects of such a violation be removed, above all via an appropriate statement, for instance one where the slander is taken back, false information is corrected or an apology is offered. Moreover, a wronged person whose personality rights have been violated may demand financial compensation or payment of an specific sum of money to a socially beneficial cause. If the violation of personality rights has led to damage to property, there is also a possibility to demand that such damage be redressed. In the latter case, however, it is necessary to prove that such damage has, indeed, occurred.

The Polish Civil Code provides that a person whose personality rights have been unlawfully undermined may demand protection (Article 24 of the CC).[35] This means that a wronged person must only indicate the existence of a personality right and the fact that it has been threatened or violated. If this is the case, it is presumed that such a violation is unlawful. If a defendant claims he/she had the right to take the action concerned, he/she must demonstrate that his/her actions were not unlawful. This is particularly important in cases which are of most interest to us here, such as impairment of dignity/

---

33 Judgment of the Supreme Court of 6 October 1969, I CR 305/69.

34 Judgment of the Supreme Court of 18 June 2009, II CSK 58/09.

35 Article 24 of the Polish Civil Code: § 1. Anyone whose personality right is threatened by actions of others may request that such action is discontinued, unless such action is not unlawful. In the event of an infringement he/she may also demand that the person who committed the violation performs the actions necessary to remove its effects and, in particular, makes a declaration of the appropriate content and in a proper form. Under the rules laid down in this Code, he/she may also demand financial compensation or payment of an appropriate amount of money for a designated social purpose.
§ 2. If damage to property has been caused as a result of violation of a personality right, the victim may demand that it is redressed under general terms.
§ 3. The aforementioned provisions shall be without prejudice to the powers provided for in other provisions, in particular in the copyright law or law on inventive activity.

honour, where defendants often speak of justified criticism. In such cases, the defendant must demonstrate that the criticism was indeed made in defence of socially important values: '*As values related to the inner life and, as such, not equally measurable, personality rights are protected under the civil law only in such cases (...) when the violation of those rights occurred as a result of an unlawful action undertaken by the violator. Criticism is a socially useful and desirable activity as long as it has been undertaken in public interest, and if it was not intended to bully another person, and if it shows attributes of reliability and reality.*'[36] In its subsequent judgments, the Supreme Court emphasised that the absence of unlawfulness can be supported by the provision of actual facts: '*Even a violation of another individual's personality right as a result of dissemination of information does not constitute an infringement if the information concerns actual facts and the informant acts in a legitimate interest, whether private or public. On the other hand, in order to prove that the information was accurate and, as such, the perpetrator's acts cannot be deemed unlawful, one must, in principle, demonstrate that the facts covered in the information did, indeed, take place.*'[37]

The Supreme Court and, following its footsteps, also appellate courts and district courts, have repeatedly invoked the concept of 'internal honour', '*understood as self-esteem and the expectation to be respected by others*'[38] and 'external honour', which '*comprises attributes or actions ascribed to a person where they can humiliate that person in public or expose that person to the risk of losing trust needed to perform a specific profession or activity.*'[39] As the Supreme Court stated, '*Damage inflicted on an individual's reputation is reflected both in the self-identification of that person and in her/his perception by others.*'[40]

Since the civil protection of personality rights can be viewed as an alternative versus the private complaints path, I made an attempt to check whether these options are viewed as alternatives in real life, and not only in the letter of the law. Such an attempt had been already made in my first research on conflict resolution (Fuszara 1988). I asked all the subjects participating in private complaint cases in three court districts if 'their' case could have been lodged also with a civil court. Although a very long time has lapsed (the research was conducted in late 1970s), the results of the research are worth quoting: at least 90% of the defendants in

36 Judgment of the Supreme Court of 19 September 1968, II CR 291/68.

37 Judgment of the Supreme Court of 5 March 2002, I CKN 535/00.

38 Judgment of the Supreme Court of 18 January 2013, IV CSK 270/12.

39 *Ibidem.*

40 *Ibidem.*

each of the analysed court districts (Warsaw-Praga District, Lesko and Kępno) either gave a wrong answer or said they did not know. Although the defendants were involved in private complaint cases, most of them claimed this was a civil case since it was not brought by a public prosecutor. Therefore, as we can see, the possibility to choose between the two paths when defending personality rights is only theoretical since poor knowledge of the law means that most of the individuals concerned were unfamiliar with the alternative procedures (without lawyer's advice) and, moreover, could not distinguish between civil cases and private complaints in the criminal procedure.

Another way to seek an answer to this question involved the analysis of case files in cases related to the protection of personality rights, heard by voivodship courts competent for the areas where the private complaints path was also studied, i.e. in Krosno, Warsaw and Kalisz. That research produced interesting results. Cases for the protection of personality rights could be described as an alternative course of action vis-a-vis private complaints only in the case of the voivodship court in Krosno: cases lodged under both procedures arose from similar conflicts, the parties remained in similar relationships, and lawsuits were brought to defend the same values. At that time, I studied a total of 76 cases lodged with the voivodship court in Krosno in 1978–1979 in connection with the violation of personality rights. Among them there were cases lodged in defence of reputation, primarily in situations when someone was accused of committing a crime (theft) or infringing on norms related to sexual mores. Other cases were connected with the violation of bodily integrity and were usually accompanied by property claims. Another group comprised property-related disputes, nearly identical with private complaints, involving adjacent land plots. As I wrote at that time, '*The conducted comparisons indicate that neither the type of conflict, the kind of values being defended nor the type of relationships between the parties determines the selection of either the civil procedure or the criminal procedure. The addresses of parties in the Krosno voivodship who opted for civil protection of personality rights suggest that that proximity of the court plays a decisive role: those cases are lodged primarily by individuals living in the vicinity of the voivodship court. This observation reveals a concern: the real choice between the two options to defend their rights is only available to citizens living in the vicinity of voivodship courts. One may doubt whether the legal regulation which creates such a variation in access to court is right.*' (Fuszara 1988, p. 93).

The cases filed with the voivodship court in Warsaw were quite different. In total, I studied 116 cases lodged with that court in 1978–1979. They were mostly filed in defence of reputation but they differed visibly from the private complaints since the defendants were mostly editorial offices of newspapers or television, and film-making teams. Typically, such cases were not lodged with other voivodship courts under study even though the seats of local newspapers were located in smaller towns. However, the cases against editorial offices were lodged in Warsaw and involved only nation-wide mass media. The defendants were primarily accused of distorting facts and formulating defamatory opinions. Apart from those cases, other common cases at the voivodship court in Warsaw were lodged against cemetery management who took actions and measures without the consent of the site owner. However, those cases were of a completely different type in comparison with those which could be resolved under the private complaints procedure.

The voivodship court in Kalisz was the third court covered by the study. I extended the time frame in my search of cases lodged to defend personality rights by adding two years. Nevertheless, I found only one such case filed there in 1976–1979. How can we assess the real choice between two ways of bringing a dispute to court? Are those paths alternative versus each other or are they mutually complementary?

The first problem lies in legal ignorance, which means that in many cases the interested parties have no real possibility to choose between those two ways of resolving a dispute. The existence of an alternative way in the law does not mean that such a possibility exists in real life: if people are to take advantage of such opportunities, they must be aware of their existence as a minimum precondition.

The choice of the civil path to protect personality rights confirmed our previous observations concerning the existence of a major regional differentiation as regards the participation in disputes. The region of Kępno turned out to have few conflicts also in this case: no cases concerning the protection of personality rights were lodged here.

On the other hand, a large number of cases in defence of personality rights were lodged with the voivodship court in Warsaw. However, those cases were quite different in nature in comparison with the private complaints lodged in the same region. The civil lawsuits lodged with this court included widely publicised cases of defamation against institutions, notably the mass media. The claimants demanded that their reputation be restored and expected the court to prevent the dissemination of defamatory opinions or biased presentation of facts. Therefore, these two paths are not alternatives since they are not used for the same types of conflicts.

The Krosno voivodship was the only one where the interested parties involved in similar conflicts resorted to both methods to defend their rights, i.e. the civil path and the private complaints method. However, the choice between those methods was also limited since the civil action was used by people who could take advantage of the geographic proximity of the voivodship court (Fuszara 1988, pp. 94–95).

In the studies conducted recently I attempted to use another method in order to check whether civil courts are actually used in conflicts which are similar to those where wronged parties instigate private prosecution. Since the list of protected personality rights listed in the Civil Code includes honour, and a violation often leads to a private complaint, I sought an answer to the question about the alternative use of either procedure in such cases. As mentioned earlier, since the competence in such cases lies with the circuit court, the web portal of court judgments will be helpful for such research. The search using the Polish word '*cześć*' ('honour') mentioned in Article 23 of the Civil Code turned out to bring very confusing results,[41] so I decided to search for relevant cases by using the Polish word '*honor*' ('honour'). The portal returned 67 cases where the word '*honor*' occurred in the content of judgments or their rationales in cases examined by civil departments of courts during the period concerned.[42] Not all of those cases were lodged in defence of reputation: as many as 19 cases ended up in the sample because 'honour' was mentioned in another context, especially in comments made by parties and in rationales for judgments. Those cases turned out to be interesting as they provided additional knowledge on the contexts where honour is invoked in court.

To supplement my research, I analysed cases heard by the Civil Chamber of the Supreme Court where judgments were issued in 2013–2016. Since there was only one case where the word 'honour' was used, I searched for relevant cases using another phrase, i.e. '*dobre imię*' (reputation, literally: 'good name'). There were a total of 37 such cases in the said period. Therefore, I finally supplemented my research with a brief analysis of 38 cases heard by the Supreme Court, some of which were instigated in defence of honour and reputation.

In a subgroup of the analysed cases honour and reputation were tarnished by the mass media: on television, in nation-wide or local press and, increasingly, on the Internet. The portal with judgments issued by common courts returned 17 such cases (35%), and 19 cases of this kind were heard by the Supreme Court (50%). In most cases there was no doubt that personality rights had been violated:

41 This happens mostly because the search engine shows thousands of judgments with the word '*część*' [Pol. part, differing in one letter from '*cześć*' – honour], which makes such search results virtually useless.

42 Access between 15 February 2016 and 15 August 2016. Judgments in those cases were issued between 2013 and 2016.

the media messages contained suppositions regarding embezzlement, financial fraud, alleged court judgments from many years ago, mismanagement, obtaining money under false pretences, blackmailing or mental illness. One example was a case brought against a television broadcaster which reported false information about a local politician's alleged links with the trade in bills of exchange issued by utility companies. The politician was also accused of selling municipal property at a price below its value. As the case had been dismissed by the public prosecutor, the television broadcaster was obliged to publish an apology.[43]

In another similar case defamatory information was disseminated via electronic media but it was targeted at a much narrower audience. A chairman of a housing association was accused by the members of the association of fraudulent financial settlements. In e-mails distributed to various recipients the chairman was described as a liar, a fraud and a man without honour. The court ordered the defendants to apologise to the claimant in a letter addressed to him personally.

Some cases, however, ended with a dismissal since the defendants managed to demonstrate that their action was not illegal since they acted in a socially legitimate interest, wanted to draw attention to an important social problem and their utterance was evaluative rather than descriptive. In one such example, a case was brought to court by a person who was described by one newspaper as someone who got his position through connections, without the needed qualifications or competence. The claimant said that this undermined his honour and took the case to court. The appellate court justified the dismissal of the claim as follows: '*(…) it is justified to believe that the defendant was acting within the legal order, to defend the public interest, which excludes the protection of the claimant, despite the infringement of the claimant's personality rights.*[44] In the statement of reasons, the court invoked the fact (also stressed in the decisions of the European Court of Human Rights) that a public person must be prepared for the possibility of being criticised and that the author of the utterance was acting in socially justified interest and wanted to draw attention to an important social problem, i.e. nepotism.

However, there also cases where claimants demand that information about them or their image be removed from the Internet. One example was a case brought against a website administrator where users posted a primary school photo with captions. The claimant argued that he had never agreed for his image to be posted online. The court decided, however, that the website administrator

43 Circuit Court in Warsaw, I ACa 436/13.

44 VI CA 1951/13, Appellate Court in Wrocław.

did not violate the claimant's personality rights since this was a regular class photo which had been posted by other people featured in that photo.

The most complex cases with the longest-running proceedings relate to the defence of reputation of people described in books (three cases among those heard by the Supreme Court, and one by common courts). All those cases related to the period of World War II and the early post-war years.

In a handful of cases, defendants were accused of violating the claimants' reputation in other widely disseminated sources of information, such as a pre-election leaflet, a referendum bulletin and a debt register. The most unusual place to bear defamatory information was a fence featuring a slandering banner. The claimant demanded that the message should be taken back and an apology should be delivered in the same manner, i.e. using a banner on the fence.

As a rule, cases lodged in defence of reputation relate to natural persons, yet legal persons also defend their reputation by invoking personality rights. In one example, a municipality sought to defend its reputation because a newspaper published a series of articles containing '*a number of false and unfounded statements about the circumstances surrounding the pregnancy of five teenage girls attending a lower secondary school.*' The municipality responsible for running the school demanded a public apology and a compensation of PLN 200,000. In the statement of claim, it argued that the students' pregnancies were individual cases, occurring at different times, whereas the authors of the article stated directly that the pregnancies resulted from an organised orgy the students participated in. The claimant argued that the news was false and, moreover, no effort was taken to establish whether the statements were true or not. The newspaper publications contained the following statements: '*secondary schools don't educate (...), instead, they deprave the kids (...) students engaged in group sex for fun*', even though not a single person was found who would have taken part in such events. The newspaper did not publish the corrections sent by the school principal. The school and the responsible municipality suffered damage not only to their image but also to their financial status because, some candidates withdrew their applications after the publication. The court took the side of the municipality and ordered an apology and a payment of a compensation of PLN 200,000, stating that the publications were '*highly damaging for the claimant's reputation*' and the compensation was considered '*adequate and moderate*' under the circumstances.[45]

Cases in defence of personality rights are relatively commonly lodged by public persons, particularly politicians and former politicians (eight cases on the portal),

45 Judgment by the Appellate Court in Warsaw, XXIV C 107/11.

whose actions in their public role were presented in an unfavourable light and, moreover, defamation or slander was sometimes used against them as a method of political fight. One example is a case brought by a mayor where a referendum was organised to dismiss him from the office. During the campaign, the 'Referendum Newsletter' published some false news, for instance that he allegedly obtained public money thanks to his connections and spent that money on a billiards table for his son. This piece of news was false and the mayor proved that the table had been bought using private money. The court ruled that the news was false and no diligence had been exercised in order to verify it. The court obligated the defendants to publish an apology in a newspaper and to pay an indemnity of PLN 6,000. Both parties claimed in court that the opponents' actions were part of a political game, attempting to influence the result of that game.[46]

There are relatively many examples with 'politics in the background', many of them related to election campaigns. One example is particularly interesting taking into account the divergent interpretations given by the courts of various instances. The case, heard by the Supreme Court, was lodged by poviat authorities to defend their reputation. In an electoral leaflet, it was claimed that people who were running for the poviat council aimed '*to put a stop to corruption and fraud in the offices and organisational units of the Poviat Office in* [...].' In the view of the Appellate Court, this statement did not violate any personality rights and was an element of an election programme, and, given the situational context, it should have been seen as part of discourse which is admissible in politics during election campaigns. Such discourse usually contains much harsher language than expressions used in ordinary human interactions. The Supreme Court interpreted the same thing differently, considering the cassation to be justified: '*Therefore, phrases which tarnish reputation are those which provide an objective assessment yet associate a legal person with incorrect behaviours, even if indirectly, and this may undermine confidence in that legal person, where such confidence is required for the legal person to operate properly and to perform its statutory responsibilities. In other words, the assessment of whether personality rights of a legal person have been violated or not must be associated not only with the assessment of activities undertaken by the members of its governing bodies but also with behaviours ascribed to local government officials whose work is also an element of the legal person's operations.*'[47]

A considerable group of cases were brought to court by natural persons against the State Treasury in defence of personality rights. They were lodged mostly

46 Appellate Court in Cracow, Ca 294/13.

47 Judgment by the Supreme Court of 28 April 2016, Case No. V CSK 486/15.

against heads of penal institutions courts and prosecutors' offices, and a handful of cases were brought against the Institute of National Remembrance and its publishing house (14 cases on the portal, 20%). The cases brought against court presidents, public prosecutors and the police are particularly interesting if we look at how those involved understand the court procedures and how they resort to court to claim their rights. The claimants are usually dissatisfied with public prosecutors' actions, dismissal of cases or judgments issued by courts. The claimants believe that actions which are against their expectations infringe their personality rights (including honour) and expect that the role of the court would be to agree with the claimant. In one example the district court did not believe a woman's statements and she decided to file a case with the circuit court to defend her personality rights since she believed the circuit court supervised the district court and the notarial office. As she put it, '*her honour was tarnished because her statements were not believed.*'[48] Cases of this kind clearly indicate that some people in legal proceedings do not understand the mechanics of court proceedings or the application of the law. Moreover, they do not understand the idea of various court instances, and they put the blame for their failures on institutions, not on their own deeds.

There is a large and homogenous group of cases brought against heads of detention centres. Some of them are brought against more than one such centre (three or even eleven) which offer very poor conditions for detainees. As the court stated in one of such cases, staying in an overcrowded cell with mouldy walls without ventilation, bearing the stench of sanitary facilities, may be likened with degrading treatment, impairing the dignity of the person who has been deprived of liberty. A detainee who stayed in such a cell for 28 days received a compensation of PLN 3,000 days for impairment of dignity.[49]

Some cases are lodged by individuals who believe their reputation was tarnished by witnesses testifying in court, prosecutors or people reporting a crime or an offense. A common behavioural pattern could be tracked in all such cases: people who were accused in a criminal case lodged a civil action in defence of their personality rights, reputation and honour, thus trying to reinforce their defence in the criminal case and reiterate that they were not guilty. In such cases, the court did not side with the individuals who were trying to defend themselves in such a way. In each of those cases it was easy to demonstrate that those who instigated the criminal case acted within the law. Such cases also ended up in the

48 Appellate Court in Gdańsk, IA Ca 324/13.
49 Appellate Court in Katowice, IA Ca 949/15.

Supreme Court, especially in situations where a person accused of committing a crime (violence, mobbing) was acquitted.

Some lawsuits brought against the State Treasury are related to actions associated with the change of the political system in Poland and the claimants find such actions unjust. For instance, someone may claim they have been unfairly accused of reporting on fellow oppositionists to the communist authorities during the martial law. In one such case the court stated: '*The claimant suffered serious injustice. During the period before 1989 he was an opposition activist and, therefore, suspecting him of reporting on a colleague who was also actively involved in the opposition movement brings him into serious disrepute.*' A similar lawsuit was brought in connection with wrong vetting decisions made in the cases of high military officials.

Despite the lapsing time, cases related to false accusations involving actions committed before 1989 (i.e. before Poland's systemic transition) have been lodged with courts of all instances. One example is a case recently adjudicated by the Supreme Court where a woman was defamed on a website and in local online television. It was claimed that she was allegedly a member of the Civic Council of National Salvation (a pro-regime body) during the martial law. She was presented as a 'comrade' and a person supporting General Jaruzelski. As it turned out (e.g. on the basis of the letters sent by social activists in her defence), she had never been a member of the Polish United Workers' Party or the Civic Council of National Salvation. On the contrary, she was an oppositionist and a Solidarity activist. Most probably, the woman was defamed because some of her personal data were similar to the data of another person for whom such accusations could be relevant. The claimant won her case in all instances. The court ordered a compensation and payments to a publicly beneficial cause and, moreover, ruled that an appropriate apology and a correction must be published by the defendant at their own expense.[50]

Cases have been also brought by private individuals against various institutions with legal personality (8 cases posted on the portal) such as banks or associations. Other cases (6) were lodged by private individuals against editorial officers, bloggers or website administrators. Sometimes (3 cases) legal persons were involved on both sides: a foundation against an association, two publishing houses, or a company against a municipality.

50 Judgment of the Supreme Court of 10 November 2016, IV CSK 42/16.

And, finally, when we analyse civil lawsuit in defence of personality rights, we will find a group of cases which are similar in their nature to those lodged with criminal courts in the private complaints procedure (24 cases). Those cases were related to protracted conflicts between neighbours or family members, conflicts between former spouses or between former and current partners, where the violation of honour and reputation was just one of many elements in a conflict between the parties. Overall, a half of those cases (12) resulted from conflicts involving claimant's relatives or partners. Three cases resulted from protracted conflicts between neighbours. It is worth pointing out that one of them was heard by both a criminal court which ruled on a punishment, and a civil court which obliged the defendant to apologise and pay compensation. Cases related to work (disputes between co-workers or business partners) were more common (9 in total) than disputes between neighbours. In one case, a former business partner mailed letters to clients in order to discourage them from using the services of his former business partner. The letters contained false information and the court ruled, among others, that the sender should circulate letters of apology, taking back the false accusations.

Only one case among those heard by the Civil Chamber of the Supreme Court was similar to those lodged with criminal courts in the private complaint procedure. The case involved family members and the evidence consisted of a recording made in the claimant's absence. He recorded the defendant's utterances with a voice recorder left in the room. She was speaking about the claimant in an offensive way, using insulting words and, among others, she said he was 'a bastard, a Lemko, and those are the worst scumbags, they would beat and torment Poles, a pimp.' This was the only case heard by the Civil Chamber of the Supreme Court that was similar to actions lodged as private complaints but also the only case involving a defence of personality rights which included an element of hatred on grounds of nationality.

Court files provide us with information on the types of accusations that are applied to defame other people and the types which are thought to be hurtful enough to make the affected person turn to court. Importantly, the cases available through the aforementioned portal are highly anonymised, which means that the charges and, in particular, the insulting words are erased in many cases. As a result, this online resource does not offer a full picture of the accusations found in court files (Fuszara 1988). However, a few types of accusations can be identified on the basis of the available data. One of them involves repeated accusations of poor performance in a public office as well as accusations of fraud and mismanagement committed by high officials, especially on a local scale. For instance, there might be accusations whereby people allegedly undersell municipal property or co-operative property, buy items for private use using their institution's money, a mayor allegedly does not collaborate with the local council, officials give permission to cut down trees, or engage in unfair financial settlements.

Another group of defamatory accusations relate to alleged crimes: paedophilia, membership in a criminal group, domestic violence combined with murder threats, contract falsification, blackmailing, extortion of money, destruction of a water meter, or illegal lobbying. A particular subgroup here involves accusations of denunciation. Sometimes those are 'false denunciations' (someone allegedly reported a fellow oppositionist to the communist authorities), whereas other people are accused of notifying the authorities of a crime or a violation of rules (whistleblowing). In one such case, the court analysed the degree of insult in such a denunciation. By referring to the historical context, the court stated that while '*many people do not view the person reporting to the authorities as a model citizen,*' however, in the case of citizens' denunciations or whistleblowing '*it seems that currently (...) the prevailing view is that such a notification is a moral duty towards the country and the public order.*'

Other accusations refer to the absence of the required competences when being hired, lack of competences to perform a job (a catechist) or to run a business (a private detective).

In three cases the phrase 'mentally ill' was used. The statement of claim in one such case reads that such a phrase '*is discrediting not only for the claimant but also for people who are actually ill (...) and they are entitled to the same social activity as people who are healthy.*'

Moreover, in individual cases the claimants brought an action since they felt insulted by references to an extramarital affair, alcohol addiction, homosexuality, work for the communist secret services or delaying the repayment of a debt.

As I wrote earlier, when queried with the word 'honour' (Polish '*honor*'), the website with court decisions issued by civil departments of common courts returns cases which were lodged in defence of reputation as well as other cases where someone referred to 'honour'. Those cases turned out to be interesting because, as Maria Ossowska suggested, they allow us to analyse 'honour' in a specific context and they indicate who is currently viewed as 'honourable' and who is not honourable, and how honour has been lost. As Maria Ossowska wrote, 'We should not ask what dignity is or what honour is. Instead, we may ask what it means when someone behaved in a dignified way or when the honour took the better of him' (Ossowska, 1970, p. 61). Therefore, on the margins of this discussion, it is interesting to take a look at the contexts where people referred to 'honour' in court also in defence of rights other than reputation.[51]

It turns out that the phrase '*unieść się honorem*' ('to behave honourably' or 'the honour took the better of him') is found quite commonly in such cases. This phrase appears often in cases brought by parents who want to amend the deed of gift which they signed with their children in exchange of care and lifelong benefits. The children who had received the gift did not fulfil their obligation to provide for their parents and the parents '*behaved so honourably that they did not stand up and demand the benefits*' or did not demand them '*as the honour took the better of them*'. Also, a son-in-law '*did the honourable thing*' when the father-in-law told him to '*get out of the house*'. Likewise, the partner of a woman who demanded financial settlement and repayment of money behaved in the same way. Such phrases were also used in a dispute between two housing associations where a major association installed entry gates into a shared road and the members of the smaller association refused to accept the gate-opening devices *in an incomprehensibly honourable behaviour, which boiled down to the statement, reiterated during the trials (...) that petty merchants were abused by a mighty capital owner.*' Therefore, when someone's honour/ambition takes the better of them, people will not demand the benefits they are entitled to, and they would also not succumb to other people's demands if considered unfounded. Notably, relatively many such cases were lodged by family members, relatives or partners. Apart from the examples mentioned earlier (parents wanting to annul a deed of gift), there was another case where a mother claimed that some of her children '*had no honour or ambition and lied in court that I, their mother, had falsified the will.*' In another one, a father would repay debts '*to save the honour of the family*' and caused the objects stolen by his son to be returned (also within the same family). Those examples indicate that 'honour' prevents people from demanding benefits from family members as long as they can survive without such benefits. Honour also obligates people to conceal negative behaviours or even crimes committed by family members and obliges people to break off contacts in the case of serious charges (a son-in-law moving out, a partner). Reactions to a violation of personality rights are close to Maria Ossowska's understanding of 'defence of one's dignity'. When someone 'takes the honourable way', they do not derive a financial benefit from it but, on the contrary, often suffer a financial

51 The following analysis does not include other uses of the word 'honour' in phrases such as 'honorary member' or names of decorations containing the word 'honour' since they do not add any additional understanding to the notion of 'honourable behaviour' or being 'a man of honour', both of which are the focus of this analysis.

loss in the name of more important values such as cohesion and unity of the family. Maria Ossowska identifies two types of virtues which she describes as a follow-up to Hobbes and Dupreel, i.e. a distinction between citizen virtues, which lead to peaceful co-existence, and personal virtues, held by people per se, and important for those who have them. She also invokes Fromm's statement from his 'Escape from Freedom', where he wrote that there is a tension between the striving to achieve smooth coexistence and to develop one's personality in full. Such peaceful coexistence is particularly important among the closest family, which is why lawsuits against family members are not brought to courts easily. Another reason may lie in the fact that an accusation against family members may be perceived as an attack on dignity ('these are my children, I raised them, they misbehaved, they did not fulfil their obligations'). Therefore, the borderline between self-defence and the defence of family members violating some rules may be vague. In order for people to take a case to court, the norms of intra-group loyalty among family members must be violated in a flagrant way.

An informal promise or giving one's word, '*a word of honour*' was another context where honour was mentioned repeatedly. Witnesses say they are not sure if the agreement was made in writing or if the parties gave their 'word of honour'. The parties claim that the other person gave their word they would not build anything on the land plot, etc. While this argument is taken into consideration to some extent when the court assesses the testimonies of parties and witnesses, it cannot provide grounds for any further claims, such as liquidated damages. Thus, trusting a business partner and taking their 'word of honour' may sometimes be risky.

Another context which uses 'honour' relates to the phrase '*ujma na honorze*' ('tarnished honour'). Slander and defamation are directly described as 'tarnishing person's honour'. In other similar cases we can guess from the context that this phrase describes the feelings of people who take the matter to court.

On the negative side, the word 'honour' is also mentioned in insulting phrases such as 'a man without honour'. On the other hand, when someone says they 'have their honour', this entitles them to claim their rights and defend their arguments, also before court. As one claimant said in a case brought against a municipality: '*I have my own honour, which I put before money*'.

Honour is also mentioned in the context of social roles: in court decisions, it was invoked with reference to a profession, the management of a club or a university student. In one case it was argued that the defendant (an architect) took on a job but did not have the right staff and, by doing this, he did not '*protect the honour of the profession*'. Moreover, honour is referred to in the excerpts of codes of ethics quoted in pleadings, for instance '*an attitude of personal dignity should be connected with care about the honour of the team*' (a footballer's code of ethics). In the words of oaths students commit themselves to '*treating teachers and the university authorities with respect, taking care of the honour and dignity of the student*'. In such cases 'honour' resembles a catalogue of virtues which must be demonstrated by a member of a group. Whenever this is violated, people can be accused of betraying the group's values and might be excluded from the group as a result.

The vast majority of civil cases in defence of personality rights are brought by private individuals against other private individuals. However, those matters are highly varied: some are brought by public officials whose position is undermined by publications that challenge their reputation, professional and moral qualifications, through defamatory letters and rumours. In many a case, defamation and slander are used in political fights and the defamed people take the matter to court as a way to defend themselves. Similarly, an attack on personality rights and lawsuits brought in defence are sometimes used in business conflicts. For instance, competitors may be slandered or accused of unfair competition and the affected parties defend themselves by resorting to court procedures.

Cases from another category are brought by private individuals against government institutions. Many of them (e.g. those brought against courts and prosecutors' offices) indicate that claimants do not understand the respective legal regulations or the application of law. On the other hand, other cases (e.g. against defamatory publications of the Institute of National Remembrance or slanders in official reports) are the only way for individuals to defend themselves when their rights have been violated.

Notably, there is a high share of cases related to someone's reputation tarnished in the mass media. Much like in the past, those cases often arise from press publications or TV broadcasts. However, with the rise of the Internet as a common medium of communication, it has also become a place where reputation may be tarnished. Removing the consequences of a violation is particularly difficult because the same message could be disseminated via different websites. While cases concerning the dissemination of an erroneous or defamatory message via other means (e.g. in a book) are easier to resolve by ordering that the relevant excerpts are removed from the publication, obliging the perpetrator to remove defamation from the Internet does not have the same effect. Even if the perpetrator is obliged to remove the message, this does not mean that the message will disappear from other websites, blogs, or other people's posts. In one case heard by the Supreme

Court,[52] someone posted a recording featuring a woman reporting a crime. The conversation was copied by various websites and the woman (the claimant) became an object of mockery and ridicule. It is easy to tell that even if the court rules that an apology must be issued and the recording must be removed from one website, this will not prevent further violation of the claimant's rights, which a successful court case should prevent.

Courts ruling in private complaints procedure, and participants in such proceedings, also grapple with similar problems, as discussed further in this publication.

52 Judgment of 14 January 2015, Case no. II CSK 747/13.

Małgorzata Fuszara

Chapter V. Private prosecution

In Polish law private prosecution, in contrast to public prosecution, has several defining characteristics. The key difference is a person who brings the charges. Instead of a public prosecutor, the case is brought to court by a victim. The public prosecutor is authorized to do so only in a very limited number of situations.[53] Thus, first of all, there is no "theft of conflict" by the state (Christie 1977), and a victim is not marginalized. Indeed, a victim remains in control of a case throughout the entire court procedure. Secondly, the objective of the proceedings is to solve a conflict between the parties. A counter-claim can be lodged, because matters typically pursued in this procedure tend to involve mutual violations of rights by the parties involved; the two cases are then investigated jointly. The court is under obligation to try to bring the parties to reconcile, and settlement remains an option throughout the trial. The court must either open the proceedings by holding a conciliatory session[54] where parties are encouraged to reconcile[55] or refer a case for mediation, where a mediator is charged with the same task: helping the parties settle the case. If a settlement is reached, the case is discontinued.[56] Further evidence of this objective of private prosecution is that the settlement reached by the parties can include elements of the conflict between the parties which were not listed in the charge sheet.[57] The private prosecutor can also withdraw the case (unilaterally until the trial begins, and with the defendant's consent at the later stages).[58] The court will only enter a ruling if the case is not withdrawn and the parties fail to reach an agreement (a settlement).

53 Article 59 § 1 of the Code of Criminal Procedure reads: "The victim may, acting as a private prosecutor, bring and support charges relating to crimes that can be privately prosecuted." Article 60 authorizes the prosecutor to lodge proceedings in such cases "if social interest so requires."

54 Article 489 § 1: "The main hearing is preceded by a conciliatory session presided over by the judge."

55 Article 490 § 1: "Conciliatory proceedings begin by asking the parties to reconcile."

56 Article 492: "If the parties reconcile proceedings are discontinued."

57 Article 494 § 1: "When reconciling, the parties may make a settlement that can also pertain to claims related to the charges."

58 Article 496 § 1: "Private prosecution cases are discontinued with the consent of the defendant if the private prosecutor withdraws the case before the proceedings end in a

This old procedure, deeply rooted in tradition, used to be very popular. Charges used to be brought by private prosecutors very often, and cases lodged in this manner constituted a large proportion of criminal cases entering the court system overall. At present, these cases are quite rare. Since the late 1980s, i.e. the political transformation of Poland, there has been an uninterrupted decline in the proportion of private prosecutions in the totality of criminal cases.

Table 1. Proportion of privately prosecuted cases in the totality of criminal cases

Year	Proportion of privately prosecuted cases	Year	Proportion of privately prosecuted cases	Year	Proportion of privately prosecuted cases
1955	35.4	1976	25.3	1997	8.8
1956	38.7	1977	24.5	1998	8.1
1957	40.5	1978	22.1	1999	6.9
1958	31.4	1979	21.3	2000	6.7
1959	26.8	1980	21.3	2001	4.2
1960	22.8	1981	25.8	2002	4.0
1961	26.3	1982	34.8	2003	3.5
1962	24.9	1983	23.7	2004	3.4
1963	25.2	1984	22.2	2005	3.1
1964	26.3	1985	15.9	2006	3.2
1965	28.2	1986	14.4	2007	3.1
1966	27.6	1987	16.1	2008	3.2
1967	27.5	1988	20.5	2009	3.6
1968	26.4	1989	23.8	2010	3.6
1969	28.0	1990	20.6	2011	3.7
1970	22.2	1991	14.9	2012	3.8
1971	21.6	1992	12.9	2013	3.8
1972	27.6	1993	10.7	2014	4.2
1973	26.8	1994	9.7	2015	4.0
1974	26.6	1995	8.4	2016	4.5
1975	26.6	1996	8.7		

Source : Statistical yearbooks published by the Polish Central Statistical Office (GUS)

final and binding manner." Article 496 § 2: "The consent of the defendant is not required if the private prosecutor withdraws the case before the trial begins at the main hearing."

Due to the number of cases it is impossible to say what types of issues are brought to court and solutions to what types of conflicts are sought there. I first attempted to address these questions in a period when private prosecutions were relatively popular and constituted approximately a quarter of all criminal cases (Fuszara 1989). I conducted research focusing on three districts, each selected for a specific reason. The first was the region of Lesko, selected because it had the highest proportion (country-wide) of private prosecutions per capita. Generally, this proportion tended to be high in rural regions, but it varied across the regions. This is why the next district I chose was Kępno. Among the rural districts, it had the lowest proportion of private prosecutions per capita. The final location selected for the study was metropolitan: I chose Warsaw's district named Praga (hereinafter: Warszawa Praga). In urban districts, the proportion of private prosecutions per capita was low and quite uniform country-wide.

The first stage of the study consisted of a review of all private prosecutions lodged with the relevant three courts in 1975. This produced 141 cases lodged in the court in Lesko, 88 in Kępno, and 150 in Warszawa Praga. In total, I reviewed 379 private prosecution cases. The review served as a basis for developing a questionnaire to interview parties to conflicts. The interviews were held in August and September 1977. The number of completed interviews with parties to privately prosecuted cases was 136 in Lesko region, 79 in Kępno region, and 157 in Warszawa Praga. In total, this produced 372 in-depth interviews with parties to conflicts which generated court cases lodged by private prosecutors.

The key findings of that study provided a foundation for analyses undertaken in subsequent years, and served as a point of reference for comparisons between the types of conflicts, solutions to conflicts, and the role of the courts therein in that period and now.

On the basis of the results of the study, conflicts were conceptually divided into simple and complex, because between these two categories the context (and thus the development and outcome) was very different. I considered conflicts to be "simple conflicts" if the charge sheet covered the entirety of the conflict between the parties: there were no prior conflicts between the same parties and also relatives, partners, etc. of the parties were not in conflict with one another. Simple conflicts were a source of less than a half of all the conflicts, but nonetheless they accounted for a significant proportion of private prosecutions: 41% in the region of Lesko, 38% in the region of Kępno, and 33% in Warszawa Praga. The majority of conflicts were "complex conflicts", i.e. situations where there had been prior conflicts (even if minor) between the parties and/or where one of the parties was also in conflict with the relatives, partners, etc. of the other party. In complex conflicts, the type of ties (relations) between the parties was the defining characteristic. The following categories of complex conflicts could be distinguished: between strangers; between acquaintances (people who know each other from work, live in the same town, etc.), between neighbours, and between family members (including former in-laws). One of the conclusions was: "The closer the ties between the parties, the higher the proportion of cases prompted by complex conflicts" (p. 133). Quite naturally, all cases involving strangers resulted from simple conflicts, as did many of the conflicts between acquaintances. Cases involving neighbours generally tended to arise out of complex conflicts. As for cases involving family members, in the region of Lesko each and every one of them was based on a complex conflict, with a great majority of them arising out of complex conflicts also in the region of Kępno (73%) and in Warszawa Praga (83%).

Another noteworthy issue is the values that are defended by means of private prosecution. What is interesting that a value-driven approach is often demonstrated not only by a private prosecutor (which is only natural), but also by a defendant who – acting against the law – is nonetheless, in his or her opinion, defending values that he or she finds important and precious. Sometimes this occurs when lawful measures have proved ineffective. In other cases, either the court is not considered the proper venue for finding resolution to a conflict, or values are not suitable for defence by institutional means. Regardless of the reasons, the defendants often feel that they have been right in taking the actions contemplated in the court case, because of the sense that they must stand in defence of a value they hold dear.

Private prosecutors typically brought cases to court in defence of values named in specific legal regulations: their good name, reputation, bodily integrity. These value are of course fully in line with the objectives stated in the legal regulations. In more complex situations, the private prosecutors (as revealed by the interviews) acted in pursuit of more general goals, such as ensuring a peaceful coexistence (e.g. with neighbours, family members, at work, etc.) These cases were characterized by multiple, repeated violations and the expectation on the part of the private prosecutors was that these violations should cease. Why there was no peaceful coexistence, how the peace was disrupted, what somebody said, etc. was often secondary and varied over time in these conflicts. The key issue was the repeated, continuing nature of the violations and the private prosecutors' desire for them to cease. Thus, the expectations extended beyond the specific event that resulted in bringing the case to court.

Sometimes, the values mentioned by the parties are not at all included in the legal system. For instance, one of these values is the right to have or retain a partner. While insults or physical attacks provide the formal grounds for filing a case, in fact private prosecutors are trying to achieve another objective: either win back a partner or get rid of a rival for their attention. Cases like this were most typically lodged by women who were willing to settle if their husband/partner agreed to return, to renounce another relationship, or to guarantee them exclusivity. The actions listed in the charge sheet, while specified in a factually correct manner, in reality serve as an excuse. Hence, focusing on them in court is unlikely to actually solve the conflict; yet it may "tame" the conflict and prevent further crimes. The ideal outcomes expected by the private prosecutors in these cases are practically impossible to achieve by means of the court system.

This is also the case with some property-related goals sometimes pursued by private prosecutors: for instance, if a request is made in a criminal court that the court should punish a debtor who is in default on a loan. There are also prolonged conflicts stemming from unsolved succession and inheritance matters as well as real-estate problems where the actions listed in the charge sheet serve only to provide a springboard for filing a case (which is often yet another case) against the opponents involved in these far-ranging conflicts.

The defendants often act out of similar motivations, with the difference that they use unlawful measures in doing so. Again, one of the values involved is the right to have or retain a partner. Respondents said in the interviews that in their opinion, this right justifies all sorts of actions, including unlawful ones, and serves as a *sui generis* defence to claims of illegality. These respondents were convinced that the court should side with them because they were right – because they had been betrayed, cheated on, left, abandoned. Based on the interviews, I wrote: "It is likely that these persons perceive the court as an institution of justice not in the sense of application of laws, but rather in the sense of determining what is just and fair, and proposing outcomes in line with >what someone is owed<". (Fuszara 1989, p. 169). Even if these persons admit to having insulted, offended, attacked the victims, etc., they believed that their actions were justified because they were in the right. These violations often targeted not just the cheating/abandoning former partner but also that partner's new partner. I was struck by how often the cheating/abandoning partner was objectified, i.e. perceived as a thing that is stolen and can be recovered, rather than a person who makes their own choices. This interpretation comes to the fore particularly in the cases where the focus in on a divorced spouse.

Yet another value also cited by defendants is peaceful and quiet neighbourly coexistence. The defendants argued that they had been harassed and attacked by the private prosecutors, or that both parties had been guilty of such conduct to the same extent, but – in contrast to the private prosecutor – they decided for whatever reason not to press charges. Somewhat similar arguments were made in cases where in a fight the defendants acted in defence of other persons. While the defendants admitted that they had participated in the fight, they argued that their intention was to "calm down", separate the parties, etc.

Some defendants were convinced that they acted in a just cause, in public interest, and that their criticism was justified – but the private prosecutors misinterpreted it as defamation. In all these cases, an analysis was necessary as to whether indeed the words spoken by the defendant constituted justifiable criticism, or whether they amounted to defamation.

Values related to property are also noteworthy here. In certain cases, the defendants resorted to "self-help", i.e. acting outside of the law in situations where they had a very clear and well-founded claim to certain property. For instance, a defendant used unlawful means to obtain payment for work he had done, and another tried to recover money he had loaned. Unlawful measures were also used by defendants trying to avoid eviction and to gain possession of a part of inheritance they believed should rightfully be theirs.

Several cases contemplated in the study were brought against defendants who had resorted to violence to defend values they found important, because they saw no other options of defending these values. These included parents of children bullied by older kids and a mother of a child harassed by a neighbour for being born out of wedlock. The parents used violence against the tormentors of their children and were fully aware that they would have to face the consequences of their actions. However, the response of the relevant institutions had been, in their opinion, insufficient, or had actually proved ineffective, and thus they found it necessary to resort to "self-help" to protect their children. These situation demonstrate the helplessness of institutions in the face of certain social problems.

After 25 years, I once again decided to study private prosecutions. This time, I focused on just one court district in the region of Bieszczady mountains. Privately prosecuted cases only accounted for less than 10% of cases at that time (down from 25%). Due to the low number of cases, I took a 2-year period under review, namely 2000–2001. This produced a total of 62 cases. Interviews with parties were also conducted, although this proved to be a difficult task. Some of the people I contacted declined to talk, and social mobility was also a factor: many persons had left (for locations in the country and abroad) and it was impossible to arrange an interview.

An analysis revealed that the change that took place over the 25-year period consisted in more than just the decline in the number of private prosecutions.

Another aspect of the change was the disappearance of certain types of cases from the courts. Cases between strangers virtually disappeared. Simple conflicts were at the root of hardly any of the cases lodged. People resorted to courts only with regard to complex conflicts, and typically where the relations between the parties were quite close. Just like in the 1970s, in the early 2000s the most heavily represented conflicts were between neighbours (in 1975–41%, in 2000–2001 – 36%), acquaintances (over 30% in both periods), while the proportion of cases involving family members increased a little (in 1975–16%, in 2000–2001 – 22%). The interviews regarding the 2000–2001 cases demonstrated that family members were involved in even a greater proportion of the cases than revealed by the court files. For instance, there were conflicts where the defendant was the private prosecutor's mother's brother, or the brother-in-law of a brother-in-law, or the son-in-law, etc. – all situations where the family relation is not immediately clear.

Two observations are particularly important as a result of the comparison of situations divided by the span of 25 years. Firstly, there is a striking similarity of some of the 1970s and 2000s cases. The cases where the defendant believed to be expressing justified criticism and the private prosecutor found the words defamatory serve as a good example. The difference is often in the means of dissemination of the words in question. In the 1970s, it was the local press, a local meeting, or simply gossip. In the 2000s, the words were often published online – it is almost a rule now that offending content is distributed via the Internet. Another difference is in the persons who are targeted by these forms of speech. In the 1970s, due to the limited civil rights, criticism towards politicians and officials was rare. A quarter of century later, it was widespread, both locally and nationally.

Secondly, some conflicts continued despite the lapse of time. A quick look into the files revealed that some conflicts between the same families (usually neighbours) that generated court cases in 1975 continued to produce them all these years later. Back in the 1970s, I posited that conflicts with neighbours are handed down through generations. One respondent explicitly said that she had seen the conflict play out among her parents and her parents' neighbours and now that her generation is involved, their children and grandchildren are witnessing the same conflict still taking place. The events that provide a springboard for the court case have changed, and the conflict is transformed, but not extinguished. Both the dispute itself and the mode of conduct is inherited by the next generation.

An important part of the study consisted in a review of the outcomes of privately prosecuted cases, and the effectiveness of the procedure in putting an end to a conflict. I will discuss this topic further herein, together with a review of contemporary outcomes of such cases.

A. Private prosecution today

I carried out the study of private-prosecution criminal cases in 4 selected district courts. In Płock, where these cases were quite numerous, 80 case files were reviewed, pertaining to the cases lodged in the two criminal divisions of the local district court in 2014. In the remaining three locations, where private prosecutions were much less numerous, the review covered cases from a period of three years: 2013, 2014, and 2015. In Węgrów, the total number of cases under review was 77, in Olesno – 13, and in the district court for the region of Bieszczady (the district court in Lesko and its branch in Ustrzyki Dolne) – 46.[59] In total, the review encompassed 216 private prosecution cases. In their great majority, the cases focused – either exclusively or to a certain extent – on violations of the right to good name (reputation) and honour. I will therefore start with these cases.

Cases brought in defence of honour and good name (reputation)

The largest proportion of crimes that are privately prosecuted[60] are crimes that infringe the right to honour and good name (reputation). The first crime of this kind consists in allegations of conduct or characteristics that can humiliate a person or jeopardize the trust of others towards them.[61] In its aggravated from, this crime is committed by means of mass media.[62] Cases like this leave a lot of room for interpretation in court. Firstly, on each occasion a court must determine

59 When the study that is referenced here was conducted in the late 1970s, the territorial jurisdiction of the district court in Lesko extended throughout the entire Bieszczady region (Fuszara 1989). In the early 2000s, the area was divided between the territorial jurisdiction of the district court in Lesko and the municipal court in Ustrzyki Dolne (Fuszara 2004). At present, the area falls under the territorial jurisdiction of the district court in Lesko and its branch in Ustrzyki Dolne, and the branch office handles a part of the private prosecution cases.

60 Private prosecution is only possible where the Criminal Code allows it specifically. This is true with regard to the following crimes: defamation (*pomówienie*); insult; infringement of bodily integrity; minor bodily harm.

61 Article 212 of the Polish Criminal Code reads: "§ 1. Whoever defames another person, group of persons, institution, legal person or organizational unit without legal personality by alleging that they engaged in conduct or that they have characteristics that may humiliate them publicly or may put them at risk of losing trust necessary at a given position, profession, or type of operation, is punishable by a fine or the penalty of limitation of freedom.

62 Article 212 of the Polish Criminal Code further reads: "§ 2. If the perpetrator commits the acts specified in § 1 above by means of the mass media, he is punishable by a fine,

whether the allegations actually posed the risk of such humiliation or jeopardized the potential trust. Secondly, in some cases allegations are not criminal. This is applicable either when the allegation was not made in public and it was true, or when it was made in public but is true and either concerns a person holding a public office or is justified by reasons of social interest.[63] Other crimes of this kind is insult (*zniewaga*)[64], and yet another – infringement of bodily integrity (*naruszenie nietykalności cielesnej*)[65]. With regard to the latter, court may refrain from punishing the perpetrator if the action was triggered by the conduct of the other party or if the other party responded in kind.

Infringement of bodily integrity, along with the crimes of insult and defamation, is placed in the chapter of the Criminal Code that deals with offenses against honour and personal inviolability, because the legislator assumed that actions constituting these crimes are generally symbolic in nature and designed to humiliate rather than be physically hurtful. I am now going to present an overview of various types of attacks against the good name (reputation) and honour that result in cases being brought to court.

Overall, the insult and defamation cases were present in the greatest proportion (just like in the past, see: Fuszara 1989, Kurczewski, Fuszara 2004) in the rural regions. In Węgrów there were 60 (78%), in Bieszczady 36 (78%), and in Olesno 12 (92%). In the urban environment of Płock there were 52 such cases (65%), a relatively low proportion. There is a certain similarity between the conflicts that led to the court cases, but region-specific characteristics are also observable. In

---

the penalty of limitation of freedom, or the penalty of deprivation of freedom for up to one year."

63 Article 213 of the Polish Criminal Code reads: "§ 1. The crime specified in Article 212 § 1 is not committed if the allegation, made otherwise than in public, is true."
§ 2. The crime specified in Article 212 § 1 or 2 is not committed if a person in public raises or disseminates a true allegation: 1) about the conduct of a person holding a public office, or 2) made in the service of a socially justified interest.

64 Article 216 of the Polish Criminal Code reads: "§ 1. Whoever insults another person in that person's presence or not in that persons presence, but in public or with the intention that the insult should reach that person, is punishable by a fine or the penalty of limitation of freedom.
§ 2. Whoever insults a person by means of the mass media, is punishable by a fine, the penalty of limitation of freedom, or the penalty of deprivation of freedom for up to one year."

65 Article 217 of the Polish Criminal Code reads: "§ 1. Whoever hits a person or otherwise disrupts that person's bodily integrity, is punishable by a fine, the penalty of limitation of freedom, or the penalty of deprivation of freedom for up to one year."

Lesko, which had a record-breaking number of such cases in the 1970s, followed by a sudden drop (Fuszara 2004), the number remains low enough to rank the region far behind the top of the table. The types of conflicts are the same in each region, but their proportions vary. Alleged defamation perpetrated online provides a good example of these differences. The greatest proportion of such cases was found in Bieszczady, which is somewhat surprising in such a rural area. There were 11 such cases, i.e. 31% of all the cases concerning alleged defamation. In the much more urban, industrial region of Płock, which also has one of the oldest secondary schools and a tertiary education institution, there were 9 cases amounting to 17% of all the cases of alleged defamation. In Olesno, there was one case of this type (8%). In the rural region of Węgrów no such cases were recorded in the period under review. These cases varied in content. There were allegations of defamation brought by local politicians and other public persons featured in critical or insulting texts published in online editions of newspapers, blogs, etc. Charges were also filed by private persons defamed online. Finally, there were cases brought by persons who suffered identity theft regarding their online accounts on Facebook and other similar social media sites.

As for the relations between the parties to cases involving alleged infringement of reputation, it appears likely that the differences in Internet use are connected with different relations between private prosecutors and defendants in each region. In Węgrów, the most frequently recorded conflicts were between persons with close ties: family members, former family members, and current and former partners (27 cases out of 60, 45%). In the region of Olesno they constituted 38% (5 cases out of 12), in Płock 29% (15 out of 52), and in Bieszczady only 22% (8)[66] of the total number of insult and defamation cases. Family conflicts very rarely spread onto the Internet. They tend to be complex and multi-layered, and often generate many competing court cases where charges are met with charges against those who have filed originally. Sometimes the conflicts involve extended families, or former romantic partners, former in-laws, or former and current

66 It is possible that the differences in relations between the parties (where the comparison is made between the Bieszczady region and the remaining two regions) were impacted by the fact that the court files proved least informative in this respect there. In Węgrów, this proved impossible to determine in 5 cases (9%), in Płock – only in 2 cases (4%), and in Bieszczady in 9 cases (25%). Some of these cases may have involved extended family members, which sometimes is only revealed in interviews (Fuszara 2004). This has no bearing on the fact that in Bieszczady there was no record of a single extensive family conflict which would give rise to several court cases, and in other regions such conflicts were recorded.

romantic partners, i.e. in relationships where the intensity of conflict had already led to divorce or separation, but where these events did not put an end to the conflict. Often both court cases and mediation attempts have already taken place. The act which triggered the private prosecution is typically only one facet of the conflict, alongside fights, invectives, allegations, actual violence, and numerous disputes involving the court system. Parties take legal action against one another and then, as they meet in the courtroom and interact in the corridors etc., they commit new violations that serve as the basis for new accusations. There was no case in the reviewed material where the conflict was simple and could be presented in full in the documentation of the case. Moreover, family secrets are often revealed in the courtroom. Issues that were private become public knowledge, and this irretrievably changes the relations within the family. The parties are often at odds regarding money (e.g. inheritance, land boundaries), personal relations (e.g. affairs, including affairs with other family members), abuse and violence (within a marriage, towards parents, in-laws, etc.) any many other issues of varying importance. It is hardly realistic to expect that a court can satisfactorily resolve a conflict of such complexity. At best, the level of aggression between the parties can be reduced.

In many ways, conflicts between neighbours resemble those between family members as far as insult and defamation issues are concerned. They were most heavily represented in the rural regions: in Węgrów they accounted for 29% of cases, in Bieszczady and Olesno – 16%, and in Płock only 10%. In the past, conflict between neighbours used to differ very clearly between rural and urban areas, which mirrored in an apparently evident manner the nature of the neighbourhoods. In the urban areas, there were noise and cleanliness conflicts, and other conflicts arising out of living in flats in the same building. In rural areas, there were boundary disputes, animal trespassing issues, etc. (Fuszara 1989). While these types of conflicts were, of course, "ideal types" to an extent, the relationship between conflict type and area type has almost completely disappeared. Noise and disorder issues are now raised in rural areas to, although they tend to arise between persons sharing one house. The similarity to family conflicts lies in the complexity, long duration, and multi-layered nature. Moreover, the infringements are often mutual and lead to multiple court cases. Consequently, there are the same difficulties in expecting the court to put an end to such a dispute.

In previous studies (Fuszara 1989, Fuszara 2004), the most frequent types of conflicts were those between acquaintances. Now, the proportion of such cases was relatively high in Płock (31%) and Olesno (33%), somewhat lower in Węgrów

(22%), and low in Bieszczady (8%). The category of acquaintances includes residents of the same town or village, persons encountered at work or school, or those met at social functions.

Even in the early 2000s, there were hardly any cases between strangers. On the occasion of the latest study, no such cases were noted in Lesko, with one in Płock, one in Węgrów, and one in Olesno. While almost extinct as a type, these cases are virtually identical to those heard by the courts decades ago. They are filed as a deterrent by persons who were insulted by strangers in the course of their daily work as a bus driver, sales assistant, etc.

The category of acquaintances would grow considerably if we included in it another group which was practically absent from the studies carried out in the past: cases filed by politicians, or more broadly speaking persons holding some type of office or position of authority, and criticized on account of how they are exercising the power arising from that office and/or position. There were regional differences in this category too. Interestingly, no cases of this type were recorded in Węgrów and Olesno. In the other two regions (and in particular in Bieszczady) there were instances of such cases filed with the courts. In Bieszczady, as many as 5 cases (14%) were filed by local politicians seeking protection of their reputation, and another 4 cases (11%) by other persons holding public office. In Płock 3 cases (5%) were lodged by politicians and another 10 (19%) by other persons holding public office. The category of "persons holding public office or in positions of authority" includes various persons defamed in relations to their position or function, such as police officers, municipal guards, a president of a foundation, a headmistress of a school, the manager of a community centre, the management of a housing cooperative, a president of a housing association. In Olesno, there was a case of this type where the private prosecutor was a trade union activist. These persons take the conflicts to court because attempts to tarnish their reputation generate problems for them in the context of professional work or public activity. The cases tend to be similar to one another, and they are often covered by local press. Politicians are accused of accepting bribes, financial mismanagement, dishonest hiring practices, wasting public funds, etc. – allegations that, if true, would indicate conduct that is sometimes criminal and sometimes just dishonest. Other persons holding public office are typically accused of abusing their power, fraud, and other misconduct. Such allegations are often disseminated online; cases of this type were particularly frequent in Bieszczady.

It is interesting to compare criminal cases filed in the private prosecution procedure in defence of honour and reputation in the past and now. Certain types of disputes have practically disappeared: those between strangers, and also those that are quite simple in nature ("simple conflicts"). "Simple conflicts" can be solved by court quite easily. Now, they are practically never taken to court. Either the parties find them to be too petty to be taken to the justice system (as the above-mentioned public opinion poll would suggest) or they are solved using other methods. The conflicts that make their way into the court system are difficult to solve, complex, and multifaceted. I argued before (Fuszara 1989) that it is easier to solve conflicts that are, using Vilhelm Aubert's (1983) distinction, conflicts of interest rather than conflicts of values (beliefs). Yet prolonged complex conflicts tend to contain elements of both: when a dispute about inheritance drags on for years, it breeds resentment, a sense of humiliation and slight, especially if there are differences in status between the parties. The previous research (Fuszara 1989) indicates that conflicts are easier to solve if the status of the parties is comparable. The most recent study is based solely on court files (not interviews) and thus renders it almost impossible to determine the status of the parties. The status difference is of course clear with regard to those in public office holders or persons in other positions of authority. It is however also observable in some family conflicts and conflict between neighbours, where differences in wealth, education, and professional position are sometimes evident.

A review of civil cases brought by claimants seeking protection of their right to honour and reputation and private-prosecution criminal cases with a similar objective reveals what attacks against one's honour (dignity) and reputation are considered severe enough to merit a court case in contemporary Poland. It is best to begin with a review of how attempts to tarnish reputation are made:

1. Words. The most typical and common form of insulting someone is the use of words generally considered offensive. The options are rather limited and generally imply that a person engages in sexual conduct that is unacceptable in a relevant social milieu. This typically includes the suggestion of promiscuity in women, certain types of sex (in particular oral sex), and the use of vulgar names for the male genitalia to insult men. This is nothing new. In fact, these terms can be found in Polish court files going hundreds of years back (Fuszara 1989). Two words seem to have been added to the repertoire in more recent years: *pedał*, *pedofil* (faggot, paedophile), often spoken together, which suggests that their meaning is not entirely clear to those who wield them. The terms are used solely in reference to men. This is a fairly significant change in that insults concerning sexual conduct were used in the past practically solely to offend women, while now men are insulted in this manner too. The two genders are now treated equally, in the sense that allegations of "wrong" sexual conduct are used to offend either of them. However, the specific terms used remain

gender-specific. The rise in the use of 'paedophile' as an insult is interesting. Paedophilia, which was a strong taboo in the past, is now widely talked about in the media. It is now applied to the everyday reality, and its derogatory connotations have probably caused its rising popularity as an insult.

Other commonly used insults refer to mental health ('idiot', 'crazy', 'mentally ill', etc.) and criminality ('thief'). All of these terms can be both insulting and defamatory, because they impute to the recipient certain conduct that is socially stigmatized. Other terms are purely insulting ('a pig', 'a brute', etc.). These words are very rarely spoken on their own. Instead, they are usually a part of a longer diatribe of insults, sometimes accompanied by physical violence. Thus, in many cases the claimants / private prosecutors claim the violation of their right to honour, reputation, physical inviolability and other rights.

2. Defamation. The long-standing philosophical division into personal virtues and civic virtues is useful in categorizing defamatory comments into those that impute personal shortcomings and those that refer to a person's conduct in society. The former include allegations of illness: mental illness (including an allegation that someone is undergoing psychiatric treatment), drug addiction, and alcoholism. Also similarity can be noticed with regard to allegations that pertain to a person's private affairs: extramarital relations, breaking up other people's marriages, promiscuity, prostitution, having children out of wedlock. These allegations are targeted exclusively at women. As for men, which I noted above, different allegations in the sexual context are made, e.g. denouncing somebody as homosexual, which in rural areas can be stigmatizing.

   Sometime, allegations of a darker type are raised against men (and men only). They are also related to sexuality, but in a criminal context. Allegations of sexual harassment are fairly common. On rare occasions, there are also mentions of having sexual relations with an underage person and even of rape, as well as domestic violence or other criminal conduct. Some of these allegations are made informally while others are verbalized in the courtroom or in official reports filed with the authorities. In the latter cases, it is easy to demonstrate that the report was made in the public interest rather than to harass the person named therein, and thus the private prosecutors tend to lose if they bring such cases to court.[67]

67 The Polish Supreme Court noted: "Even a violation of another person's legally protected personal rights as a result of disseminating certain information is not unlawful if the information is true and the person who disseminates it is acting out of justified private or public interest" (judgment of the Polish Supreme Court dated 5 March 2002, case no. I CKN 535/00).

There is also a separate group of cases where the claimants have been accused of having been an informant ('a snitch'). Some cases are clear-cut where the claimant was wrongly accused of 'snitching' on his colleagues during the martial law in Poland, generally being an informant for the communist regime, and other similar allegations which courts find to be insulting and defamatory. However, in other situations, notifying the authorities of suspected crimes (domestic violence, theft, disorderly behaviour) is referred to as 'informing on someone' and 'snitching'. The reports may be made to the public prosecutor's office, the police, the municipal guard, the town hall, etc.

Other allegations that the claimants found to be defamatory in nature and which have a community dimension rather than a private one are generally found in lawsuits brought by persons holding a public office or working in another similar capacity. These include allegations of misuse of public funds (of a commune, town, a foundation, etc.), fraud, wasting public money on unacceptable expenditures (e.g. teambuilding trips described as 'bunga bunga trips'), bribery and corruption, and nepotism.

3. Images. Giving offence by using images is primarily an Internet phenomenon. It consists in generating memes, transforming images and films (especially those with an intimate connection), or putting together collages that are offensive to those pictured in them. Interviews with judges suggest that these cases are often heard by youth and family courts, because they typically involve very young persons. There are also private-prosecution criminal cases like this, e.g. a case of a politician whose ties to the communist regime were suggested by publishing his image next to the image of Trybuna Ludu, a newspaper associated with the communist party. In another case, the claimant argued that somebody 'set my profile picture to a hippo to compare my face to that animal'.
4. Gestures. There are only a few mentions of offensive gestures in the court files under review. They include a suggestion of mental illness (in Poland, the gesture consist in knocking a finger against one's forehead) or in 'giving somebody the finger'.
5. Physical violence. Insulting physical acts have appeared in three forms. The most typical one was a slap in the face. Another was kicking somebody's backside. Yet another (typical in one of the regions in particular) was spitting, both at someone and under their feet, as accompaniment to invectives. Finally, in a few cases women took legal actions because they had been slapped on their buttocks, which they felt was insulting, even though the offenders appeared clearly 'amused' (according to the claimants). While such cases were not numerous, they deserve attention. In the past, these behaviours never led to legal

action. This may point to shifting social customs and indicate that women are putting much clearer boundaries and fighting against violations of their physical integrity they find unacceptable.

Bodily integrity protected in privately-prosecuted cases

The next group of private prosecutions are cases brought by persons who have suffered so-called "minor bodily harm".[68] These cases are now relatively less numerous because of recent changes in the law; if an assault took place against a close family member, the crime is prosecuted by the public prosecutor, either on this prosecutor's own initiative or following a relevant application of a victim. Under the legal regime in force during the previous studies, these matters required private prosecution. Even today, some mistakes occur and attempts are made to prosecute these matters privately. Typically, courts refer the charges to the public prosecutor's office.

Physical violence usually occurs together with verbal abuse, and constitutes just one element in a larger pattern of abuse in complex conflicts. This is why the cases in this category cannot be contemplated in complete separation from those discussed above in connection with infringements of the right to honour and reputation. However, it proved possible to isolate 55 cases in which bodily harm was either the sole charge or the main charge. The largest number of them was recorded in Węgrów (26–34%), followed by Płock (20–25%), Lesko (8–17%), and a distant last – Olesno (1–8%). There are two sub-categories here. The first is assault with only a flimsy excuse, often by a drunk perpetrator, for no reason at all, sometimes to the point of the perpetrator mistaking the victim for another person. The second is physical abuse in complex, on-going, long-term conflicts between neighbours or family members. Victims and perpetrators in these scenarios

---

68 Article 157 § 2 of the Polish Criminal Code reads: "Whoever causes impairment of functioning of a part of the body or disruption of health lasting no more than 7 days, is punishable by a fine, the penalty of limitation of freedom or deprivation of freedom for up to 2 years. § 3. If the perpetrator of the act specified in § 1 or 2 above acted unintentionally, he is punishable by a fine, the penalty of limitation of freedom, or the penalty of deprivation of freedom for up to one year. § 4. The crime specified in § 2 or 3 above, if the impairment of functioning of a part of the body or the disruption of health lasted no more than 7 days, is subject to private prosecution, unless the victim is a person with whom the perpetrator has a close relationship and who occupies the same residence as the perpetrator. § 5. If the victim is the person in a close relationship with the perpetrator, prosecution of the crime specified in § 3 above takes place following an application lodged by that person."

include divorcing spouses, feuding neighbours, and extended family members arguing about inheritance issues. Physical abuse takes the form of hitting, shaking, dragging, hair-pulling, attempts to suffocate, use of a stunt gun, hitting someone with a car (or with a moving piece of farm equipment), etc. Yet another category that could be placed somewhere in between the former two, is violence directed against noisy children of the perpetrator's neighbours. The conflicts in which this takes place are drawn out over time; these are not single incidents. Nonetheless, there is clearly an excessive tendency towards "taking matters into one's own hands" in these situations. Cases involving physical violence were recorded in all regions contemplated in the study. Most likely they reflect the general reality in which the skills necessary to solve conflict without resorting to violence are observed to be sorely lacking.

Resolutions in the private-prosecution criminal cases

Response to crime differs across time and takes a variety of forms. This is influenced by a number of factors that include the strength of the state as an actor responding to the violation of the norm but also the ideas popular at any given time with regard to guilt, objective of punishment, and effectiveness of measures that help reinstate social order. J. Braithwaite argues that Western culture has gone through the following stages of response to a violation of the norms:

1) A pre-state stage where restorative justice and banishment is dominant, 2) A weak state stage where corporal and capital punishment dominate, 3) A strong state stage where professional police and penitentiaries dominate, 4) A Keynesian welfare state stage where new therapeutic professions such as social work colonize what becomes probation-prison-parole, 5) A contemporarily evolving new regulatory state phase of community and corporate policing (with a revived restorative justice) (J. Braithwaite 2002, p. 7).

Since the 1970s, the concept of restorative justice has been gaining popularity both in criminology and in dispute resolution. J. Braithwaite posits the enormous importance of the subsequent shift from "regulatory activities having individuals and their bodies as their objects to a world where more of the wrongdoing is done by organizations that are regulated in a mostly restorative fashion" (*ibidem*, p. 8). There are two reasons behind this shift. Firstly, there is a belief that a victim must have an adequate role in the response to crime. Secondly, the social order which is disrupted by the crime must be restored by means of a process which will give the victim a sense of justice and the perpetrator an option to return to the society. Tony F. Marshall notes:

"Restorative Justice is a problem-solving approach to crime which involves the parties themselves, and the community generally, in an active relationship with statutory agencies.
It is not any particular practice, but a set of principles which may orientate the general practice of any agency or group in relation to crime. These principles are:

- making room for the personal involvement of those mainly concerned (particularly the offender and the victim, but also their families and communities)
- seeing crime problems in their social context
- a forward-looking (or preventative) problem-solving orientation
- flexibility of practice (creativity)" (T. F. Marshall 1999, p. 5).

This approach to crime has its roots in the practises of small, tightly knit communities, where the members come into direct contact with one another and the entire group develops a mode of response to the violations of group norms by group members. The procedure has a twofold aim: to give satisfaction and compensation to the victim, and to return the perpetrator back to the fold of the community, e.g. by having a celebration in order to put an end to the dispute (Kurczewski 1973, Kurczewski 1982, Braithwaite 2002). The original ideas behind traditional court proceedings, including private prosecution, were similar. The legal construct of the private prosecution procedure, where a settlement is encouraged, gives it a philosophical similarity to the concept of restorative justice. What makes them different is that the settlement is reached with the assistance of an institutionalized third party: either a judge acting as mediator, or simply a professional mediator (and not the community). Another difference is a range of possible outcomes. In the private prosecution procedure, a settlement is encouraged, but if it cannot be reached, a judgement is entered. The third party (i.e. a court) acts in a twofold capacity: firstly, to foster reconciliation, but secondly, to decide on crime and punishment. Which of these prerogatives predominates in practice? An answer can be glimpsed from the resolutions to private prosecution cases.

Table 2. Resolutions in private-prosecution criminal cases

Type of resolution	Number	Percentage
Settlement	46	21%
Fees not paid	61	28%
Private prosecutor's failure to appear in court	12	5%
Case withdrawn	19	9%
Conviction	21	10%

Type of resolution	Number	Percentage
Acquittal	8	4%
Judgment: case discontinued due to insignificant social harm	7	3%
Judgment: case conditionally discontinued for 1 or 2 years	10	5%
Other (statute of limitations has run out, no filing by an authorized prosecutor, inability to identify an IP address, etc.)	32	15%
Total	216	100%

As demonstrated by these numbers, only in 22% of cases did the courts actually enter a ruling, i.e. act as an institution that provides a resolution to the conflict. In the remaining cases, there was no need for a ruling: either there was no trial (failure to pay the required fees, failure to appear in court) or the parties reached a settlement. Overall in more than 40% of cases the court issued no decisions because the prosecutors failed to meet the formal requirements: pay the fees, amend the documents as directed, appear at a sitting (which is tantamount to dropping the charges). Most frequently – in more than half of the cases – this occurred in the rural region of Węgrów. While the number of cases filed with the court there was relatively high, many of them ended without an actual trial. Filing the case often marks the beginning of informal negotiations and a private, behind-the-scenes agreement or settlement, which is the reason why court proceedings are abandoned (Fuszara 1989). Case files suggest that particularly frequent informal settlements are the reason why charges are dropped; the file then contains a note to the effect that the reason for dropping the charges is an apology, reconciliation, or clarification of the case. In procedural terms, a case can be withdrawn unilaterally by the private prosecutor only until the trial begins. Later, the defendant's consent is necessary.

Formal settlements reached in the courtroom account for just above 1/5 of all the case resolutions, but that proportion is higher in the urban region (26%). In that region private prosecutions were also most often referred for mediation. Interestingly, no cases at all were referred to mediators in the region of Bieszczady. It is difficult to assess the effectiveness of mediation. Case files sometimes carry an annotation that parties are unwilling to undergo a mediation attempt because they had already settled via mediation but the dispute continues and the relations between parties have not improved. Thus, despite formally attempted mediation leading to a settlement, mediation was unsuccessful. Sometimes things work out the other way round too: despite reaching no formally mediated settlement, the case has an amicable resolution. In one case, the mediation attempt was declared unsuccessful, but the parties arrived at the trial with a draft of a settlement to be approved by the court. The mediation attempt was likely a contributing factor in reaching this outcome. These examples illustrate why it is difficult to assess the effectiveness of mediation in the longer perspective. Mediators can certainly serve to take some burden off the judges' shoulders, but they are not more effective than judges who attempt to mediate between the parties.

Court-based settlements are not a mere formality or a dry statement of the fact that the parties have reconciled. They are typically quite ceremonial, and the case files contain records of how the defendant apologised to the private prosecutor and asked that their apology be accepted, while the private prosecutors accepted the apology and withdrew their request that the defendant be punished. Sometimes there is also a note in the file stating that the defendant and the private prosecutor shook hands, which is a clear symbol of reconciliation. Where the alleged infringements of rights were mutual, the parties apologise to each other and promise to act better and build good neighbourly relations in the future. For example, in one settlement the defendant apologised and said "he will do his best to make sure that such incidents on his part do not happen in the future", and the private prosecutor formally forgave him. Occasionally, the notes reference less formal events of reconciliations, e.g. in one case a party said: "let's get back to how things were before", to which the other party replied: "let bygones be bygones", and they shook hands. These little ceremonies are very important socially. They are similar to the ceremonies that small communities hold as part of the restorative justice processes, where the emphasis is on making up for the infringement by apologising to the victim, revoking the charges, and the victim formally forgiving the perpetrator. On just a few occasions, and only in cases where physical violence was involved, the settlements are accompanied by an obligation to pay compensatory damages (*zadośćuczynienie*). Where the conflict is a conflict of interest, damages or compensation can be paid. In conflicts of values, the emphasis is on a formal apology, often offered publicly so that the persons who heard the offending allegations could now also be reached by the news of the apology.

Settlements, whether formal or informal, meet the parameters of restorative justice, and the rituals serve to further emphasise it. The guilty party must apologise, but this in itself does not suffice: the acceptance of the apology by the victim is necessary for the cycle to be complete.

Earlier research suggests that a settlement as a resolution to a court case is the most effective route towards actually putting an end to the conflict. Firstly, this is due to the fact that the parties themselves have worked out the conditions of the settlement and that one party apologized and the other accepted the apology. Secondly, a settlement is the only resolution that can be interpreted by both parties as a victory, or at least – as something other than a loss (Fuszara 1989).

Where cases proceed through a trial all the way to sentencing, the matter is very different. Unsurprisingly, there are very few of these cases in the rural region (Węgrów – 8%) where many cases were dropped. In the other regions decidedly more cases end with a ruling (Bieszczady – 24%, Płock – 27%). The largest proportion of cases that end with a ruling is in Olesno (54%), which suggests that in that region, cases are brought to court as a last resort, when the parties see no option for either giving up on their claims or reaching an agreement, but hope that an impartial court can find a solution to a conflict.

Some of the rulings recorded in the court files raise a lot of questions. The category of 'case conditionally discontinued' is of particular interest here. In these cases, the judgment finds the defendant guilty of the alleged infringement of rights, and the defendant's conduct is found to meet the definition of the crime, but the trial is discontinued because the crime does not meet the threshold of being detrimental to the society. The content of these rulings is often cursory; in their majority, they fail to meet the requirement set by the Polish Supreme Court: "When assessing the degree of social harmfulness of an act or omission, it does not suffice to generally cite the *actus reus* and *mens rea* of the crime. Instead, it must be demonstrated which elements of this *actus reaus* and *mens rea* support the claim that the act or omission is socially harmful only to a negligible degree".[69] The courts very rarely specify exactly why the contemplated conduct should be considered socially harmful only to a small degree. This is of great importance in private prosecutions. The entire case hinges here on the decision of the victim who believes that his or her rights (e.g. the right to honour and good name) have been infringed. Under these circumstances, where the court finds that the crime was not detrimental to the society, the private prosecutor may perceived this as hurtful – especially in cases regarding matters as delicate as honour and reputation. However, even when this judgment is entered, the private prosecutor may consider it a victory. After all, the court clearly states that the defendant committed a crime.

69 Supreme Court judgment of 8 February 1984, V KRN 2/84, OSNPG 1984, no 6, item 51

Finally, it is interesting to compare civil cases brought in defence of honour and good name (reputation) with private prosecutions. The latter tend to be filed more often in long-term conflicts, in particular those involving family members or neighbours, in situations where the same conflict generates multiple court cases over time. There is a very high proportion of cases where the claimant alleges that the conduct of the defendant amounted to an insult. The Polish Supreme Court has ruled that certain words can constitute both defamation and criminal insult, and must be treated correspondingly. Using a very common Polish swearword (which literally means 'a prostitute') as a name to call a woman is an insult, but at the same time may impute marital infidelity (and thus defame). Calling someone 'pedał' ('faggot') can either be interpreted as an insult or as an attempt to impute homosexuality. However, a review of case files suggests that private-prosecution criminal cases are often filed when insulting words are spoken as part of a longer unkind utterance and serve to insult rather than defame. In civil courts, this is a less frequent occurrence.

Another difference is in the parties involved. Private-prosecution criminal cases are filed almost exclusively by private persons on their own behalf. While civil cases are also more often filed by private persons, there is a larger proportion of them brought in defence of the reputation of a legal person. Yet another difference concerns the defendants. While in civil cases the State Treasury (the public prosecutor's office, the courts, the police, directors of penitentiary facilities) is sometimes named as the defendant, this does not happen in criminal cases pursued by private prosecutors. The civil procedure is often used by private citizens defending their rights against infringements caused by institutions.

Part III. And in the Living Law

Jacek Kurczewski and Małgorzata Fuszara

Chapter VI. Popular patterns of dispute settlement

The data we discuss here were collected through the nation-wide survey made in Poland on our request sponsored by NCN research grant by public Centre for Social Opinion Research (CBOS) in May 2014[70]. The questionnaire included six general questions on law and dispute settlement, as well as questions on personal experience with disputes of various (ten) kinds and the courses of action taken. It also asked about personal experience with courts, its assessment, reactions to a series of hypothetical (eight) vignette-types of disputes taken from everyday life (referred to as 'scripts' in this publication), and finally about the dispute settlement patterns recommended for use at the collective level of action, within a state as well as between states. In this chapter, our focus is on statistical analysis of the aggregate indicators of the exposure to potentially judiciable disputes, general attitude to courts as dispute settlement agencies, and to other ways of dispute management in the case of the inter-personal disputes.

I. Institutionalized or informal way of settlement

The crucial question posed in the opening part of the questionnaire concerned the choice between, on the one hand, an official institution (e.g. a court) that has the power to impose a settlement, and, on the other hand, an informal way of mediating a dispute. This was followed by a series of general questions on law and justice, including two structurally similar questions asking the respondents to choose between a settlement fully satisfying the claims of one of the disputants at the expense of the opponent versus a mutually agreed compromise, and to choose between a settlement strictly in line with the law versus a flexible compromise. These questions had been posed already in the survey on all-Polish representative sample in 1976 (Kurczewski and Frieske 1978) using a methodology similar to that applied

70 Research carried out within the project *Patterns of Dispute and Dispute Settlement in Popular Legal Culture (National Science Committee research grant No. 203744 OPUS HS6).* by CBOS Public Opinion Research Center, and 1061 CAPI interviews were collected using random route sampling method. For further analysis, we adjusted these data to the most recent figures to match national Polish statistics of age and sex. This left us with 1031 full interviews as the basis for the statistical analysis.

in 2014. The results repeated after 40 years look symptomatic: the largest change consists in the increase in popularity of the authoritative official settlement (court and similar institutions) and the decrease in popularity of informal settlements.

Table 1. Patterns of dispute settlement in national public opinion polls 1974–2014

Patterns of dispute settlement		**1974 (n= 974)**	**2014 (n=1031)**
1.What is better	a. Full satisfaction of claims made by one party	12%	10%
	b. Mutual agreement	79%	85%
2.What is better	a. Strictly according to law	28%	39%
	b. Mutual compromise	60%	54%
3.What is better	a. Official settlement e.g. by a court	32%	52%
	b. informal mediation	52%	38%

Apparently, the shift from a totalitarian regime (in which the independence of the judiciary was reduced to the individual conscience of a judge) to a democratic rule of law (in which the judiciary is constitutionally an independent branch of power) resulted in an increase in willingness to rely on the courts rather than resort to informal ways of dealing with violations of legally protected rights. It might therefore be argued that amicable resolutions, based on the concept of restorative justice, are particularly popular not only when some of the roles of the state are taken over by various organizations as part of the state's reconfiguration (Banaszak, Beckwith and Rucht 2003), but also when the state and its legal system are not particularly trusted by the citizens.

It is important to note, following the argument proposed by J. Braithwaite (2003), that a belief in restorative justice can also produce rather dangerous outcomes. For example, it can empower a community to such an extent that its members will feel authorised to employ drastic solutions going far beyond the law, such as corporal punishment or even lynching. In the scripts we presented to the respondents, 'self-help' – including the use of physical force – was often described as justified in response to a prior conduct of a victim. This is not a community that has this feeling of being excessively empowered, just individual perpetrators. However, there is acceptance for such conduct, which means that the fears expressed by J. Braithwaite might actually materialize.

At the other end of the spectrum, there is a concept of legal empowerment. It posits that a reliance on law and legal procedures may be used to improve the situation of those who are underprivileged or marginalized. In this case, the law is used as an instrument of pursuing their interests and improving their position: 'Legal empowerment occurs when poor or marginalised people use the law, legal systems and justice mechanisms to improve or transform their social, political or economic situations' (Pilar and O'Neil 2014:4). While self-help and mediation reflect a departure from strictly legal procedures, legal empowerment and legal mobilisation favour the opposite approach. Studies conducted in this framework focus on demonstrating 'how and why the law and legal entitlements are employed, often strategically, by and on behalf of marginalised groups and minorities as well as by various kinds of actors who seek to influence social change on their behalf' (Anagnostou 2014: 205). These two concepts match the two sets of attitudes towards the law as an instrument of conflict resolution that we take into account in our research. One consists in the reliance on law to pursue one's interests; the other consists in the reliance on other instruments, such as amicable methods of conflict resolution, mediation, and ultimately self-help.

II. Between authoritative settlement and friendly mediation

Historically, this issue is of primary importance. Thus we begin the statistical analysis from the logistic regression creating three sets of independent variables and three simple models to explain the variance of the binary variable of choice between the official authoritative settlement of dispute and settlement offered informally by the third persons.

Table 2. *In your opinion, what is better: (0 – settlement imposed by an official institution that has authority, like a court; 1 – settlement mediated by third parties that can only advise)*

MODEL 1: Socio-demographic variables:	**Odds ratio**	**p**
Constant	1.01	.945
Gender (0–female, 1-male)	0.95	.722
Age (0-younger up to 50 yrs, 1-elder than 50 yrs)	1.17	.279
Education (0-up to certified secondary, 1-post-secondary and more)	1.08	.652
Financial status (0–bad or very bad + as average, 1–good or very good)	**0.56**	**.001** ***
Employment status (0–no employment, 1–employment permanent, part-time and sporadic)	0.76	.060
Size of locality of residence (0-up to 20,000, 1- above 20,000)	**0.76**	**.049** *
Levels of significance: *** p<0.001, ** p<0.01, * p<0.05		

*Wald's x^2 (6) = 23.52, p=0.001 ***, Nagelkerke's R^2 = 0.03, Hosmer & Lemeshow's test p =0.073.*

MODEL 2: General Attitudes:	**Odds ratio**	**p**
Constant	1.16	.856
Social control (0 – yes, 1 – not)	0.79	.559
Trust in others (0 – never trust the others, 1 – trust the others unless they fail)	1.10	.851
Religiosity (0 – practicing at least once a week, 1 – practicing less often or not at all)	0.58	.197
Political orientation (0 – left, 1 – right)	1.57	.856
Levels of significance: *** p<0.001, ** p<0.01, * p<0.05		

Wald's x^2 (4) = 3.29, p=0.511, Nagelkerke's R^2 = 0.04, Hosmer & Lemeshow's test p =0.178.

MODEL 3: Socio-legal variables	**Odds ratio**	**p**
Constant	20.24	.010
Evaluation of law in Poland (0 – requires serious change, 1 – all other answers)	1.10	.699
Purpose of law 1 – social change, development (0 – all other purposes, 1 – Purpose of law: social change, development)	0.62	.195
Purpose of law 2 – dispute settlement (0-all other purposes, 1- dispute settlement)	0.65	.255
Purpose of law 3 – securing public order (0-all other purposes, 1- securing public order)	**0.45**	**.010** **
Purpose of law 4 – satisfaction of needs and interests (0 – all other purposes, 1 – satisfaction of needs and interests)	0.60	.120
Abidance by the law (0-all other answers, 1- should be obeyed even if unjust)	**0.59**	**.051** *
Right claims to be fully satisfied (0 – compromise, 1- right claims of a party fully satisfied)	0.46	.091
Strict legality of verdict (0-both sides satisfied, 1-strictly according to law even if only one side satisfied)	**0.56**	**.042** *
Civil court experience (0-none , 1-yes)	0.81	.511
Criminal court experience (0-none , 1-yes)	0.77	.403
Knows unjust verdict (0 – doesn't know, 1 – knows)	1.46	.184
Court unpleasant (0 – not, 1 – yes)	1.07	.821
Mediation by neighbors (1-yes, 2- not + it is hard to say)	0.65	.100
Knows expert in law (0 – not, 1 – yes, knows whom to ask)	**2.57**	**.038** *

MODEL 3: Socio-legal variables	Odds ratio	p
Personal experience of just court verdict (0 – none, 1 – yes, had experienced just verdict)	0.77	.313
Confidence in family matters (0 – don't use court for family disputes, 1 – family disputes not the obstacle for using court)	**0.49**	**.010** **
Levels of significance: *** p<0.001, ** p<0.01, * p<0.05		

Wald's x^2 *(16) = 51.17, p=0.001 ***, Nagelkerke's* $R^2 = 0.19$*, Hosmer & Lemeshow's test p =0.836.*

As for the socio-demographic variables, the correlation of choice of authoritative settlement with better than average self-assessment of one's living standard and living in the cities suggested the further checking with the aggregate index of social position where positive (1) scores count: age between 34 and 60; living in the cities; male gender; tertiary education; recent employment and better than average relative self-assessment of one's living standard. The results of the bi-variate logistic regression on such index and the choice of the ideal settlement procedure show both the significance of the correlation and its drastic weakness measured by Nagelkerke's $R^2 = 0.02$:

Table 3. Social Position As Independent Variable

Social Position As Independent Variable in Bi-Variate Regression:	Odds ratio	p
Constant	1.45	.063
Social Position Index (0–lower than Me, 1 – Me and higher)	**0.63**	**.000** ***
Levels of significance: *** p<0.001, ** p<0.01, * p<0.05		

Wald's x^2 *(1) = 12.23, p=0.000 ***, Nagelkerke's* $R^2 = 0.02$*, Hosmer & Lemeshow's test p =0.484.*

The social position index as already used in the 1970s was adjusted from then influential Johan Galtung's scale of Centre – Periphery. The simplicity of the scheme that accorded the scores according to the prevalent concept of what is the better social capital, as it is said nowadays, should not blind us to the fact that the index itself is heterogeneous and not exactly correlated. The structure of the index has been disclosed with help of the main components analysis using orthogonal rotation:

Main Components of Social Position Index

	Components:		
	1	2	3
Social habitat (1 – cities > 20,000)	.580	.038	-.079
Employment (1 – permanent or sporadic)	.259	-.725	.349
Living conditions (1 – above average)	.391	.132	.629
Education (1 – above secondary)	.793	-.137	.107
Age (1 – middle 35 to 59 years)	.121	.822	.212
Gender (1 – male)	-.388	-.123	.776

Varimax method with Kaiser's normalization in 5 steps, K-M-O test = .443, Bartlett's test = 310.103, df = 15, p < .000

The Main Components Analysis isolated three factors explaining about 63% of variance. Evident heterogeneity of the Social Position index helps to measure different aspects of a social position – component 1: middle age and employment, component 2: social habitat and education and component 3: gender and satisfaction with living standards. The extensive statistical analysis of correlations between the SP index and all dispute settlement indices led to conclusion that people in the social Centre are more prone to choosing court as an authoritative dispute settlement agency while people on the social Periphery tend to opt for more informal ways.

III. Between courts and informal settlement in everyday conflicts

Case Scripts

In the questionnaire we included a number of case scripts that could be considered controversial, even if, legally, the situations described therein are quite clear. The observation of social practice and the analysis of court files suggest that on many occasions, parties to such conflicts refrain from taking legal or other formal steps, resorting instead to 'self-help' or simply choosing not to act on their claims. Previous research suggests that some persons declare they would never go to court at all, or they would never go to court against some categories of persons, e.g. family members (Fuszara 1988). We compiled several short, potentially controversial vignettes ('case scripts') and asked the respondents what they believed the victims should do in each case. The respondents had to choose between the following reactions: (a) Don't react, do nothing; (b) Reach agreement and compromise; (c) Use self-help to achieve in private what one considers as due; (d) Go to court (e) Go to another public agency. The first three case scripts concerned conflict between non-related individuals, the subsequent three were conflicts between an institution and an individual, and the last two – between spouses.

In the first case script, an adult inflicted corporal punishment on their neighbour's children because they had been generating a lot of noise under his windows. Legally, there is no doubt that the parents can go to court in defence of their children. However, people in Poland are generally quite accepting of corporal punishment of children, and the children did misbehave by playing noisily. We were therefore curious what reactions this case script would generate.

Somebody's children were beaten by a neighbour as he could not rest after work due to their noisy behaviour. In your opinion, what should the parents of the beaten children do?

1. Don't react, do nothing n=20 (2.0%)
2. Reach an agreement and compromise with the man n=613 (59.1%)
3. Use self-help to achieve in private what one considers as due n=66 (6.4%)
4. Go to court n=174 (16.8%)
5. Go to another agency n=141 (13.6%)

For this question (and all the subsequent questions about the suggested response in the case scripts), we ran a binomial logistic regression on preference for compromise, taking into account choice of compromise (generally dominant) vs other choices as independent variable in turn. The result is as follows: the choice of compromise is predicted (in a statistically significant manner) by gender (female) – Odds ratio = 0.72, $p<0.01$, age (middle-aged and elderly) – Odds ratio = 4.45, $p<0.001$, education (lower) – Odds ratio = 0.52, $p<0.001$, self-assessment of one's own financial status (poorer) – Odds ratio = 0.57, $p<0.001$, place of residence (rural areas) – Odds ratio = 0.54, $p<0.001$, summary index of social position (lower) – Odds ratio = 0,38, $p<0.001$, the community control (yes) – Odds ratio = 0.76, $p<0.05$, and religiosity (higher) – Odds ratio = 0.43, $p<0.01$.

In the second case script, a person responded to defamation (in the form of being gossiped about) by slapping the person who was spreading the gossip. This case script is less clear-cut in a sense that both parties are victims and both have the right to bring a case either to a civil court (in defence of their legally protected personality rights) and to a criminal court in the private prosecution procedure. Previous research on private prosecution criminal cases indicates that in practice these cases often involve situations where both parties file claims with the court, in particular if a conflict is complex and has continued for a long time.

An acquaintance of Mr K. was gossiping about him among their friends, so Mr K. slapped him in the presence of others. In your opinion, what should the acquaintance do?

1. Don't react, do nothing n=62 (6.0%)
2. Reach agreement and compromise with the friend n=701 (67.7%)
3. Use self-help to achieve in private what one considers as due n=170 (16.4%)
4. Go to court n=45 (4.3%)
5. Go to another agency n=16 (1.5%)

In this case script, very few independent variables proved to predict significantly the choice of compromise. They included sex (female) – Odds ratio = 0.67, $p<0.01$ and summary index of social position (low) – Odds ratio = 0.78, $p<0.05$, and in psychosocial terms, trust in other people (one sgould trust always the other people, yes) – Odds ratio = 1.57, $p<0.01$ and religiosity (higher) – Odds ratio = 0.71, $p<0.01$.

The final case script that involves a conflict between two individuals is between a lender and a borrower. When the loan was not repaid on time, the lender took an item that belonged to the borrower, and that was equal in value to the amount of the loan. Legally speaking, the lender had no right to do so: he should have sought the repayment of the loan, either by means of mediation or in court. However, since the debt is not substantial, and the costs of court proceedings (fees, absence from work, transportation, etc.) can be considered large, filing a formal claim in court is rare in cases like this. This is why we asked about 'self-help' in such cases where it can serve as a preliminary step towards negotiations. It is important to remember than none of these considerations in any way undermine the fact that what the lender did was unlawful.

A friend borrowed 250 euros and failed to repay the debt despite repeated demands. The lender came to the debtor's house and took something of that same value. In your opinion, what should the borrower (from whose house the item had been taken) do?

1) Don't react, do nothing n=67 (6.5%)
2) Reach agreement and compromise with friend n=673 (64.9%)
3) Use self-help to achieve in private what one considers as due n=103 (9.9%)
4) Go to court n=117 (11.3%)
5) Go to another agency (WHICH?) n=43 (4.1%)

The following variables predict a compromise in this case script: age (middle-aged and elderly) – Odds ratio = 1.38, $p<0.05$, self-assessment on one's own financial status (lower) – Odds ratio = 0.55, $p<0.001$, social position (lower) – Odds ratio = 0.78, $p<0.05$, and trust in other people – Odds ratio = 1.38, $p<0.05$.

Where the conflict presented in the case scripts is with official institutions, the image arising out of the study results is more complex.

In the next case script, an employer asks a hospital to reveal information about a patient's health status. This information, once revealed, is used against the patient. This is a clear breach of confidentiality, and the doctors bear criminal, civil, and disciplinary responsibility for this breach. What is probably crucial from the point of view of the victim (the patient) is that he is entitled to compensation covering the full spectrum of losses he suffered. One may wonder whether seeking an agreement would not offer an easier way to ensuring that compensation is paid. In recent years there has been a rise in the number of law firms that help victims obtain compensation for medical malpractice and other issues in the doctor-patient relationship. It is therefore likely that the public awareness about the possibility of pursuing claims in such situations is also on the rise.

An employer asked the hospital for information about the illness for which one of his employees was treated. The hospital provided the information, which was then used against the patient. In your opinion, what should the patient do?

1) Don't react, do nothing n=35 (3.4%)
2) Reach agreement and compromise with employer n=271 (26.2%)
3) Use self-help to achieve in private what one considers as due n=70 (6.7%)
4) Go to court n=525 (50.7%)
5) Go to another agency (WHICH?) n=64 (6.2%)

Statistically significant predictors of the choice of compromise include in this case script: age (middle-aged and elderly) – Odds ratio = 2.13, $p<0.001$, education (lower) – Odds ratio = 0.53, $p<0.001$, self-assessment of one's own financial status (poorer) – Odds ratio = 0.69, $p<0.05$, currently being unemployed – Odds ratio = 0.52, $p<0.001$, place of residence (rural area) – Odds ratio = 0.48, $p<0.001$, social status (lower) – Odds ratio = 0.47, $p<0.001$, and also religiosity (higher) – Odds ratio = 0.65, $p<0.01$.

The next case script concerns an abuse of power by the police intervening during a brawl. The intervening police officers used their batons, which hit not only the brawlers but also innocent bystanders. Situations like this do sometimes occur in real life. Depending on the resulting harm to victims' health, prosecution can be either private or public. Under the Polish law, if the disruption to the health of the victim lasts for more than 7 days, the offence is prosecuted by the public prosecutor, and if it lasts for a shorter period, only private prosecution is possible. The victim can also seek compensation from the State Treasury for the actions of the police. On the one hand, since the events described in the case script took place in public, most likely the victims are able to find witnesses to the events. On the other hand, the victims may be reluctant to come into conflict with the police. We thought the case script was also interesting because the victim must have weighed the arguments in favour of legal action (punishment, apology, compensation) and against it (difficulty in collecting and presenting evidence, necessity to confront the testimony of the police officers saying they acted towards everybody in the crowd, etc.).

In the evening, a brawl started close to a restaurant. A police patrol was called in to calm the situation. Police officers used batons not only against the brawlers but against innocent bystanders as well. In your opinion, what should those bystanders do?

1) Don't react, do nothing n=50 (4.8%)
2) Reach agreement and compromise with police n=315 (30.4%)
3) Use self-help to achieve in private what one considers as due n=51 (4.9%)
4) Go to court n=487 (47.0%)
5) Go to another agency (WHICH?) n=69 (6.6%)

The analysis produced results for this case script that are similar to the previous one. Statistically significant predictors of the choice of compromise are: age (middle-aged and elderly) – Odds ratio = 1.93, $p<0.001$, education (lower) – Odds ratio = 0.69, $p<0.05$, currently being unemployed – Odds ratio = 0.76, $p<0.05$, place of residence (rural area) – Odds ratio = 0.72, $p<0.05$, social status (lower) – Odds ratio = 0.55, $p<0.001$, and religiosity (higher) – Odds ratio = 0.49, $p<0.001$.

The last case script that involves an individual and an institution concerns an order to demolish a house. The reason for the order is that the local area development plan (the masterplan) has changed. An order like this can only be issued in very limited circumstances. It is naturally very burdensome to the owner of the house. The situation of the owner depends on a number of factors, e.g. whether a specific permit has been issued for the construction of the house, and whether its construction was allowed under the previous masterplan. Again, we asked the respondents what they believed to be the best solution to the conflict.

Somebody built a house but due to a change in the local area development plan, the authorities ordered him to demolish it. In your opinion, what should the person who built the house do?

1) Don't react, do nothing n=9 (0.9%)
2) Reach agreement and compromise with authorities n=359 (34.7%)
3) Use self-help to achieve in private what one considers as due n=34 (3.2%)

4) Go to court n=533 (51.4%)
5) Go to another agency (WHICH?) n=53 (5.2%)

This time, there are only four statistically significant predictors of compromise: currently being unemployed – Odds ratio = 0.68, $p<0.01$, place of residence (rural area) – Odds ratio = 0.55, $p<0.001$, social status (lower) – Odds ratio = 0.72, $p<0.05$ and religiosity (higher) – Odds ratio = 0.79, $p<0.05$.

The final two case scripts concerned conflicts within a marriage. The first one is financial. The wife has inherited a sum of money and has deposited it on her own private account rather than in the spouses' joint account. In terms of the law, she was fully within her rights to do so: funds that are inherited form part of the heir's private property are not automatically included in the community property. Therefore, the husband would have no chance in court if he argued that the money was part of the community property. Nonetheless, in the popular perception spouses who have agreed to the community property regime should share all the money each of them comes into, regardless of the laws, which is why we proposed this case script.

A dispute arose between spouses when the wife inherited 10 000 euros and placed the funds on her own account, rather than contributing it to the family budget. In your opinion, what should her husband do?

1) Don't react, do nothing n=234 (22.6%)
2) Reach agreement and compromise with wife n=741 (71.5%)
3) Use self-help to achieve in private what one considers as due n=18 (1.7%)
4) Go to court n=20 (2.0%)
5) Go to another agency (WHICH?) n=3 (0.3%)

In this case script, the choice of compromise was more frequent among women – Odds ratio = 0.76, $p<0.05$ and younger persons Odds ratio = 0.58, $p<0.001$. This was an exception to the rule: generally, compromise was favoured by those who were older (and by this virtue also more religious).

In the last case script, evidently a crime is committed: a jealous husband beats up his wife. This is of course a crime, and one that is liable to be prosecuted by the public prosecutor. However, practice demonstrates that cases of violence under such circumstances are only rarely reported. Testimony concerning domestic violence appears in courts not only in cases of abuse or assault but also in divorce cases. This is why we asked the respondents who suggested going to court in this case script whether they would suggest a criminal court (to punish the perpetrator) or a divorce case (with no crime report filed).

A husband battered a wife suspecting her of secretly meeting with another man. In your opinion, what should the woman do?

1) Don't react, do nothing n=49 (4.7%)
2) Reach agreement and compromise with husband n=574 (55.4%)
3) Use self-help to achieve in private what one considers as due n=69 (6.7%)
4) Go to court n=138 (13.3%)
5) Go to another agency (WHICH?) n=128 (12.4%)

Many respondents believe that the scale of this conflict is beyond domestic privacy. The predictors of compromise in this case script included: age (middle-aged and elderly) – Odds ratio = 2.21, $p<0.001$, education (lower) – Odds ratio = 0.47, $p<0.001$, financial status (poorer) – Odds ratio = 0.69, $p<0.05$, being currently unemployed – Odds ratio = 0.69, $p<0.01$, place of residence (rural area) – Odds ratio = 0.59, $p<0.001$, generally lower social status – Odds ratio = 0.55, $p<0.001$ and religiosity (higher) – Odds ratio = 0.67, $p<0.001$.

The distribution of answers in the above eight cases shows that they may be conveniently divided into three types:

a) Where majority of respondents support the mutual negotiations as the best possible option while important minority (from one fourth up to one third) opts for moving conflict already at this phase as described in the case story on the public forum, whether in court or another public office (from police to the local counselors or head of the local government).All private disputes belong here, including the use of physical violence as an element..
b) The opposite case where majority selects the third party public forum and only minority opts for the choice of informal direct negotiations with the opposing party, here are all the three cases of conflict with a corporate actor such as hospital, police or local government belong.
c) The case where the informal direct negotiations are selected as the dominant preferred solution while the dispute is kept by overwhelming majority off the public forum. This includes all private disputes from the set presented in the survey that do not involve the physical violence as such.

All this leads to the question: what are the socio-demographic characteristics of people who prefer particular types of reaction, are those reactions correlated with the court experience and is the choice of reaction in the particular types of conflicts correlated with the general attitudes towards the dispute settlement?:

Table 4. The Multiple Regression Analysis of the Aggregate Indices of Preference for Compromise, Court and Other Institutional Dispute Settlement (beta values) [71]

	Choice of informal compromise in 8 cases (0 – in no case, 3/5 – in all cases)		**Choice of court in 8 cases (0 – in no case, 3/5 – in all cases)**		**Choice of any institutional settlement in 8 cases (0 – in no case, 3/5 – in all cases)**	
Socio-demographic variables :	Private	Public	Private	Public	Private	Public
Age in years	**0.20** ***	**0.14** ***	**-0.22** ***	**-0.20** ***	**-0.30** ***	**-0.22** ***
Employment (0-none, 1- permanent, part-time and sporadic)		**-0.08** **		**0.11** ***		**0.13** ***
Social habitat (0- up to 20,000 inhabitants, 1- above 20,000)	**-0.13** ***	**-0.17** ***		**0.16** ***	**0.09** **	**0.18** ***
Model 1 – fitness	n=1035, F (2; 1033) = 31.46 p= 0.000***, R^2= 0.06	n=1035, F (3; 1032) = 25.03 p= 0.000***, R^2= 0.07	n=1035, F(1; 1034) = 51.81 p= 0.000***, R^2 = 0.05	n=1035, F(3; 1034) = 51.81 p= 0.000***, R^2 = 0.05	n=1035, F(2;969) = 61.16 p= 0.000***, R^2= 0.16	n=1035, F(3;1032) = 48.22 p= 0.000***, R^2= 0.12
General attitudes:						
Religious practices (0-at least once a week, 1-less often and never)	- **0.15** ***	**-0.12** ***	**0.10** ***	**0.17** ***	**0.12** ***	**0.17** ***
Model 2 – fitness	n=1035, F(1;1034) = 23.31 p= 0.000***, R^2 = 0.03	n=1035, F(1;1033) = 14.47 p= 0.000***, R^2 = 0.03	n=1035, F(1;1034) = 10.95 p= 0.000***, R^2 = 0.07	n=1035, F(1;1034) = 30.78 p= 0.000***, R^2 = 0.03	n=1035, F(1;1033) = 12.82 p= 0.000***, R^2 = 0.02	n=1035, F(1;1034) = 31.96 p= 0.000***, R^2 = 0.03
Socio-legal variables:						
Official pattern of dispute settlement (0-informal mediation, 1- public body like a court)	**-0.07** *	**-0.15** ***	**0.17** ***	**0.17** ***	**0.16** ***	**0.17** ***

71 In the Table 4 only the statistically significant predictors were left.

	Choice of informal compromise in 8 cases (0 – in no case, 3/5 – in all cases)		Choice of court in 8 cases (0 – in no case, 3/5 – in all cases)		Choice of any institutional settlement in 8 cases (0 – in no case, 3/5 – in all cases)	
Civil court experience (0-none , 1-any)						
Criminal court experience (0-none , 1-any)	-0.09 **	-0.07 *	0.07*	0.07 *	0.09 **	0.08 *
Knowledge of unjust verdict (0-doesn't know, 1-knows)						
Model 3 – fitness	n=1035, F (2;926) = 3.27 p= 0.000***, $R^2 = 0.01$	n=1035, F (2;926) = 6.57 p= 0.000***, $R^2 = 0.02$	n=1035, F (2;926) = 8.85 p= 0.000***, $R^2 = 0.03$	n=1035, F (2;926) = 8.61 p= 0.000***, $R^2 = 0.03$	n=1035, F (2; 926) = 8.08 p= 0.000***, $R^2 = 0.03$	n=1035, F (2; 926) = 8.73 p= 0.000***, $R^2 = 0.03$
Levels of significance: *** p<0.001, ** p<0.01, * p<0.05						

To begin with the socio-demographic variables the pattern in findings is clear and consistent:

A. Age. Independent of type of dispute – private or public – the younger age predicts significantly the choice of court or another public referral body as the way out of conflict situation, while the elder age predicts significantly the choice of directly negotiated compromise with the opponent, which assumes personal contact. As obvious reason one may invoke the different value of time for the elder and younger, the informal personal contact is still assumed quicker and, additionally, cheaper or cost-free. The in-depth interviews with participants in the disputes of various sorts and of various social categories should in the future be the basic way to test such an interpretation.
B. Employment. When it comes to employment or the lack of it, full or part-time employment predicts significantly the choice of court or another public body for dispute settlement and rejection of informal direct compromise in dispute with public bodies.
C. Social habitat. Finally, as for the socio-demographic variables, the social habitat matters. In Chapter 7 the local surveys made in the mid-2010s in three small (under 20.000 inhabitants) towns are compared with a metropolitan area of Warsaw. The patterns of advised ways out of the conflict situation differ

alongside countryside township – metropolitan area dimension. The role of social habitat emerges in the MLA as it is also the significant predictor with a large urban habitat predicting the choice of a public agency and rejection of personal compromise independent of the type of dispute and the choice of court in public disputes.

These findings have made us look again into the aggregate Social Position Index as the predictor of dispute settlement patterns:

Table 5. The Multiple Regression Analysis of the Aggregate Indices of Preference for Compromise, Court and Any Institutional Dispute Settlement and Social Position As Predictor

	Court in private disputes (0 – none, 5 – in all cases)		**Court in public disputes (0 – none, 3 – in all cases)**		**Com-promise in private disputes (0 – none, 5 – in all cases)**		**Com-promise in public disputes (0 – none, 3 – in all cases)**		**Any in-stitutional in private disputes (0 – none, 5 – in all cases)**		**Any in-stitutional in public disputes (0 – none, 3 – in all cases)**	
	Beta	**p**	**Beta**	**p**	**Beta**	**p**	**Beta**	**p**	**Beta**	**p**	**Beta**	**p**
Constant		.001		.000		.000		.000		.000		.000
Social Position Index (0–low, 6-high)	0.17	.000 ***	0.21	.000 ***	-0.22	.000 ***	-0.17	.000 ***	0.29	.000 ***	0.24	.000 ***
Levels of significance: *** p<0.001, ** p<0.01, * p<0.05												

*$F(1;1034) = 31.59$, $p=.000$ ***; $R^2 = 0.029$; $F(1;1034) = 46.48$; $p = .000$ ***; $R^2 = 0.042$; $F(1;1034) = 51.41$; $p = .000$ ***; $R^2 = 0.046$; $F(1;1034) = 28.66$; $p = .000$ ***; $R^2 = 0.026$; $F(1;1034) = 97.49$; $p = .000$ ***; $R^2=0.085$; $F(1;1034) = 63.93$; $p = 000$ ***; $R^2 = 0.057$*

Evidently higher social position in general (aggregate index discussed above) predicts significantly the preference for the choice of court and other authoritative dispute settlement agencies and the lack of preference for informal dispute settlement by the third parties.

D. Religiosity. We must pay more attention to religiosity as widely agreed as the important factor influencing beliefs and patterns of behaviour in Poland. The question may be posed as to whether religiosity should be considered a type of „legal sub-culture" in Podgórecki's terms (Podgórecki 1991), influencing also attitudes towards law and dispute practices. We are inclined to follow this line of reasoning and to deal with religiosity as cultural factor in the context of the socio-legal controversy over the effective role of sub-cultures or cultural factor in general in shaping the functioning of law in society (Blankenburg 1991, Murayama 2011, Murayama 2016).

Our hypothesis is that religiosity is a significant element in Polish popular consciousness, and that it is partially independent of other social factors. In our survey, two questions concerned religion: one dealt with the declared intensity of religious belief and the other with the declared frequency of attendance at religious practices. They are strongly correlated (rho and tau = .880, p<.000), and thus in further analysis we decided to only take into account the frequency of church-going divided (for the purpose of regression analysis) into the following categories: (a) practicing frequently: once a week or more often; (b) practicing not more than twice a month or not at all. Measured by these criteria, religiosity is not independent of social factors. It is at bi-variate analysis level significantly related with age (Ref. 50 years +; Odds ratio = 0.58, p<.000), size of locality (Ref. cities > 20,000; Odds ratio = 2.01, p<.000), and gender Odds ratio = 1.83 p ref. men Odds ratio = 1.54, p<.000). On the other hand, it is not related significantly with the employment status, social status, and education. The lack of relationship with education supports our hypothesis that, at least partly, religiosity exerts influence on people with better education and higher social status. The conventional opinion that religiosity is a marker, if not a result, of lagging behind the shift in beliefs and opinions does not hold, at least not fully. Why? There are cases where it is 'pre-modern', and this can be observed if one looks into the tri-variate relationships. The simplest and the least assuming one in here is the comparison of statistical significance and the strength of the bivariate phi coefficients when controlling the socio-demographic variables one after another. The following conclusions can be drawn:

1) Almost unconditionally within the set of our socio-demographic variables, age is related to higher religiosity independent of other variables except for the size of locality, and vice versa. These two variables – age and size of locality – are interacting so that in the urban areas age is related to higher religiosity while amongst the younger respondents living in rural areas, it increases the level of religiosity. In the rural areas (understood as villages and small towns up to 20 000 residents) age has no bearing on church-going, while in larger towns the elderly are more religious than the youth. Amongst the youth the social habitat is related to religiosity, while among the elderly it is not.

2) Certain partial correlations point to the conservative character of religiosity. Respondents who consider themselves poorer or average in terms of relative assessment of their own and their family's financial status are more religious, but this has been observed only among the youth (phi = -.115, $p<.05$) and in the rural areas (phi = .112, $p<.01$). In the cities, better education is significantly related to lower religiosity (phi = .091, $p<.05$).
3) Gender is significantly related to religiosity: women tend to be more religious regardless of age and size of locality. It is thus to be considered an independent factor at the primary level of analysis. On the other hand, the relationship between gender and religiosity is not significant amongst respondents who are employed, who assess their relative financial status as better than average, and who are better educated.
4) At this stage of analysis, given our hypothesis that 'religiosity' entails two components – first, pre-modern traditionalism and second, the new religious revival component – then the relationships with sex, age and rural area of residence point in the first direction. However, there is still a lot of religiosity amongst men, youth, and urbanites that cannot be so easy explained. The level of education seems to be the most acceptable indicator of pre-modern traditionalism. The first-order relationship between religiosity and education is insignificant. If one introduces political orientation from Left to Right, it is also – as expected – significantly related to religiosity (phi = .229, $p<.000$), Right being more often religious. Importantly, this relationship remains significant regardless of the level of education (.202 among less and .303 among better educated, both $p<.000$). The strength of the relationship between religiosity and politics is even slightly higher among those who are better educated. Therefore, apparently, for those with a better education, religiosity is a matter of convictions rather than a habit. This reasoning fails when it comes to the regression of religiosity on the choice of courts as controlled by education, but it holds true for the choice of compromise which is most strongly related to religiosity. We have also checked partial correlations between religiosity and dispute settlement pattern keeping under control the feeling of political alienation as indicated by the agreement with statement that "most of our politicians think only how to exploit common people" and this has led us to reject the correlation between the choice of compromise and religiosity as statistically insignificant.

Table 6. The Multiple Regression Analysis of the Aggregate Indices of Preference for Compromise, Court and Other Institutional Dispute Settlement Including Socio-Demographic Variables and Religiosity

	Court in private disputes (0 – none, 5 – in all cases)		**Court in public disputes (0 – none, 3 – in all cases)**		**Com-promise in private disputes (0 – none, 5 – in all cases)**		**Com-promise in public disputes (0 – none, 3 – in all cases)**		**Any in-stitutional in private disputes (0 – none, 5 – in all cases)**		**Any in-stitutional in public disputes (0 – none, 3 – in all cases)**	
Socio-demographic variables:	**Beta**	**p**	**Beta**	**p**	**Beta**	**p**	**Beta**	**p**	**Beta**	**p**	**Beta**	**p**
Constant		.000		.000		.000		.000		.000		.000
Gender (0–female, 1-male)	0.03	.309	-0.04	.221	-0.72	.024 *	0.06	.045 *	-0.02	.589	-0.03	.406
Age (0-up to 50 yrs, 1-elder)	-0.20	.000 ***	-0.18	.000 ***	0.18	.000 ***	0.13	.000 ***	-0.29	.000 ***	-0.20	.000 ***
Education (0-up to secondary, 1-post-secondary)	-0.03	.397	0.02	.505	-0.06	.092	-0.02	.653	0.09	.006 **	0.04	.278
Financial status (0 – bad + average, 1–good)	0.11	.001 ***	0.03	.289	-0.06	.041 *	-0.01	.875	0.09	.005 **	0.02	.623
Employment (0–none, 1– perma-nent ful lor part-time and sporadic)	-0.03	.347	0.10	.004 **	0.04	.199	-0.10	.008 **	0.02	.522	0.11	.001 ***
Social habitat (0-up to 20,000 inhabit-ants, 1-above 20,000)	0.09	.005 ***	0.13	.000 ***	-0.12	.000 ***	-0.15	.000 ***	0.13	.000 ***	0.15	.000 ***
Religiosity (0 – practicing at least once a week,1 – practicing less often or not at all)	0.06	.083	0.13	.000 ***	-0.09	.006 **	-0.11	.000 ***	0.07	.017 *	0.12	.000 ***
Levels of significance: *** p<0.001, ** p<0.01, * p<0.05												

*$F(7;999) = 11.16$, $p=.000$ ***, $R^2 = 0.066$; $F(7;999) = 18.06$, $p=.000$ ***, $R^2 = 0.106$;*
*$F(7;999) = 13.18$, $p=.000$ ***, $R^2 = 0.078$; $F(7;999) = 13.02$, $p=.000$ ***, $R^2 = 0.077$;*
*$F(7;999) = 28.91$, $p=.000$ ***, $R^2 = 0.163$; $F(7;999) = 22.34$, $p=.000$ ***, $R^2 = 0.129$*

As seen in the Table 6 when religiosity is included with the basic set of socio-economic variables its significance holds aside the significance of age, financial self-assessment, education, social habitat and employment. So, the components of the higher social status seem to relate independently of low religiosity to the preference for the authoritative dispute settlement patterns.

IV. Dispute settlement patterns

The eight dispute scripts were next subjected to the cluster analysis by A. Wichrowski, aiming at distinguishing the social categories that differ as to the patterns of reaction to dispute as in the respective scripts.

At first, the missing data was replaced using the hot-deck imputation method. Dataset was sorted by sex, year of birth, voivodship and size of town. Then, missing values ("hard to tell", "refusal") were replaced with the data from prior cases. Then the data transformed these multiple nominal into dummy variables, on which the hierarchical cluster analysis was performed, using squared euclidean distance as a distance measure and Ward's method as a criterion of clustering. This led to the emergence of six clusters. The centroids of five most meaningful clusters were then used as starting points in k-means hierarchical analysis that simply classified all the cases into these five clusters.

1. SELECTIVE – that is those who prefer a private compromise in private disputes and authoritative official settlement in case of disputes with public bodies. They do not differ significantly on any account from the total sample.
2. INFORMAL – elder, less educated, countryside dwellers with lower income, people who in all – private and public type of dispute – prefer an informal compromise.
3. BASE DEFENDERS, people who are compromise-minded except when it comes to the hypothetical threat posed by the authorities to the home they have built. In the latter case they would go to the court. This group also includes more pensioners but it does not differ in terms of age, income or social habitat from the whole sample. 'Base defenders' slightly more often declare right-wing political views, and have slightly more court experience.
4. COWBOYS, much more than others, prefer either a way out of a conflict situation through a private pursuit, whatever it may mean in practical terms, or an option of withdrawal. Significantly more men and less educated people belong to this group. 'Cowboys' do not want to abide by the laws they consider unjust, more often they declare political sympathy for the libertarian politicians.

5. AUTHORITATIVE – who sometimes opt for a compromise but much more than the others choose a judicial settlement of disputes. The 'Authoritative' are the youngest in our sample, best educated and living in the larger cities[72].

As a follow up of the remarks made when the results of MLA on the aggregate indices of preference for one of three such types of reaction in the hypothetical cases have been presented, we want here to point at two potential factors that seem to influence the preferred pattern of dispute settlement – personal experience of court proceedings and religiosity as a general attitude. A. Court experience. As for the role of personal experience in the court the results are complex. The AUTHORITATIVE, the SELECTIVE and the COWBOYS significantly less often had such experience than the BASE DEFENDERS (cf Table 1 in Appendix B).

However, the experience may be specific as to the type of law. In fact in the questionnaire there are three types of the possible court cases reported as personally experienced – civil, criminal and the other – and here the complexity is found. Leaving aside the "other" as heterogeneous and smallest in numbers we checked that the civil case experience is among the AUTHORITATIVE and COWBOYS the lowest (35%) and among the former significantly lower than among the INFORMAL who have the highest level of civil court experience (77%) (cf. Table 2 in Appendix B).

But when asked about the participation in criminal case, the order is opposite, the AUTHORITATIVE (and COWBOYS) have significantly more criminal case experience (44%) than the SELECTIVE (26%), INFORMAL (31%) and BASE DEFENDERS (25%) (cf. Table 3 in Appendix B).

The obvious suspicion is that while the reporting of civil court experience does not blame any of the opponents, it is different in a criminal case when only happy ones – not found guilty – are ready to acknowledge taking part in the proceedings. This assumption may be tested on our original data. Two sub-sets of data were created, one of those who declared personal experience of at least one civil case in their life – n = 313, the second composed of those who declared to experience the criminal proceedings at least once (n = 172). It is important as only minorities in the sample had the actual court experience and the effect of it should be established within these sub-sets. In both sub-sets the multivariate regression analysis was performed with the patterns of dispute settlement as the dependent variable and socio-demographic variables as independent predictors. Those who assessed the verdict issued in the case by court as just or at least partially just were coded against those

72 In Appendix A the distribution of types of the preferred reaction in each of the 8 hypothetical dispute cases along these clusters is presented.

who assessed the verdict as unjust or were unable to judge the court's judgment. Such a variable was then added and removed from the regression models. For all possible comparisons only once the effect of the assessment of the court verdict as just was significant – the justness of the civil verdict allows to predict the preference to withdraw from dispute (beta = -.115, $p<.05$) together with age (beta = .148, $p<.05$) and the model with justness of the civil verdict fits slightly better (corrected R square = .048) than the model without the verdict justness (corrected R square = .031). We conclude then within the scope of our data the assessment of a judicial decision as experienced personally does not relate to the preference for choosing court or the alternative dispute settlement procedure. The other factors seem to matter here.

B. Religiosity. Now we may resume the issue of religiosity raised in connection with MLA findings pointing to religiosity as the only significant predictor in the Model 2 including general attitudes.

Table 7. Distribution of religiosity across the clusters

Do you take part in religious practices such as Mass, religious services or meetings ?						
	TOTAL	**SELECTIVE (2)**	**INFORMAL (3)**	**BASE DEFENDERS (4)**	**COWBOYS (5)**	**AUTHORITATIVE (6)**
Usually several times a week	5%	2%	7,6% (2,6)	4%	4%	4%
Once a week	48%	50,9% (6)	53,2% (6)	61% (T+,5,6)	44%	34,8% (T-)
On average, once or twice a month	12%	10%	13%	9%	12%	15%
Few times a year	22%	25%	18%	19%	18%	28,8% (T+,3,4,5)
AND do not practice at all	13%	12%	8,5% (T-)	6,5% (T-)	21,3% (T+,2,3,4)	17,8% (T+,3,4)
BASE	1 035	179	297	175	122	262
Weighted Base	1 036	173	288	162	129	283
'Base: Qualified						
a. Sig. level=0,05						

As seen in the above Table the AUTHORITATIVE who considerably more often choose the authoritative dispute settlement, significantly more often abstain totally from religious services than the sample as a whole and the INFORMAL and the home defenders in particular. Among the BASE DEFENDERS – 65%, among the INFORMAL – 61% and among the SELECTIVE – 51% attend church services at least once a week in contrast to the AUTHORITATIVE of whom 39% practice religiosity so often. The significance of religiosity measured by frequency of church-going was also established as a result of the multivariate discrimination analysis including the variables from all the three sets (socio-demographic, socio-legal and general attitudes).

Summary

In 2014 all-Polish representative survey of 1061 people two types of questions were posed concerning the preference for the type of dispute settlement procedure. The first question was about the ideal general pattern pressing to choose between the settlement by an authoritative official body such as a court and the settlement by mediation of other people. The second one concerned the choice between court and other authoritative bodies and an informal direct compromise with the opponent in 8 hypothetical dispute scripts, ranging from the intra-family conflict through private conflicts with friends and neighbors to conflicts with public bodies like the police and municipality. The regression analysis disclosed, among others, a positive, though very weak, influence (if a causal link is to be assumed) of personal court experience on a decision to choose court as the ideal institutional agency to apply to in the case of dispute settlement. Other two significant independent non-attitudinal predictors are: (lower) age and (better) self-assessment of one's and his/her household living conditions relative to the average in the locality of residence.

As for the ways out of a conflict situation declared as best in the hypothetical dispute cases if we begin with the socio-demographic variables the pattern in findings is clear and consistent. Regardless of the type of dispute – with a private or public opponent– younger age predicts significantly the choice of court or another public referral body as the way out of a conflict situation, while elderly age predicts significantly the choice of a directly negotiated compromise with an opponent, which assumes personal contact. The role of a social habitat is also significant with a large urban habitat predicting the choice of a public agency and the rejection of a personal compromise independent of the type of dispute and the choice of court in public disputes. In the context of the fundamental controversy within the sociology of law about the role of institutional factors and attitudes or the culture factor, our findings speak in favor of the first as MLA have pointed to the predictive insignificance of the attitudinal variables. The cluster analysis executed on the 2014 data indicated, however, that there are 5 clusters of respondents that differ significantly with regards to their attitudes towards the ways of the hypothetical dispute settlement under discriminative analysis, but fail to produce strong results. The clusters were respectively labelled as the SELECTIVE, INFORMAL, BASE DEFENDERS, COWBOYS AND THE AUTHORITATIVE. The AUTHORITATIVE choosing courts more often than other groups are the youngest, inhabit the larger cities and are best educated while the INFORMAL ones who choose INFORMAL personal compromise independent of the character of dispute – private or public – are the oldest, inhabit the countryside and are the least educated in the sample. The SELECTIVE group does not differ significantly from the sample as the whole, while BASE DEFENDERS who will defend in court their home against the authorities are also similar as to the socio-demographic characteristics but significantly more likely to declare the right-wing political orientation. The specificity of the COWBOYS who are more often male lies in the fact that they more often than others follow a private pursuit or resort to self-help and redress the wrongs suffered and are more libertarian in stressing the dominance of their judgment over the law of the country.

The extremely low discriminative value of these cluster classification is in our view the argument for general conclusion that at least within the scope of our variables the attitudes matter but not enough to provide the safe base for predicting the declared legal practices. This is the case of religiosity that significantly relates to skepticism towards the use of courts and the preference for informal compromise.

The most general conclusion is that in Polish legal culture informality and compromise retained their popularity despite a marked increase in the choice of the court settlement of disputes during consolidation of the legal democratic state. Even though the preference for a compromise with the opponent is more popular among the elderly, people living in countryside and non-employed (pensioners, retired etc.) or generally people in the social periphery, there is also the cultural factor of religiosity which partially reinforces the trend to settle disputes amicably. However, the institutional context of dispute seems to be of the paramount importance – whether it is a dispute with the institution where going to court prevails or with an individual person, in the case of which direct negotiations are most often advised.

Appendix A. Clusters and the reaction patterns in 8 hypothetical case scripts

Script Case No 1

Noisy kids beaten by the neighbor	TOTAL	Cluster Number of Case				
		SELECTIVE (2)	INFOR-MAL (3)	BASE DE-FENDERS (4)	COWBOYS (5)	AUTHORI-TATIVE (6)
Do not react, give up	2%	0%	2%	1%	2%	3%
Arrive at agreement and compromise with opponent	59%	95,4% (T+,3,4,5,6)	83,7% (T+,5,6)	83,2% (T+,5,6)	54,1% (6)	0,6% (T-)
Pursue on your own what is owed	6%	1,3% (T-)	1,5% (T-)	4,6% (3)	22,9% (T+,2,3,4,6)	8% (2,3)
Go to court	17%	1,2% (T-)	6,2% (T-,2)	5,7% (T-,2)	4,9% (T-)	49% (T+,2,3,4,5)
Go to another institution	14%	0,5% (T-)	4,4% (T-,2)	4% (T-,2)	11,3% (2,3,4)	37,5% (T+,2,3,4,5)
Difficult to say	2%	1%	2%	1%	4,8% (T+,2,3)	2%
Refusal to answer	0%	0%	0%	0%	0%	0%
BASE	1 035	179	297	175	122	262
Weighted Base	1 036	173	288	162	129	283
Base: All respondents who answered the question.						
a. Sig. level=0,05						

Script Case No 2

Friend publicly slapped in face for slander	TOTAL	Cluster Number of Case				
		SELEC-TIVE (2)	INFOR-MAL (3)	BASE DEFENDERS (4)	COWBOYS (5)	AUTHORI-TATIVE (6)
Do not react, give up	6%	4%	6%	8%	6%	6%
Arrive at agreement and compromise with opponent	68%	89,2% (T+,5,6)	82,8% (T+,5,6)	84,2% (T+,5,6)	0% (T-)	60,7% (T-,5)

Friend publicly slapped in face for slander		Cluster Number of Case				
	TOTAL	SELEC-TIVE (2)	INFOR-MAL (3)	BASE DEFENDERS (4)	COWBOYS (5)	AUTHORI-TATIVE (6)
Pursue on your own what is owed	16%	0% (T-)	3,4% (T-,2)	1% (T-)	90,8% (T+,2,3,4,6)	14,4% (2,3,4)
Go to court	4%	2%	2%	0,3% (T-)	1%	11,7% (T+,2,3,4,5)
Go to another institution	2%	1%	0%	3,6% (3,5)	0%	2,5% (3)
Difficult to say	4%	4%	5%	2%	2%	4%
Refusal to answer	0%	0%	0%	1%	0%	0%
BASE	1 035	179	297	175	122	262
Weighted Base	1 036	173	288	162	129	283
Base: All respondents who answered the question.						
a. Sig. level=0,05						

Script Case No 3

Friend took an item from home as pledge for the debt		Cluster Number of Case				
	TOTAL	SELEC-TIVE (2)	INFOR-MAL (3)	BASE DE-FENDERS (4)	COWBOYS (5)	AUTHORI-TATIVE (6)
Do not react, give up	7%	6%	6%	6%	10%	6%
Arrive at agreement and compromise with opponent	65%	55,9% (T-,5)	81,1% (T+,2,5,6)	74,5% (T+,2,5,6)	35% (T-)	62,3% (5)
Pursue on your own what is owed	10%	8,6% (3)	3,4% (T-)	8%	39% (T+,2,3,4,6)	5,4% (T-)
Go to court	11%	22% (T+,3,4,5)	3,8% (T-)	7%	7%	16,7% (T+,3,4,5)
Go to another institution	4%	7% (3,4)	2%	1%	3%	6,9% (3,4)
Difficult to say	3%	1%	3%	3%	5,3% (2)	3%
Refusal to answer	0%	0%	0%	1%	1%	0%

Friend took an item from home as pledge for the debt		TOTAL	Cluster Number of Case				
			SELEC-TIVE (2)	INFOR-MAL (3)	BASE DE-FENDERS (4)	COWBOYS (5)	AUTHORI-TATIVE (6)
	BASE	1 035	179	297	175	122	262
	Weighted Base	1 036	173	288	162	129	283
Base: All respondents who answered the question.							
a. Sig. level=0,05							

Script Case No 4

Hospital gave confidential information to patient's em-ployer		TOTAL	Cluster Number of Case				
			SELEC-TIVE (2)	INFOR-MAL (3)	BASE DE-FENDERS (4)	COWBOYS (5)	AUTHORI-TATIVE (6)
Do not react, give up		3%	2%	4,8% (6)	4,8% (6)	5,9% (6)	0,8% (T-)
Arrive at agreement and compromise with opponent		26%	15% (T-,6)	52% (T+,2,4,5,6)	34,8% (T+,2,5,6)	19,6% (6)	5% (T-)
Pursue on your own what is owed		7%	8,7% (6)	4%	12,1% (T+,3,6)	12,4% (T+,3,6)	2,2% (T-)
Go to court		51%	63,3% (T+,3,4)	21,8% (T-)	34,5% (T-,3)	55,3% (3,4)	79,6% (T+,2,3,4,5)
Go to another institution		6%	3%	6,5% (5)	7,7% (5)	0,5% (T-)	9,4% (2,5)
Difficult to say		7%	8% (6)	10% (6)	6%	6%	3% (T-)
Refusal to answer		0%	0%	0%	1%	0%	0%
	BASE	1 035	179	297	175	122	262
	Weighted Base	1 036	173	288	162	129	283
Base: All respondents who answered the question.							
a. Sig. level=0,05							

Script Case No 5

Innocent bystanders beaten by police pacifying tumult outside the pub	TOTAL	Cluster Number of Case				
		SELECTIVE (2)	INFORMAL (3)	BASE DEFENDERS (4)	COWBOYS (5)	AUTHORITATIVE (6)
Do not react, give up	5%	3%	6%	4%	9,7% (T+,2,6)	3%
Arrive at agreement and compromise with opponent	30%	0% (T-)	49,5% (T+,2,5,6)	76,6% (T+,2,3,5,6)	18,3% (T-,2,6)	8,6% (T-,2)
Pursue on your own what is owed	5%	0,4% (T-)	4,6% (2)	9,9% (T+,2,3,6)	9,6% (T+,2,6)	3%
Go to court	47%	83,7% (T+,3,4,5,6)	25% (T-,4)	0% (T-)	51,3% (3,4)	71,7% (T+,3,4,5)
Go to another institution	7%	6%	7,6% (4)	2,2% (T-)	4%	10,2% (T+,4,5)
Difficult to say	6%	7,7% (6)	7%	7%	7%	3%
Refusal to answer	0%	0%	0%	1%	0%	0%
BASE	1 035	179	297	175	122	262
Weighted Base	1 036	173	288	162	129	283
Base: All respondents who answered the question.						
a. Sig. level=0,05						

Script Case No 6

Authorities order to dismantle the house	TOTAL	Cluster Number of Case				
		SELECTIVE (2)	INFORMAL (3)	BASE DEFENDERS (4)	COWBOYS (5)	AUTHORITATIVE (6)
Do not react, give up	1%	0%	0%	1%	2,9% (T+,2,3)	1%
Arrive at agreement and compromise with opponent	35%	6,3% (T-,4)	90,5% (T+,2,4,5,6)	0% (T-)	20,8% (T-,2,4)	21,6% (T-,2,4)

Authorities order to dismantle the house	TOTAL	Cluster Number of Case				
		SELECTIVE (2)	INFORMAL (3)	BASE DEFENDERS (4)	COWBOYS (5)	AUTHORITATIVE (6)
Pursue on your own what is owed	3%	3%	0,8% (T-)	6,5% (T+,3,6)	8,4% (T+,2,3,6)	2%
Go to court	51%	82,5% (T+,3,5,6)	0% (T-)	84,3% (T+,3,5,6)	60,1% (3)	61,8% (T+,3)
Go to another institution	5%	5%	4%	2%	4%	8,7% (T+,3,4)
Difficult to say	4%	3%	5%	5%	3%	5%
Refusal to answer	0%	0%	0%	1%	0%	0%
BASE	1 035	179	297	175	122	262
Weighted Base	1 036	173	288	162	129	283
Base: All respondents who answered the question.						
a. Sig. level=0,05						

Script Case No 7

Inherited legacy kept by wife for herself	TOTAL	Cluster Number of Case				
		SELECTIVE (2)	INFORMAL (3)	BASE DEFENDERS (4)	COWBOYS (5)	AUTHORITATIVE (6)
Do not react, give up	23%	20%	25%	22%	28%	20%
Arrive at agreement and compromise with opponent	72%	77% (5)	70,9% (5)	74% (5)	59,1% (T-)	73% (5)
Pursue on your own what is owed	2%	1%	2%	0%	7,2% (T+,2,3,4,6)	1%
Go to court	2%	1%	0%	1%	3,5% (3)	3,9% (3,4)
Go to another institution	0%	0%	0%	0%	0%	0%
Difficult to say	2%	1%	1%	2%	2%	1%
Refusal to answer	0%	0%	0%	1%	0%	1%

Inherited legacy kept by wife for herself		Cluster Number of Case				
	TOTAL	SELEC-TIVE (2)	INFOR-MAL (3)	BASE DEFENDERS (4)	COWBOYS (5)	AUTHORI-TATIVE (6)
BASE	1 035	179	297	175	122	262
Weighted Base	1 036	173	288	162	129	283
Base: All respondents who answered the question.						
a. Sig. level=0,05						

Script Case No 8

Woman battered by the jealous husband		Cluster Number of Case				
	TOTAL	SELEC-TIVE (2)	INFOR-MAL (3)	BASE DEFENDERS (4)	COWBOYS (5)	AUTHORI-TATIVE (6)
Do not react, give up	5%	4%	4%	6%	9,4% (T+,3,6)	3%
Arrive at agreement and compromise with opponent	55%	56,9% (6)	71,2% (T+,2,5,6)	71,1% (T+,2,5,6)	50,2% (6)	31,8% (T-)
Pursue on your own what is owed	7%	3%	4%	7,7% (2)	15,5% (T+,2,3,4,6)	7,5% (2,3)
Go to court	13%	20,1% (T+,3,4,5)	7% (T-)	3,7% (T-)	10,3% (4)	22,4% (T+,3,4,5)
Go to another institution	12%	10,3% (3,4)	3,1% (T-)	4,5% (T-)	7%	30,1% (T+,2,3,4,5)
Difficult to say	7%	5%	10,6% (T+,2,6)	6%	8%	5%
Refusal to answer	1%	1%	0%	1%	0%	1%
BASE	1 035	179	297	175	122	262
Weighted Base	1 036	173	288	162	129	283
Base: All respondents who answered the question.						
a. Sig. level=0,05						

Appendix B. Distribution of various types of Court experience across the clusters

Table 1. General life court experience distribution among the clusters

Had you ever appeared before the Court in whatever role (party, accused, witness etc.)?							
		TOTAL	SELEC-TIVE (2)	INFOR-MAL (3)	BASE DEFENDERS (4)	COWBOYS (5)	AUTHORI-TATIVE (6)
No, never		50%	51,3% (4)	50%	40,4% (T-)	55,1% (4)	53,4% (4)
Yes		50%	49%	50%	59,6% (T+,2,5,6)	45%	47%
	BASE	1 035	179	297	175	122	262
	Weighted Base	1 036	173	288	162	129	283
'Base: Qualified							
a. Sig. level=0,05							

Table 2. The life civil court experience across the clusters

Have you ever appeared before the Court in a civil case?							
		TOTAL	SELEC-TIVE (2)	INFOR-MAL (3)	BASE DEFENDERS (4)	COWBOYS (5)	AUTHORI-TATIVE (6)
Not		29%	30%	22%	28%	35%	34,5% (3)
Yes		69%	68%	77% (5,6)	69%	64%	65%
Difficult to say		2%	2%	1%	3,1% (6)	2%	0%
Lack answers		0%	0%	0%	0%	0%	1%
	BASE	536	92	153	108	58	125
	Weighted Base	516	85	145	97	58	132
'Base: Qualified							
a. Sig. level=0,05							

Table 3. The life criminal court experience across the clusters

		Have you ever appeared before the Court in a criminal case?				
	TOTAL	SELEC-TIVE (2)	INFOR-MAL (3)	BASE DEFENDERS (4)	COWBOYS (5)	AUTHORI-TATIVE (6)
Not	65%	71,7% (5,6)	67,3% (6)	73,5% (5,6)	55%	55,5% (T-)
Yes	34%	26%	31%	25%	45,1% (2,4)	44,5% (T+,2,3,4)
Difficult to say	1%	2%	1%	1%	0%	0%
BASE	536	92	153	108	58	125
Weighted Base	516	85	145	97	58	132
‘Base: Qualified						
a. Sig. level=0,05						

Jacek Kurczewski

Chapter VII. Four Local Studies of Transformation[73]

Although Maria Ossowska when founding the new Science of Morality kept her construction as far as possible from the lawyers whom she suspected of futile verbalism, she was actually interested in various aspects of law – as a citizen she criticized capital punishment, the repressive so-called Little Penal Code supplementing the normal one with an elaborated list of capital and petty political crimes all punished severely, and as the academician she pointed. to the class character of the penal law and moral elements in the English laws addressing poverty, devoting to this subject a whole socio-legal chapter in her *Moral Thought of English Enlightenment*. She welcomed the socio-legal interest of her young staff member Adam Podgórecki, though her resistance to using mass interview techniques in this area as well as in the area of moral beliefs was elegant but invincible.

In this chapter we focus on the issue that seems far from the sociology of morality, but which we think is in fact very much related to some of its basic topics, that is the ideal of social relations. We are so accustomed to hearing disputes on differences between law and morality, the dispute that Ossowska once described as basically verbal and not substantial, that we forget that law is morally evaluated as one of the mechanisms of social conflict and cooperation. To choose between law and non-legal judgments, to choose between courts of justice and informal negotiation and mediation reflects two different normative models of social life. This is best exemplified in a debate on the supposed Japanese ethos of conciliation that was promoted by founder of the Japanese sociology of law T. Kawashima and undermined in the course of sophisticated statistical research by Masayuki Murayama. If there is such a conciliatory base in Japanese culture this is a question for the anthropology of ethics in a general sense, a discipline that Maria Ossowska, pupil both of Bronisław Malinowski and the British philosophers most admired among the modern-day social scientists.

The main thesis here is that there are two ways of social life, apart from the Law of the Strong, which is in essence no law at all but the Order of Power. There

73 Previously published as J. Kurczewski and P. Orzechowski, Dispute Settlement Patterns in Polish Public Opinion – Four Local Studies of Transformation in: Societas/Communitas 2, 2016. Mr Orzechowski prepared the regression analysis for this chapter.

are two other ways for social life, one through the development of certain ideally impartial rules and powers that act in no other interest than support for the common good; second, the mutual interaction of social actors together with all their affiliates. In the senior author's juvenile exploration into the anthropology of law (Kurczewski 1973) several cases of native systems of sociologically understood law operating in traditional societies were presented and in most of them no authoritative dispute cutting mechanism, equivalent to our courts of law, is present. Courts were a discovery in the course of societal evolution. But law can exist without courts if, following Petrażycki, we will view law as the interpersonally interacting reciprocal attitudes of righteous claiming and obedient fulfilling of an obligation bound, as Roman lawyers used to say, in *nexus iuris*. If claims conflict, a dispute may emerge (Kurczewski 1982) and this conflict may be then either fought with force or avoided, which is the opposite, or develop into a dispute that is the use of arguments aiming at ending the conflict in question. Two ways of ending a dispute are then, first of all, an attempt to change the expectations of the other side based upon the free will of both parties; secondly, a voluntary involvement by at least one of the opposing parties with a third party to act as neutral arbiter whose authority is a priori acknowledged. Our publication deals with the micro-study of circumstances in which one or another way of dispute management is chosen.

Description of research

In the 1970s a series of studies was initiated that aimed at the description of the ways in which Polish society dealt with its everyday conflicts. The techniques used were exactly the ones which Ossowska found abominable– questionnaires with many close-ended questions asked in a survey of a random or quota sample. Financial limitations imposed a limit on the sample size to ca. 200 people. In all the areas it was an exactly random address sample. Altogether 334 interviews were made by students in Warsaw-Ursynów (1977/8), 229 in Olesno (1977) and 211 in Lesko (1978). The outcome was two books published in the next decade (Kurczewski. 1982; Fuszara 1988). The position of the judiciary in democratic Poland has changed totally since 1989, while its personnel remained largely the same at the beginning, except for a few cases of blatant overzealousness with which many judges implemented the martial law regulations. Following the Italian model, the Supreme Council of the Judiciary has been set up, and judges are independent of the Ministry of Justice while courts remain within its organizational and financial domain. The panoply of supreme courts, Constitutional Tribunal, Supreme Court, Supreme Administrative Court and even a separate Tribunal of State to deal with cases against the President and involving the constitutional responsibility of the Prime Minister and other ministers. In addition, there is a function of the Ombudsperson, who in Poland played a significant role in the transition years 1988–1993 and who partially took over the role played in this respect by the Constitutional Tribunal in Hungary. After 25 years it was time to compare the patterns of disputes and the role of courts in everyday life in democratic Poland with that in the Polish People's Republic. The research was made possible with the support of KBN Grant 1H02A 01218 and was conducted in 2001–2003 in seven judicial districts . Warsaw- Ursynów, Lesko, Olesno, Węgrów, Kutno, Płock, and Włodawa (Kurczewski and Fuszara 2004), the first four of which were also the loci of our investigations in the 1970s. The sampling model was replicated except for the metropolitan area where the quota scheme had to be applied as a result of the dramatic rise in the inaccessibility of randomly selected respondents (see Appendix A at the end of the book). In 2014–2016 this research model was used for the third time within the frame of a new research project on Dispute and Dispute Settlement Patterns in Popular Legal Culture (National Science Center research grant No. DEC-2012/07/B/HS6/02496) making it possible to draw the comparison over time. As it turned out later, it was the last moment to study the dispute patterns as they functioned within the democratic legal state as it was shaped after 1989 and before the beginning of the wholescale change of the justice system in Poland by the Law and Justice Party government starting with changing the position of the Constitutional Court.

The purpose of this chapter is to describe the changes in the perception and the use of courts or alternative ways of dispute management in that historical context using the four cases for which we have data starting from late 1970s until the recent times. Such historical scope has its price. Apart from the obvious change in the meaning of institutions, the original research model has become obsolete. It was our conscious decision that it would be an obvious loss for the sociology of law if this opportunity for such a comparison with all its faults and weaknesses were to be missed. After all, progress in the research methodology is so continuous that all research done today will be inevitably downgraded in the face of new models and new techniques. It does not mean, however, that in some corner of our discipline the old descriptions cannot be used even if one does not, as in our case, have original data to be re-analyzed. After all, in the 1970s, when the first round of research was done there were no microprocessors, technology that made the sophisticated statistical analysis of data possible, and which is so common today. In effect, we have to present a mixture of qualitative case analysis with quantitative data that should be viewed with caution as an indication of a possible relationship rather than its measure in the strict sense.

One should start by saying that Poland is divided into a few hundred judicial districts covering the national territory in an even geographical pattern. This means in practice that these regions differ in terms of their demographic density and sociological characteristics. Most of the district seats are also county seats, though, to the despair of the researcher the boundaries do not coincide, making sociographic comparisons impossible. Taking into account the fact that the majority of the seats are small towns, the author thought in the 1970s that the proper way of taking this variety into consideration is, on the one hand, to collect the relevant information in the capital, the Warsaw-Ursynów metropolitan area, and on the other one, to do a study in small localities where the traditional model of the small court and personal knowledge of the local judges and lawyers, not to mention of some clients, prevailed. This is why in three small towns, each with a population more than 10,000 inhabitants, the questionnaire was administered to random samples of all the adults listed in the electoral register.

The four social habitats

These three small towns represent three historically distinct Polish territories. Olesno (9,648 inhabitants in 2015) with most of Silesia came in the mid-18th century from under Austrian to Prussian rule and remained part of the German state until 1945. Its inhabitants, the local people, were Silesians of Slav or German origin and had different linguistic and ethnic orientations. After the war, when Poland took over the formerly German part of Silesia, many Silesians could and did in fact claim Polish citizenship, in contrast with those parts of formerly German Silesia where no Polish minority had been registered prior to the war. With the arrival of democracy in 1989 most of them, however, reclaimed Silesian-German identity as a strongly organized local political grouping which, despite the fact that in the town itself they were a minority, had been effectively ruling the town until 2006.

There is another dramatic past behind the two remaining small towns under study. Lesko (5,615 inhabitants in 2015) in the southeast corner of the post-war Poland, for centuries used to be a busy little commercial center on the route between Poland and the Polish-controlled Ukraine as well as between Poland and Hungary and Hungarian-controlled Slovakia. After the partitions of Poland it belonged to Austrian Galicia until Poland regained independence in 1918, most of the time with great local autonomy including the justice administration. The town was in 1939 occupied by the Soviet Union, by Germany after 1941 and eventually restored to Poland. During World War II, the Jews (63% of inhabitants in 1923) were exterminated and after the War, Ukrainians were expelled to the East and Westwards, while some Poles expelled from the East were re-located here.

Węgrów (12,641 inhabitants in 2010) used to be a Polish-Jewish town east of Warsaw under Russian rule throughout the 19th century until 1918. In 1939–1945 it came under German occupation, several thousands of Jews (5.148 Jews registered in 1923) were exterminated and the half-empty town was partially re-settled by Polish peasants from the countryside.

As a counterpart to the small towns, the metropolitan district of Warsaw – Ursynów was chosen as the fourth research area. A middle class housing district (149 167 inhabitants in 2015) of the metropolitan city built on the outskirts of the Polish capital starting from 1977 and slowly modernized after 1989, well-linked with courts at all levels.

In terms of the legal culture one may say that apart from the countryside-metropolitan dimension each of the three small towns under study represents a historically different legal tradition despite the fact that the law personnel have been trained everywhere in the unified Polish professional legal culture. If one takes into account the fact that the modern justice administration was established on the Polish territories under foreign rule in the 19th century it might be said that at least some of Olesno dwellers interviewed in the 1970s had personal recollections of German (Prussian) legal order, in Lesko the Galician Polish justice and in Węgrów the Russian administration of justice were already in the remote past. The regional legal differences ended with World War Two and the national legal unification started in 1918 and ended in 1946.

Table 1. Main social characteristics of the four localities under study (in %)

Social characteristics of local societies	**Lesko**	**Olesno**	**Węgrów**	**Warszawa Ursynów**
Median years in town	37	34	×	**17**
Willing to leave	39	32	×	32
Knowing majority of passers-by	74	61	×	**26**
Taking account of majority	26	27	×	**13**
Feeling neighbours know	69	62	×	**35**
University level education	31	31	27	**59**
Satisfied with relative material standard	29	28	34	33
Economically active	41	47	×	**52**
Total 100%=N	346	322	61	267

The first row indicates how settled the inhabitants of a given locality are, the median years of life in Olesno being 34 and in Lesko 37 in contrast to the metropolitan area which started to develop in 1977 and where the median length of residence is only 17 years (In Węgrów we have not collected data on this and several other social indicators as marked by X in the respective cells of the Table 1). Surprisingly, the localities do not differ much as to the percentage of those willing to migrate, nowhere is it more than 39% (the smallest Lesko) or less than 32% (both in Olesno and in the metropolitan area). This might be explained by the next to the bottom row of the Table 1 where the frequency of those who assess their living standard as slightly or much better than average in a respective locality is given. It ranges from 28% in Olesno to 34% in Węgrów.

Despite the obvious differences in the economic opportunities (in none of these small towns under study industry has even been developed), technological infrastructure and type of the labor market, the main difference between the small towns and the metropolitan area is not in the subjective well-being but in the climate of life. Two questions concerned informal social control: *Do you know somebody in your neighborhood whose opinion you take into account?* and *Do you feel that most of the neighbours know what is happening at your home?* Neighbourhood control does not necessarily go together with neighbour authority. In the early 2000s In Lesko 25% and in Węgrów 24% of those interviewed said they took into account the opinion of the majority of their neighbours, while in both small towns majorities of 45% and 53% did not have any neighbor of authority. A different climate prevailed in Olesno where both categories equaled roughly one-third of the sample (35%). Olesno, though more anonymous, is thus more integrated. The internal ethnic division into native Silesians (who mostly define themselves also as Poles) and non-Silesian Polish newcomers may account for this difference. The dwellers from the two ethnic groups may not know each other as the social ties between them are less intense. The instances of Polish-Silesian marriage in the town are rare despite attending the same school and the same church and potential couples are even dissuaded by the priests who claim that intermarriage leads to broken homes in the future. The Silesians more often pay attention to the opinion of their neighbours while the non-Silesians know some selected reference persons. In the metropolitan area the indicators of social control are about twice as low, though, it must be stressed that even here about one third of inhabitants feel they are being monitored by neighbors.

The strength of social control in small towns may be taken as a symptom of the strength of social capital. It was surprising, however, that even though all the three small towns appear to be socially well-knit and cohesive, at least within their two ethnic-cultural halves as in Olesno, in fact, rarely did those interviewed mention anybody to whom people come for assistance in disputes if they do not want to go to court. In most cases, the authority of neighbours seems to be dispersed and unstructured.

In the mid-2010s surveys there was a question included which measured personal dispute settlement capital: In case of a conflict is there anybody to whom you would go for advice and help? Are any such persons, organizations, agencies available to you?

The frequency of people without such knowledge was relatively low (about one third of the samples) and surprisingly alike in the small towns of Lesko (31%) and Olesno (37%) and the metropolitan area (32%) with the exception of Węgrów where only 15% did not mention anybody who would offer such advice and where access to professional lawyers was remarkably high (40%) in contrast to Lesko (17%). Olesno (14%) and the metropolitan area (23%). With gender, age and education in our sample kept under control we may look into Appendix A to check the respective comparison. The second difference is between the cultural capital of the localities as measured by the level of education. The metropolitan area dwellers have completed university education almost twice as often as small town dwellers.

While a declaration of the dispute experience is, in fact, intangible and we cannot do more than speculate about the interpretation made by our respondents when answering this question, which suggests departure from this part of the findings as for quantitative analysis, the approach to an official institution, especially the court with its developed administrative recording procedures makes focusing on courts as the dispute organizing agencies more substantial. The problem is, however, that the decision to approach a court is so rare that in our small local samples there are not enough cases to be put to the further analysis.

The only figure of substance is general: Had a Person ever had any experience of Court ?

Table 2. Personal court experience in four localities (in %)

Has a Respondent Had any Court Experience in His/Her Life?				
Had You any Court Experience in Your Life?	Lesko	Olesno	Węgrów	Warsaw Ursynów
Never	34	58	58	40
Yes, civil case only	24	25	24	41
Yes, criminal case only	11	16	11	11

Has a Respondent Had any Court Experience in His/Her Life?				
Had You any Court Experience in Your Life?	Lesko	Olesno	Węgrów	Warsaw Ursynów
Yes, other type of case only	3	1	3	8
Yes, other combination of cases	4	×	4	×
Total 100%=N	152	189	178	210

The total reported experience does not reveal a lot, but when a subjective definition of the type of case is introduced, it becomes clear that small towns uniformly differ from the metropolitan habitat as to the frequency of civil disputes.

Other statistics available from our data concern overall satisfaction with the court experience:

Table 3. Satisfaction with court in four localities (in %)

Overall satisfaction with the court experience [%]				
Overall satisfaction with the court experience	Lesko	Olesno	Węgrów	Warsaw-Ursynów
On the whole satisfied	61	51	58	49
Satisfied with some aspects, dissatisfied with others	9	14	19	11
On the whole dissatisfied	29	33	23	38
Total 100%=N	198	185	178	206

Lesko, where frequency of declared court experience is higher than in other localities under study has also the highest percentage of those who are satisfied, but on the whole the differences seem trivial except that in metropolitan area the degree of satisfaction is (very slightly) the lowest and the degree of dissatisfaction slightly the largest. Perhaps, then, the above described differences in the structure of court experience may be responsible. However, upon checking if the type of court experience is correlated with satisfaction, one encounters the problem of small numbers, the chi-square values in all four cases are statistically insignificant. One may here collect data from another, nation-wide survey made in 2014 for us by CBOS on a random sample of 1035 people to check the relationship. We found that 61 percent of 359 clients of civil justice had judged the decision rendered by court just, 9 percent as just on some aspects and unjust on others and 13 percent as totally unjust, while in 177 criminal cases the figures were: 47 percent referring to a just decision and 17 percent- to unjust with 21 percent judging it ambivalent, respectively. The larger share of civil cases in the experience of metropolitan court should rather work towards better judicial performance. We cannot explain at this stage why this is not the case.

Table 4. Success in court factoes in four localities (in %)

Success factors [%]								
Success factors	**Lesko**		**Olesno**		**Węgrów**		**Warsaw-Ursynów**	
	2010	**2014**	**2010**	**2014**	**2010**	**2016**	**2010**	**2015**
Merits of case	23	31	20	38	25	44	7	37
Person of judge	14	8	8	5	9	10	5	7
Good lawyer	23	21	29	27	31	23	40	26
Evidence/Witnesses	17	4	15	3	20	3	11	1
Contacts	12	16	12	7	8	3	2	7
Bribes	X	7	1	7	4	5	X	8
Luck	2	2	2	2	1	1	2	3
other	X	9	X	7	X	4	4	9
DK	X	2	X	4	X	X	6	2
Total 100%=N	234	199	258	189	224	170	192	206

The consolidation of democracy in Poland coincided in all four localities studied with remarkable improvement in the rating of justice. Pointing to the merits of the case as the factor determining success in court, positive scoring increased from early 2000s to the mid-2010s by 8 percent in Lesko and Olesno through 19 percent in Węgrów to 14 percent in the district of Warsaw. The other factors remained at a similar level, except for help of a good lawyer, which went down notably in Warsaw-Ursynów (by 14 percent) and slightly in Węgrów as well. In general, the negative factors such as bribery and informal "contacts" were rarely mentioned at either time (pointed mostly by less than 10 percent), except for "contacts" in the smallest of the towns – Lesko and also for "contacts" in Olesno, but only at the beginning of consolidation. Although ideally bribes and contacts should not be mentioned at all, given the widespread suspicion of corruption, cliques and arranging schemes, our findings generally seem to demonstrate the integrity of the local judiciary in all four cases under study. This is supported by the direct assessment of agents of justice, and order as to their performance. Except for the metropolitan area, the majority of interviewees rated the performance of local judges as very good or good. In Warsaw-Ursynów ambivalent judgment was the most frequent but here as well as in the other places the negative option ("bad" and "very bad") was the least frequent. In general, the police are at the top of good assessment, except for Lesko where prosecutors and lay assessors are at the bottom, though it does not mean that they have been so poorly assessed.

Court experience and assessment

Another issue that might be clarified here is the evaluation of the local court, closest to the respondent. But does this type of court matter in their experience? When asked if they had ever had a court experience in life people answer as follows.

The experience is, however, to a varying degree, linked with how much contact there is with the local court. In the metropolitan area only 16 percent report any experience with local (Mokotów Dolny) courts as opposed to small Lesko where the local court experience is reported by almost half – 49 percent of the interviewees. In the middle place are two other small towns – Olesno and Węgrów – where about the same fraction – 30 percent and 28 percent respectively – reported having direct experience with local justice. This should be taken into account when looking at the comparisons that follow.

Table 5. Assessment of justice agents in four localities (in %)

Citizens' assessment of local justice agents												
Citizens' assessment of local justice agents	Lesko			Olesno			Węgrów			Warsaw-Ursynów		
	positive	intermediary	bad	positive	Intermediary	bad	positive	intermediary	Bad	positive	intermediary	bad
Judges	39	24	13	39	17	8	42	26	6	21	33	7
Lay assesors	31	21	9	27	11	3	33	23	4	17	32	4
Prosecutors	30	24	15	29	19	8	27	23	10	14	30	20
Police	30	30	34	51	23	16	42	38	13	38	27	22
Lawyers	42	19	10	42	19	8	44	23	9	24	29	5
Total 100% = N	172	118	81	188	89	43	188	133	42	114	151	58

The map described above does interact with the knowledge about the agents of justice and order. As seen in Table 6 below, in all the localities a large proportion of interviewees withheld their opinion. This may come from distrust towards researchers, however, we do not know of any fact that would corroborate this interpretation. It might be simply be the result of lack of knowledge. As an indirect supportive evidence to that we may consider the fact that the lowest number of answers were given to questions on lay assessors. The fact is that their role in justice has always been marginal and has become even more marginal since the consolidation of the judiciary and lawyers as self-governing corporations. In all the courts we visited, the judges do not know the names of all the lay assessors except for a few who due to their cooperativeness, intelligence and loyalty to professional judges are most often called on to perform their duties in the courtroom. Local police forces are, not surprisingly, those agents of law and order with whom the local people have most often the contact and whose performance they most often have the opportunity to judge.

Table 6. Inability to assess the justice agents in four localities (in %)

Not having an opinion about local justice agents [%]				
Not having opinion about local justice agents	Lesko	Olesno	Węgrów	Warsaw Ursynów
Judges	23	35	25	38
Lay assessors	**38**	**59**	**40**	**46**
Prosecutors	31	44	30	36
Police	**4**	**11**	**7**	**13**
Lawyers	28	33	25	42
Total 100%=N	124	182	127	175

Table 7. Accessibility of justice agents in four localities (in %)

Access defined as "easy" in [%] of citizens samples				
Access defined as "easy" in [%] of citizens samples	**Lesko**	**Olesno**	**Węgrów**	**Warsaw Ursynów**
Court	74	67	70	**54**
Prosecutor's office	65	56	59	**46**
Police	**83**	**80**	**84**	**77**
Lawyers	75	67	73	**53**
Total 100%=N	297	270	286	230

Readiness to use courts

The strategic weapon to be used in everyday disputes is the use of courts or, at least, the threat of its use. One of the aspects of public attitudes towards courts that may be discussed in a comparative way is the readiness to use courts in 15 hypothetical dispute cases that were presented in 1978, 2002 and in 2014 to samples interviewed in Lesko:

Looking further into the frequency with which various types of reactions are advocated in hypothetical dispute situations, one sees that on average both the tendency to approach courts and other official agencies and the tendency to withdraw and surrender rightful claims have decreased.

Withdrawal was on average advocated in 1978 by 26% of the sample, in 2002 by 18% and in 2014 by 18% . A compromise with the second party was advocated by 20.4% in 1978, 36% in 2002 and 43% in 2014; private satisfaction was recommended by 11% in 1978, 15% in 2002, and 13% in 2012 while the official way of advancing one's claims was advocated on average by 30% of the respondents in 1978, 20% of the respondents in 2002 and 24% in 2014. As for courts, they were not separated from other official agencies in 1978. We know, however, that the average advocacy of judicial settlement was 17% in 2002 and the same (17%) in 2012.

Table 8. Preferred patterns of reaction in different types of conflict in Lesko 1978, 2002, and 2014 (Means in %)

<table>
<tr><th colspan="9">Lesko – Preferred patterns of reaction in conflict situation (Mean %)</th></tr>
<tr><th>Type of dispute</th><th></th><th>With-drawal</th><th>Private com-promise</th><th>Private pursuit</th><th>Court only</th><th>Total official pursuit</th><th>Total 100%=N</th></tr>
<tr><td rowspan="3">In family</td><td>1978</td><td>27</td><td>30</td><td>13</td><td colspan="2">20</td><td>90</td></tr>
<tr><td>2002</td><td>17</td><td>52</td><td>9</td><td>6</td><td>10</td><td>94</td></tr>
<tr><td>2014</td><td>19</td><td>56</td><td>9</td><td>7</td><td>14</td><td>105</td></tr>
<tr><td rowspan="3">Between friends</td><td>1978</td><td>22</td><td>23</td><td>11</td><td colspan="2">37</td><td>93</td></tr>
<tr><td>2002</td><td>18</td><td>41</td><td>18</td><td>10</td><td>14</td><td>101</td></tr>
<tr><td>2014</td><td>14</td><td>48</td><td>17</td><td>9</td><td>15</td><td>103</td></tr>
<tr><td rowspan="3">Between neighbors</td><td>1978</td><td>21</td><td>40</td><td>6</td><td colspan="2">22</td><td>89</td></tr>
<tr><td>2002</td><td>16</td><td>52</td><td>20</td><td>2</td><td>5</td><td>95</td></tr>
<tr><td>2014</td><td>17</td><td>55</td><td>14</td><td>1</td><td>13</td><td>100</td></tr>
</table>

<table>
<tr><th colspan="8">Lesko – Preferred patterns of reaction in conflict situation (Mean %)</th></tr>
<tr><th>Type of dispute</th><th></th><th>With-drawal</th><th>Private com-promise</th><th>Private pursuit</th><th>Court only</th><th>Total official pursuit</th><th>Total 100%=N</th></tr>
<tr><td rowspan="3">As consumer</td><td>1978</td><td>38</td><td>31</td><td>15</td><td colspan="2">31</td><td>115</td></tr>
<tr><td>2002</td><td>29</td><td>25</td><td>18</td><td>6</td><td>11</td><td>89</td></tr>
<tr><td>2014</td><td>35</td><td>34</td><td>13</td><td>7</td><td>15</td><td>104</td></tr>
<tr><td rowspan="3">As citizen</td><td>1978</td><td>26</td><td>4</td><td>5</td><td colspan="2">55</td><td>90</td></tr>
<tr><td>2002</td><td>8</td><td>10</td><td>9</td><td>52</td><td>62</td><td>141</td></tr>
<tr><td>2014</td><td>5</td><td>19</td><td>11</td><td>54</td><td>63</td><td>152</td></tr>
</table>

The frequency of giving answers as well as the frequency of withdrawal from a dispute were generally higher in Lesko under communism in 1978. After the regime change there was a marked increase in an interpersonal compromise and negotiations in all relations except for consumer relations. In personal and consumer relations the transition to democracy meant also the decrease in the frequency to approach an official agency. In neighbourly relations it meant also an increased tendency to take conflict into one's own hands, perhaps literally too. A second general observation to be made is that privatization did not apply to disputes with official institutions. Here the average reference to a court or another official agency in cases involving town, hospital and police increased from 55% in 1978 to 63% of the answers in 2002 and remains 63% in 2012. On the other hand, there is an obvious substitution of withdrawal with active attempts at defending one's rights in direct personal contact with the representatives of the public body in question. Withdrawal in those conflicts has fallen from 26% down to 8% of answers to 1% on the average, while the choice of compromise has risen from 4% to 19% to 19%. People are evidently less afraid of raising their claims against perceived abuses on the part of public agencies (N.B. the majority of hospitals in the country have not been privatized) and additionally they have dramatically increased their sense of their rights against those agencies.

What strikes us most in these figures is that, even when it comes to family matters, radically more often today than under communist rule people are willing to keep their domestic disputes within the confines of their homes. It is not welcome to see that even in the case of wife-beating, the attempt at compromise is more often suggested today, and an appeal to such outside forces as the police occurs less frequently. But if combined with the increase in advocacy of compromise with a gossiping wife it may suggest that this privatization of disputes does not refer to internal family matters. Here family coherence and the ideal of mutual forgiveness, and perhaps the otherwise unobserved influence of decades of papal moral teachings, seem to be at work.

As Lesko is the only case for which we have data from the 1970s, we must leave the question open as to whether it is idiosyncratic – see Fuszara (1988) on how it was then in the area where most private criminal accusation were made. In all the four localities – Lesko, Olesno and Warsaw-Ursynów – we have the data for the next historical period, early 2000s and mid-2010s, that is the period of the consolidation of parliamentary democracy under the rule of law.

Table 9. Mean frequencies (in %) of different types of reaction in different types of conflict situation in four localities (A: 2003–2004, B: 2014–16)

Mean frequencies (in %) of different types of reaction in different types of conflict situation in the four localities under study (A: 2003–2004, B: 2014–16)											
Town	**Relationship in the dispute**	**With-drawal**		**Private compromise**		**Private pursuit**		**Court only**		**Other official pursuit**	
		A	**B**	**A**	**B**	**A**	**B**	**A**	**B**	**A**	**B**
Lesko	Family	17	19	52	56	9	9	6	7	4	7
	Friend	18	14	41	48	18	17	10	9	4	6
	Neighbour	16	17	52	55	20	14	2	1	3	12
	Consumer	29	35	25	34	18	13	6	7	5	8
	Citizen	8	5	10	19	9	11	52	54	10	9
	Total N = 100%	88	90	180	212	74	64	76	78	26	42
Olesno	Family	X	16	X	55	X	10	X	10	X	6
	Friend	X	11	X	53	X	19	X	10	X	5
	Neighbour	X	13	X	49	X	15	X	9	X	6
	Consumer	X	25	X	43	X	9	X	11	X	9
	Citizen	X	5	X	18	X	8	X	57	X	9
	Total N = 100%	X	70	X	218	X	61	X	97	X	35
Węgrów	Family	17	14	62	54	10	26	3	9	5	8
	Friend	16	9	51	43	17	24	9	9	5	8
	Neighbour	17	15	51	47	15	17	5	12	3	8
	Consumer +	36	22	25	35	18	20	8	9	1	7
	Citizen	10	4	11	12	12	11	55	61	12	8
	Total N = 100%	96	64	200	191	72	98	80	100	26	39

Mean frequencies (in %) of different types of reaction in different types of conflict situation in the four localities under study (A: 2003–2004, B: 2014–16)											
Town	**Relationship in the dispute**	**With-drawal**		**Private compromise**		**Private pursuit**		**Court only**		**Other official pursuit**	
		A	**B**	**A**	**B**	**A**	**B**	**A**	**B**	**A**	**B**
Warsaw Ursynów	Family	15	18	42	39	9	15	7	9	10	7
	Friend	10	15	45	35	23	19	10	12	7	7
	Neighbour	25	15	46	42	9	17	3	8	10	8
	Consumer +	29	13	24	34	14	24	8	13	18	14
	Citizen	5	5	6	8	8	8	61	62	16	8
	Total N = 100%	84	66	163	158	63	83	89	104	61	83

+ In Węgrów and in Warsaw by mistake one of the consumer dispute cases was missing in the questionnaire.

As shown in table 9 above the period of over dozen years between the first and the second series of local surveys did not result in any remarkable changes. Nor was there a great difference over time between the localities (only two larger than 10 percent). There is also no systematic increase or fall in any of the categories except consumer disputes in which the privately negotiated compromise was on the rise at the expense of withdrawal or a private pursuit (the evidently unclear category kept from the 1970s). These four observations seem to be justified by the above data.

Firstly, uniformly in public disputes, irrespective of the type of social habitat (small town vs metropolitan area) the formal approach to the court is most preferred way of acting.

Secondly, in the metropolitan area dissatisfaction with services or goods offered is most often disregarded, whereas in the small town where business is still conducted with personal acquaintance, the failed seller or service person will most likely be approached directly in person by the aggrieved customer.

Thirdly, in all personal relations, an informal compromise is most likely to be advocated, though less so in the metropolitan area.

Fourthly, the choice of reaction in a personal conflict dispute within the confines of the types of conflict selected for the scripts in the questionnaire in most of the cases were similar and thus independent of the type of personal relationship with the opponent (family, friend, neighbor).

Ideal settlement patterns

Three questions have been repeatedly asked on the ideal ways to deal with conflicts: satisfaction of claims according to rights versus compromise satisfying partly both parties; settlement strictly according to law versus settlement satisfactory to those concerned; authoritative judicial verdict versus non-authoritative advice.

Table 10. Ideal patterns to deal with conflicts (in %)

	Lesko			Olesno			Węgrów			Warsaw-Ursynów		
Year of research	**1978**	**2002**	**2014**	**1977**	**2001**	**2014**	**1978**	**2003**	**2016**	**1977/8**	**2001/22**	**2015**
Full satisfaction of right claims	9	4	10	8	7	10	X	9	X	20	20	19
Compromise satisfying partly both parties	89	94	90	91	88	90	X	88	X	79	79	81
Settlement strictly according to law	21	24	34	17	18	41	X	21	X	33	26	41
Settlement satisfactory to all concerned	79	73	66	80	75	59	X	75	X	67	69	58
Authoritative judicial verdict	27	18	43	22	17	45	X	31	46	45	22	39
Informal mediation	72	75	57	73	70	55	X	65	54	53	73	61
TOTAL 100% = N	211	258		299	234		X	224		334	214	

Obviously, Polish society as represented in our study of the localities holds dominantly the ideal settlement of a dispute to be a voluntarily accepted compromise satisfying both parties at the expense of full satisfaction of the claims and the official law. When it comes to the choice between compromise and the authoritative dispute management, the option for informality has been decreasing in two small towns since early 2000s while the choice of an official agency has been rising. The same may be said of the rise in support for strict legalism in dispute settlement at the expense of flexible compromise agreements both in small towns and in the metropolitan area. Ultimately over the years, once the consolidation of the democratic legal state proceeded, the popularity of an informal compromise began to decrease. In the metropolitan area the pattern is different insofar as the already relatively high degree of popularity of an official agency was at similar level in 1970 as in the mid- 2010s. One is left to speculate that in the middle class-dominated Ursynów the formal authoritative dispute management pattern was already popular in the relatively quiet conditions of mid-1970s and was disrupted in the turmoil of the summer strikes of 1980, Solidarity, martial law persecutions and transformation. The fall in the popular evaluation of administration justice developed especially at the turn of the 1990s and 2000s. In this milieu the level of support for courts as authoritative dispute settlement is in fact returning to its pre-transition level after the temporary withdrawal of support from courts into the informality of personal negotiations while, on the other hand, in the small towns we have been observing a surge in support for authoritative dispute settlement since transformation.

Such a speculation is related to the importance of the problem but the only argument in favour is that of the sudden decline in support for legalism that occurred in the 1980s and ended in 1992 (Kurczewski 2004b:256). As for the prevalence of the informal compromise ideal, traditionally it has been attributed to the Oriental, and specifically Japanese legal culture ever since T. Kawashima's writings (Cf Chiba 1989). M. Murayama has put a lot of work into arguing against such an interpretation arguing for an institutional explanation of the differences. In fact, it may be universal when framed in objective terms; the question is to what degree it is felt applicable in one's own case when it actually happens. However, due to the lack of comparative studies we still do not know if that is the result of the collectivism officially imposed during 45 years of the communist rule in Poland. Contrary to such an explanation one may point to the increase in the acceptance of such an ideal in the metropolitan sample after 1978. Kurczewski in 2004 (a; b) wrote that "The transition coincided with the growing distrust of law and courts as the best methods of dispute settlement". This is supported by the mass of systematic public opinion polls conducted through the transition years starting from 1989 into the 2000s (cf. Borucka-Arctowa and Pałecki 2003; Kurczewski 2004(b); Skąpska and Bryda 2013). But the growth in support for the official authoritative dispute settlement observed in the four localities under our study after the consolidation of the democratic legal state in the mid-2010s may be explained not so much by the withdrawal from the ideal of personal negotiated settlement but by the institutional pressure requiring the use of court by individual and collective actors (Kurczewski 2004:b).

Court versus other settlements

On the basis of all the four sets of data collected in Lesko, Olesno, Węgrów and Warsaw – Ursynów the MLA (Multiple Linear Analysis) was performed in which the predictors to be used as first were the independent socio-demographic variables: gender (1 – woman, 2 –man), age measured on the ratio scale, education (1 – elementary, 2 – junior high, 3 – high and 4 – university degree), relative living standard as compared with the local average one (1 – much better, 2 – slightly better, 3 – average, 4 – slightly worse, 5 – much worse), employment (1 – full, 2 – part-time, 3 – irregular, 4 – none) and marriage status (0 – other than married, 1 – married). Next to these six the three other independent variables of general attitudes relevant in the socio-legal context were added: trust in other people (never trust the others – 1, trust only those already tested – 2 and trust everybody until this fails – 3), ideal pattern of dispute settlement (authoritative, like a court – 1 and compromise by others – 2), law abidance (0 – responses other than 1- one should abide by the law even if unjust), and two variables of court experience, first, the lifelong experience (0 – lack of it, 1 – an experience), second, in the last three years (0 – lack of experience, 1 – an experience). At the third stage two new variables were introduced as a product of satisfaction with court and experience in order to control the interaction effect between satisfaction with court decision and both measures of court experience. As in all the equations they were statistically insignificant we had them removed, but satisfaction and court experience were left for further analysis presented in Appendix A below.

- Three additional indices were dependent criteria: a) reported dispute experience in last 3 years (0 –none, 12 times reported as maximum value in Węgrów and Warsaw-Ursynów and 13 times in Lesko and Olesno), b) strength of preference for court measured by number of cases when it was advocated (0 – none, maximum value 14 [Węgrów and Warssaw- Ursynów] or 15 [Lesko and Olesno] if court was advocated in all cases presented in the interview) and c) strength of preference for private compromise (0 – compromise advocated in no case, maximum 14 [Węgrów and Ursynów] or [Lesko and Olesno] 15 times compromise advocated in the interview). The difference in the maximum values results from the difference in number of cases presented in the interview questionnaires.
- As for the general reported dispute experience in the last 3 years in Lesko significant predictors are age (beta = -0.24; $p<0.01$), employment (beta = -0.27; $p<0.001$) and recent court experience (beta = 0.46; $p<0.001$). In Olesno it is only recent court experience (beta = 0.62; $p<0.001$); in Węgrów only age (beta

= -0.39; $p<0.001$) and in Warsaw-Ursynów age (beta = -0.16; $p<0.01$), satisfaction with relative standard of living (beta = 0.22; $p<0.001$), trust in other people (beta = – 0.15; $p<0.05$), lifelong (beta = 0.17; $p<0.01$) and recent court experience. In Lesko the model fits well data F (3;170) = 19.97; $p<0.001$ and explains 25% of variance of the dispute experience (R^2 = 0.25). In Olesno model is well-fit F (1;150) = 95.74; $p<0.01$ and explains 39% of variance of the dependent variable (R^2 = 0.39). In Węgrów though model was also well-fit F (2;159) = 6.80; $p<0.001$ it explains drastically less (7% , R^2 = 0.07) of variance of dispute experience. In Warsaw-Ursynów model is also well-fit and explains as well as in Olesno more than one-third (F (5;164) = 21.85; $p<0.001$, R^2 = 0.38) of variance in dispute experience.

- As mentioned, in all the localities the incidence of disputes is relatively well predicted by age as younger people declare it more often. In the metropolitan area one should add here self-assessment of relative standard of living as those who feel poor are more likely to report disputes. The relationship between the incidence of disputes and reported recent court experience is to a certain degree spurious as not all disputes go to the court.
- As for the indices of preference for court and for compromise as ways to settle a dispute in several different cases as described in the questionnaire no statistically significant predictors were found in Lesko. In Olesno, preference for courts is significantly predicted by age only (beta = -0.28; $p<0.001$) and no significant predictor of choice of compromise was found. In Węgrów both preference for court and for compromise, though in the opposite direction from the independent variable as significantly predicted by age (for choice of a court beta = -0.39; $p<0.001$ and for choice of the compromise beta = 0.21; $p<0.01$). In Warsaw-Ursynów preference for court is significantly predicted by age (beta = -0.32; $p<0.001$), satisfaction with relative standard of living (beta = -0.20; $p<0.01$) and gender (beta = 0.17; $p<0.05$), while the preference for compromise by age (beta = -0.19; $p<0.01$), education (bata = -0.2; $p<0.01$), marriage status (beat = 0.24; $p<0.001$) and satisfying experience with court (beta = 0.25; $p<0.001$).
- As for the fitness with data all models fared well in Olesno F (1;150) = 95.74; $p<0.01$ explaining 39% of variance of the preference for courts (R^2 = 0.39), in Węgrów for courts F (2;159) = 6.80; $p<0.001$ explaining 7% of variance (R^2 = 0.07) and for Compromise F (1;160) = 7.27; $p<0.01$ explaining 4% of variance (R^2 = 0.04) and in Warsaw-Ursynów for courts F (3;183) = 12.96; $p<0.001$) explaining 16% of variance (R^2 = 0.16) and for compromise (F (4;187) = 9.00; $p<0.01$) explaining 14% of variance (R^2 = 0.14). Evidently, prediction of the

dispute settlement preferences went much worse than in the case of dispute experience, especially in Lesko where no statistically significant predictor was found. The exception is Olesno where the percent of variance explained is almost equal to 40%.

- As for the substance it may be said that in all the cases if age is a predictor of dispute settlement it is the elderly who are less likely to advocate going to court (Węgrów, Warsaw-Ursynów) and more likely to ask for compromise (Olesno, Węgrów). In the metropolitan area also the low assessment of one's own living standard in comparison with others makes choice of court less likely, while better education and male gender makes the choice of compromise less likely. It seems therefore that within the metropolitan area that social position, low or high, influences the choice of the authoritative versus dispute settlement procedures which may be explained by the anonymity of the social and public relations context in which disputes develop and official institutions like court function.

As seen above, in all the four localities the indices of preference for court or for compromise are best predicted by age, then by court experience and the least often by gender. The general ideal pattern of dispute settlement as well as attitude towards respecting the law do not influence these indices directly but through their correlations with other predictors. Our conclusion is that one needs to maintain a distinction between the ideal and the practice in the area of law and conflict as well as in the others. Although the pattern of informal settlement of an issue through negotiation and mediation has lost its popularity and the open pursuit of one's own rights before the court or any other official body has become widespread not only in the countryside but also in the middle class metropolitan habitat, still the choice of an informal or official way of dispute settlement depends on the circumstances of conflict, above all, the perceived seriousness and the type of an opponent. At this stage of research we must reject the working hypothesis of a peculiar culture of compromise and informality. Our data point also to the lack of any clear difference between the four localities under investigation. It thus seems that under contemporary conditions the uniform national institutional court structure interacts with the uniform national legal culture. This does not mean, however, that contrary to sentimental expectations the intra-institutional professional culture of court cannot differ locally. This could have been experienced by members of the research staff when contacting the respective courts. Certainly the metropolitan court has a different „climate" from the small court in a small town. This is, however, another research issue not to be tackled by this one focusing on the representations of justice in a popular, common way of thinking about law, justice and disputes. On the other hand, similarly to the knowledge of unjust verdicts that comes mostly from the media of national scope, in the metropolitan area the inhabitants have much less contact with the local court than in the small towns, The metropolitan middle-class urbanite's legal experience is shaped by contacts with a much larger variety of official agencies and lawyers than it happens in the case of the small city dweller, who knows the available lawyers in the area better and finds access to the local justice agencies more easily. In some way Węgrów is in the intermediate position as its inhabitants travel often daily to work in Warsaw, and the size of the local intelligentsia also makes it easier to find legal advice at the place or in the capital through family and other personal ties.

Having said that, it must be stated that the longitudinal communities study in 4 localities has not rejected the hypothesis of the different local legal cultures but pointed to the growth of similarity. They were much more diverse 40 years ago than during the transformation, if the attitude towards the courts is taken into consideration. In the late 1970s , the metropolitan area dwellers were much more often in favour of choosing the authoritative dispute settlement agency than small city dwellers who were more often pro private compromise. This difference disappeared first during the transformation in the early 2000s when metropolitan people came close to small town people in privatizing the dispute settlement as ideal, and then again in mid-2010s when all groups moved towards the authoritative dispute settlement model. The growing role of the official law in the everyday life of Poles has affected all, and until legal formalization of interactions ceases to be a requirement of daily life. The homogenization of popular legal culture determined by the official legal culture will follow.

Appendix A. Multiple Regression Analysis

Table 1: Court Experience in Last 3 Years (0-none, 12/13 – all dispute types experienced) (beta values)

Predictors:	Lesko	Olesno	Węgrów	Warsaw – Ursynów
Gender (1-woman, 2-man)	-0.01	-0.24	0.06	0.00
Age (continuous)	-0.24 **	0.39	-0.21 **	-0.16 **
Education (1-elementary, 4-university degree)	0.01	0.30	-0.05	-0.10
Relative living standard (1-much better, 5-much worse)	-0.17	0.45	0.02	0.22 ***
Employment (1-full, 4-lack)	-0.27 ***	-0.06	NA	0.05

Predictors:	Lesko	Olesno	Węgrów	Warsaw – Ursynów
Marriage status (0-other, 1-married)	0.00	-0.32	NA	0.04
Trust in others (1-distrustful, 3-trustful)	-0.14	0.29	NA	-0.15 *
Ideal dispute settlement (1-authoritative, 2-informal)	0.03	-0.15	0.13	-0.01
Law abidance (1-other responses, 2-strict)	0.20	-0.10	0.12	0.03
Lifelong court experience (0-none, 1-yes)	-0.11	-0.02	0.26 **	0.17 **
Court experience in last 3 years (0-none, 1-yes)	0.46 ***	0.62 ***	0.21	0.51 ***
Satisfaction with court (0-not, 2-yes)	0.04	0.16	0.39	0.11
Model – Summary	F (3;170) = 19.97 p= 0.000***, R^2 = 0.25	F (1;150) = 95.74 p= 0.01**, R^2 = 0.39	F (2;159) = 6.80 p= 0.000***, R^2 = 0.07	F (5;164) = 21.85 p= 0.000***, R^2 = 0.38
Levels of significance: *** p<0.001, ** p<0.01, * p<0.05				

Table 2: Preference for dispute settlement by court or another authoritative body and through private compromise (0-lack of choice, 14/15 – choice of the court resp. compromise in all cases) (beta values)

Predictors:	Lesko		Olesno		Węgrów		Warsaw – Ursynów	
	Court – cases (0 – never, 15 – in all cases)	Compromise – cases (0 – never, 15 – in all cases)	Court – cases (0 – never, 15 – in all cases)	Compromise – cases (0 – never, 15 – in all cases)	Court – cases (0 – never, 14 – in all cases)	Compromise – cases (0 – never, 14 – in all cases)	Court – cases (0 – never, 14 – in all cases)	Compromise – cases (0 – never, 14 – in all cases)
Gender (1-woman, 2-man)	0.12	-0.03	0.28	-0.18	-0.04	0.07	0.17 *	-0.19 **
Age (continuous)	-0.21	0.05	-0.28 ***	0.14	-0.39 ***	0.21 **	-0.32 ***	0.07
Education (1-elementary, 4-university degree)	0.01	-0.03	0.35	0.07	0.04	-0.01	0.07	-0.20 **

Predictors:	**Lesko**		**Olesno**		**Węgrów**		**Warsaw – Ursynów**	
	Court – cases (0 – never, 15 – in all cases)	**Compromise – cases (0 – never, 15 – in all cases)**	**Court – cases (0 – never, 15 – in all cases)**	**Compromise – cases (0 – never, 15 – in all cases)**	**Court – cases (0 – never, 14 – in all cases)**	**Compromise – cases (0 – never, 14 – in all cases)**	**Court – cases (0 – never, 14 – in all cases)**	**Compromise – cases (0 – never, 14 – in all cases)**
Relative living standard (1-much better, 5-much worse)	0.13	-0.03	-0.19	0.42	0.04	-0.09	-0.20 **	-0.17
Employment (1-full, 4-lack)	-0.13	-0.10	0.35	-0.08	NA	NA	0.12	0.07
Marriage status (0-other, 1-married)	-0.07	0.00	-0.58	0.65	NA	NA	-0.14	-0.24 ***
Trust in others (1-distrustful, 3-trustful)	-0.02	-0.25	-0.01	0.10	NA	NA	-0.03	-0.01
Ideal dispute settlement (1-authoritative, 2-informal)	-0.11	0.16	-0.24	-0.09	-0.09	0.13	-0.09	0.09
Law abidance (1-other responses, 2-strict)	-0.10	0.18	0.08	0.13	-0.12	0.03	-0.06	-0.08
Lifelong court experience (0-none, 1-yes)	0.56	0.33	0.33	-0.24	0.01	-0.13	0.20	-0.10
Court experience in last 3 years (0-none, 1-yes)	0.30	-0.21	-0.04	-0.08	-0.15	-0.01	-0.08	0.08
Satisfaction with court (0-not, 2-yes)	0.95	0.73	0.67	0.50	-0.21	0.19	0.05	0.25 ***
Model – Summary			F (1;150) = 13.09 p=0.000 ***, R^2 = 0.09		F (1;160) = 29.12 p=0.000 ***, R^2 = 0.15	F (1;160) = 7.27 p=0.01 **, R^2 = 0.04	F (3;183) = 12.96 p=0.000 ***, R^2 = 0.16	F (4;187) = 9.00 p=0.000 ***, R^2 = 0.14
Levels of significance: *** p<0.001, ** p<0.01, * p<0.05								

Appendix B. Distribution of answers to the hypothetical conflict case scripts in %

LESKO (Total N = 175)

Hypothetical situation	With-drawal	Private compro-mise	Private pursuit	Courts only	Official pursuit	Lost	NA	Total N = 100%
1. Neighbour telling gossip	37	46	14	2	1	0	0	175
2. Beating children by neighbour	2	49	17	12	18	1	1	175
3. Taking things from garden by neighbour	21	60	10	6	1	1	1	175
4. Face slapping by friend	18	58	18	1	2	1	2	175
5. Taking item by friend	10	43	18	17	10	1	1	175
6. Refusing to pro-mote friend	14	44	21	10	6	2	3	175
7. Waiving confiden-tiality by hospital	3	17	13	59	6	1	1	175
8. Beating by police	7	17	12	47	14	1	2	175
9. Expropriation by town	5	22	8	55	7	1	2	175
10. Random check-up in shop	43	26	11	6	11	1	2	175
11. Restrictions on sale	45	37	10	2	3	0	3	175
12. Putting picture on show	17	40	19	13	9	0	2	175
13. Inheritance kept by wife for herself	38	58	2	1	0	0	1	175
14. Wife beaten by jealous husband	2	46	14	19	18	0	1	175
15. Wife gossiping about husband	18	65	12	1	2	1	1	175

OLESNO (Total N = 152)

Hypothetical situation	With-drawal	Private com-promise	Private pursuit	Courts only	Official pursuit	Lost	NA	Total N=100%
1. Neighbour telling gossip	34	47	15	1	1	1	1	152
2. Beating children by neighbour	7	38	18	17	17	1	2	152
3. Taking things from garden by neighbour	7	63	13	10	1	3	3	152
4. Face slapping by friend	7	62	21	7	3	0	0	152
5. Taking item by friend	10	55	16	12	3	4	0	152
6. Refusing to promote friend	15	41	20	12	8	3	1	152
7. Waiving confidentiality by hospital	5	14	10	60	9	1	1	152
8. Beating by police	5	12	10	59	11	1	2	152
9. Expropriation by town	6	27	4	53	7	2	1	152
10. Random check-up in shop	34	29	8	12	15	1	1	152
11. Restrictions on sale	36	41	5	7	8	1	2	152
12. Putting picture on show	6	59	13	15	4	3	0	152
13. Inheritance kept by wife for herself	31	60	4	2	1	1	1	152
14. Wife beaten by jealous husband	5	38	10	26	17	3	1	152
15. Wife gossiping about husband	12	66	15	3	1	1	2	152

WĘGRÓW (Total N = 162)

Hypothetical situation	With-drawal	Private com-promise	Private pursuit	Courts only	Official pursuit	Lost	NA	Total N=100%
1. Neighbour telling gossip	38	46	14	1	1	0	0	162
2. Beating children by neighbour	1	30	18	27	22	1	1	162
3. Taking things from garden by neighbour	6	64	18	8	2	1	1	162
4. Face slapping by friend	13	45	28	4	6	2	2	162
5. Taking item by friend	9	46	17	18	6	3	1	162
6. Refusing to promote friend	17	38	27	6	6	4	2	162
7. Waiving confidentiality by hospital	3	14	12	61	6	3	1	162
8. Beating by police	7	8	10	58	12	4	1	162
9. Expropriation by town	3	13	12	64	5	2	1	162
10. Random check-up in shop	38	22	18	9	9	3	1	162
11. Putting picture on show	7	49	22	10	6	4	2	162
12. Inheritance kept by wife for herself	20	56	20	1	1	1	1	162
13. Wife beaten by jealous husband	2	36	9	23	22	5	3	162
14. Wife gossiping about husband	14	60	19	2	1	3	1	162

WARSAW (URSYNÓW) (Total N = 192)

Hypothetical situation	With-drawal	Private com-promise	Private pursuit	Courts only	Official pursuit	Lost	NA	Total N=100%
1. Neighbour telling gossip	43	34	21	0	0	1	1	192
2. Beating children by neighbour	3	31	21	17	21	5	2	192
3. Taking things from garden by neighbour	8	62	10	8	4	5	3	192
4. Face slapping by friend	18	35	32	6	3	1	5	192
5. Taking item by friend	8	47	17	15	7	2	4	192
6. Refusing to promote friend	18	22	31	12	11	2	4	192
7. Waiving confidentiality by hospital	2	5	8	72	4	5	4	192
8. Beating by police	7	7	10	54	17	2	3	192
9. Expropriation by town	5	12	7	60	4	3	9	192
10. Random check-up in shop	36	17	9	5	22	5	6	192
11. Putting picture on show	8	34	22	17	7	5	7	192
12. Inheritance kept by wife for herself	31	50	7	2	1	1	8	192
13. Wife beaten by jealous husband	5	22	16	20	24	7	6	192
14. Wife gossiping about husband	18	46	22	1	1	6	6	192

Jacek Kurczewski

Chapter VIII. Ethnic dimension

Apart from checking the continuity over time and the structure in dispute patterns, the third main purpose of our research was to check the role of ethnic differences in the dispute settlement patterns. In the Polish context the issue seems of marginal importance as is the minorities issue as such. It is obvious that Poland is an unusually difficult place for such a test as during World War Two and afterwards due to the Holocaust and forced ethnic resettlements, being the pre-war country in which ethnic Poles constituted over a 60% majority it became an almost homogeneous country. Suffice it to say that until dual ethnic identity was introduced in the census in 2002 ca. 96% declared themselves as Poles, 1,23% (471,000 people) gave their nationality different from Polish and 2,03% (774,900 people) did not identify their nationality at all. Once the opportunity to declare dual nationality by choice was inserted into the interview schedule in the latest National Census of 2011 run by the Main Statistical Office, Polish nationality was declared by 97.09% of those interviewed, of whom 871,500 people (2.26% of the total) declared two nationalities – including Polish, and other nationalities by 596,000 people (1,55% of the total).

The Polish Law on National and Ethnic Minorities and Regional Language of January 6, 2005 enumerates the national and ethnic minorities that are granted several rights, and above all securing the right to education in their own language. Interestingly, the ethnic group of Cassubians was not recognized as minority but still was granted the right to cultivate Cassubian language as their own "regional language". Nevertheless, the Law granted all the ethnic minorities the cultural rights that enable them to apply for State funds and sponsorship of cultural and educational activities. A special case, however, is that of the "Silesians", who before World War Two were designated as Upper Silesians (Górnoslązaki, Oberschlesier) but under German rule were characterized as a German ethnic minority with their own regional language (Wasserpolnisch) combining old Polish dialect with German intrusions. Silesians had lived in the area since late Middle Ages, first under the rule of the Czechs, then Luxemburg, Habsburgs and in the mid-18th century mostly under Prussian rule and duc to the fact that their history was not part of the Old Polish-Lithuanian Rzeczpospolita (Commonwealth) that flourished in Central-Eastern Europe until the partitions at the end of the 18th century. The National Polish movement started to influence the natives of Upper Silesia in the mid-19th century and when with the end of the First World War the German empire started do disintegrate, fierce battles between the armed partisans of the unification of Upper Silesia with the reborn Poland and the German state loyalists erupted which ended in 1920 with a plebiscite under the rule of the League of Nations. This Plebiscite divided Upper Silesia into Polish and German parts until World War Two which brought an end to German rule over the whole of Silesia and the resettlement of the Germans to Germany with its new borders. But due to the history of the organized Polish minority in Upper Silesia that survived the plebiscite the Silesians in the former contested territory – in contrast to Lower Silesia unequivocally Germanized throughout the centuries – the native population was given the choice whether to opt for Polish nationality and remain or to opt for German nationality and leave.

It is not difficult to imagine the complexity of the individual identities and social relations under such critical conditions even though the religious factor so characteristic of many other "ethnic" conflicts e.g. as the one in Northern Ireland, was not important here as the Upper Silesians were and are mostly Roman Catholic independent of their national creed. The national divide was cutting through families and other primary groups. The use of the local Silesian vernacular was also prevalent in both warring sides. Inevitably, a group of separatists emerged who tried to keep themselves apart from the division, proclaiming their own Silesian identity distinct from both the German and the Polish ones. This separatist movement administratively persecuted (as well as the German national movement) under Communist rule burst out on a previously unprecedented scale after the political emancipation of Polish society in 1989. Interestingly, separatists felt relatively well in this part of Upper Silesia which was Polish between the wars, while in the part that was annexed in 1945 the native population in 1989 identified themselves as a German minority.

The fear of Silesian separatism is at the heart of the refusal to recognize officially the "Silesians" as an "ethnic minority" despite numerous attempts by the Movement for Silesian Autonomy.(RAŚ). The "autonomists", on the other hand, refuse to recognize Silesian as the regional language as they consider it to be a fully-fledged language providing the basis for the ethnic independence or autonomy. Paradoxically, the "Silesians" though not listed in the law came to the fore in 2012 National Census with 846,719 people. So the largest Polish ethnic (?) minority totaling almost one million people (and more than one million if 375,635 Polish-Silesian bi-nationals are added) has no recognized legal status at all.

Interestingly, despite several attempts to develop ethnic identity across the country, only two groups were large enough to enter the Census statistics – Kociewiaks, the native group of Polish-speaking inhabitants of Pomorze area and "Gorole", Tatra Highlanders among whom a minority separatist movement was supported as "Goralenvolk" by the Nazi Germany occupation administration during World War Two. Both of these identities attracted about 3,000 people each, certainly not much for the Silesians.

Our study of disputes at local level began in 1977 in a small town in Upper Silesia that belonged to Germany until 1945. In the 1970s it was officially forbidden to speak of an ethnic difference. The division between Silesians and people who arrived here after 1945 was expressed in terms of the "autochthones" and the "newcomers". We have twice asked the representative sample of Olesno people about their identity, offering up to four options between regional, ethnic and national identities and the results are naturally complex as Polish identity very often coincides with Silesian or even German identity (Kurczewski 2007; 2014a). In the common stereotype Silesians characterize themselves as law abiding citizens accustomed to German (read: Prussian) strict order. The attachment to traditional values of patriarchal domestic culture is also mentioned. Above all, however, to be 'Silesian" means attachment to "Silesian culture". So the question arises, is there something like Silesian legal culture? One could expect that being a minority, Silesians would tend to keep their disputes to themselves and to use court less often than the Polish "newcomers". One should keep in mind, however, that being in a minority Silesians have been heard to complain about the "Silesian trauma" of being exploited by outsiders ruling them from Berlin and then from Warsaw and neglecting their peculiar identity, but in the late 20th century their position was already economically privileged thanks to the right to a German passport and to participate in the German labor market. Having a hundred thousand relatives who had been gradually leaving Silesia (mostly West), Germany was also the reason for feelings of inferiority for Polish newcomers arriving in the region witnessing the relative wealth of their neighbors.

Quite the opposite was the position of another minority included in our study, namely the Polish Ukrainians. To tell their story we would need another lengthy chapter but as this is not the focus of our book we will limit ourselves to the basic facts. The Ukrainian population in pre-war Poland was large and in the South-East it formed a majority in the countryside but not in the cities and towns where Jews and Poles jointly outnumbered the Ukrainians. Polish-Ukrainian antagonism has a social background, as Ukrainian peasants had been subject to Polish or Polonized gentry of Ukrainian origin for centuries. There was a religious divide as Ukrainians belonged the East Orthodox Church while the union with Rome effected in the 17th century was persecuted by the Russian authorities on a par with embryonic Ukrainian nationalism once the Eastern part of former Polish-Lithuanian Rzeczpospolita was taken under their rule. A part of the Polish-Ukrainian lands were however taken through partitions of Rzeczpospolita by the Catholic Austrian monarchy and the Habsburgs protected the Ukrainian Uniate church. The Polish-Ukrainian antagonism in the Austrian-held part of Poland called Galicia continued and was reinforced as in the late 19th century relative freedom of speech and press gave fertile conditions to the development of the Ukrainian nationalism that soon entered into open conflict with Polish nationalism. The area with its capital of Lwów (Lviv) became contested by two nationalisms, Polish and Ukrainian. At the end of World War 1 independent Ukraine in Galicia was proclaimed, but the Poles won militarily and Ukrainian irredentism went into the underground until World War 2. The German Nazi occupation of Poland allowed Ukrainians to consolidate their military power and when the Holocaust of Jews was ending, the next bloody ethnic cleansing broke out in 1943 starting with the genocide of Poles by Ukrainian nationalists in the Volhynia region. This provoked a spiral of bloody revenge as Ukrainian nationalists were forcing Poles to leave the whole area defined by them as Ukraine and the Polish national underground army was fighting to keep Poland within the pre-war borders. Whatever the wishes of both sides, the new Soviet-Polish border in 1945 shifted Poland several hundred miles west and the mass ethnic resettlement in both directions – East to Soviet Ukraine and West to communist Poland followed – but tens of thousands of Ukrainians remained in their homes in Poland to the west of the new border and because of the assumed collaboration with the Ukrainian nationalist insurgent army (UPA) they were forcefully resettled in 1947 into the new Northern and Western territories acquired by Poland from Germany as a compensation for territorial losses in the East. The resettlement policy deliberately aimed at dispersing the Ukrainians in their new locations so they would never outnumber the designated proportion, education in Ukrainian was forbidden, the Uniate (Greek-Catholic) church service was forbidden as well as any forms of even cultural self-organization until 1956 when with the general liberalization the Ukrainian minority was administratively recognized and it gained some rights allowing it to cultivate their own culture (cf. Wojakowski 2014).

The lasting effect of this policy is that until today the open acknowledgement of Ukrainian identity has been rare despite the fact that about 300,000 people were re-settled in 1947. In the 2011 National Census only 51,000 Ukrainians were recorded declaring their nationality as the only one with 27,630 declaring themselves both Poles and Ukrainians. It is also rare to find compact Ukrainian settlement areas except for dispersed villages. One of the few exceptions is Górowo Iławeckie in North-East Poland (former East Prussia) where Ukrainians are a minority in the town populated also by Poles resettled after World War II from Byelorussia and Lithuania. The small town is surrounded by villages in which

Ukrainians often form the majority of inhabitants. Górowo Iławeckie is one of the few cultural centres of the Ukrainian community dispersed throughout Poland as it is the seat of one of three Ukrainian secondary educational institutions in Poland. Even such a brief history provides the argument for our hypothesis that as a repressed minority Ukrainians will refrain from using a (Polish) court as the dispute settlement mechanism. The technical difficulty in collecting mass interviews with a dispersed minority is obvious, we had to use the snow-ball mechanism asking the first Ukrainian respondents to contact the student interviewers with further Ukrainian respondents constantly checking the age and gender parameters in order to construct the approximate quota sample. With all these shortcoming this is the first research into the legal beliefs and practices of the Polish Ukrainian minority and we feel right in presenting the results with a warning to readers that it should be treated as pilot reconnaissance and not the final solid knowledge.

Results of the Olesno and Górowo Ilaweckie studies are presented in two ways. First, the means of the variables already discussed in the preceding chapters will be checked as for the statistical significance of differences between Polish and (Polish) Silesian and Polish Ukrainian groups in each of the bi-ethnic towns made by P. Orzechowski. This is a rough way of treating the data and we do it only in order to have something to move to the proper statistical analysis using the hierarchical regression analysis model prepared for us by Z. Karpiński.

Table 1. Student's t test values for significance of difference between ethnic groups in Olesno and Górowo-Iławeckie

City	**Górowo Ilaweckie**			**Olesno**		
Ethnicity	**Poles**	**Ukrainians**	**(1 – Ukrainians, 2 – Poles)**	**other ethnicities**	**Poles**	**(1 – Poles, 2 – others)**
Ideal dispute settlement (1 – court, 2 – mediation))	1.51 (0.50)	1.74 (0.44)	**t(163) = -2.21** *	1.55 (0.50)	1.55 (0.50)	t (147) = 0.04
Dispute experience in last 3 years (0 – none, 13 – in all cases	5.56 (3.72)	5.29 (0.91)	**t (165) = -2.12** *	1.02 (1.48)	0.90 (1.42)	t (150) = 0.49
Lifelong court experience (0 – none, 1 – at least once)	0.63 (0.48)	0,52 (0.50)	t(164) = 1.43	0.42 (0.50)	0.39 (0.49)	t (150) = 0.43
Court experience in last 3 years (0 – none, 1 – at least once)	0.01 (0.02)	0.01 (0.03)	t (165= -0.07	0.16 (0.52)	0.10 (0.35)	t (150) = 0.78
Court chosen in case scripts (0 – never, 7/8 – in all cases)	2.21 (2.07)	1.58 (1.47)	t(165) = 2.30	3.07 (2.17)	3.06 (2.18)	t (150) = 0.01

City	Górowo Ilaweckie			Olesno		
Ethnicity	**Poles**	**Ukrainians**	**(1 – Ukrainians, 2 – Poles)**	**other ethnicities**	**Poles**	**(1 – Poles, 2 – others)**
Compromise chosen in all script cases (0 – never, 7/8 – in all cases)	4.92 (2.50)	5.82 (2.73)	t(165) = -1.62	5.84 (2.69)	5.90 (2.41)	t (150) = -0.14
Court chosen in private case scripts (0 – never, 4/5 – in all cases)	0.63 (1.03)	0.37 (0.73)	**t(165) = 1.93** *	1.00 (1.15)	0.90 (1.13)	t (150) = 0.51
Court chosen in public script cases (0 – never, 3/4 – in all cases)	1.59 (1.35)	1.23 (1.08)	**t(165)= 1.97** *	2.11 (1.42)	2.18 (1.24)	t (150) = -0.27
Compromise chosen in private script cases (0 – never, 4/5 – in all cases)	4.30 (1.90)	4.97 (2.10)	t(165) = -1.69	4.63 (2.13)	4.82 (1.81)	t (150) = -0.57
Compromise chosen in public script cases (0 – never, 3/4 – in all cases)	1.26 (1.16)	1.40 (1.30)	t(165) = – 0.36	1.84 (1.41)	1.79 (1.24)	t (150) = 0.24
Withdrawal chosen in all case scripts (0–0 – never, 7/8 – in all cases)	2.68 (2.30)	2.60 (1.97)	t(153) = 0.21	1.96 (2.36)	2.53 (2.18)	t (123) = -1.37
Private pursuit chosen in all case scripts (0–0 – never, 7/8 – in all cases)	2.74 (2.29)	2.92 (2.46)	t(153) = – 0.49	2.15 (1.90)	1.63 (2.05)	t (123) = 1.46
Other official institutions chosen in all case scripts (0–0 – never, 7/8 – in all cases)	4.02 (2.50)	3.11 (2.24)	**t(153) = 2.29** *	4.19 (2.39)	4.12 (2.25)	t (123) = 0.17
Withdrawal chosen in private case scripts (0 – never, 4/5 – in all cases)	1.48 (1.43)	1.26 (1.21)	t(156) = 0.81	1.16 (1.65)	1.55 (1.56)	t (130) = -1.37
Withdrawal chosen in public case scripts(0 – never, 3/4 – in all cases)	1.20 (1.21)	1.34 (1.17)	t(159) = – 0.66	0.88 (0.99)	0.96 (1.04)	t (134) = -0.51
Private pursuit chosen in private case scripts (0 – never, 4/5 – in all cases)	1.76 (1.58)	1.89 (1.79)	t(156) = -0.49	0.64 (1.00)	0.45 (0.78)	t (134) = 1.20
Private pursuit chosen in public case scripts(0 – never, 3/4 – in all cases)	1.06 (1.07)	1.03 (1.14)	t(159) = 0.07	1.51 (1.45)	1.18 (1.55)	t (130) = 1.23

City	Górowo Ilaweckie			Olesno		
Ethnicity	Poles	Ukrai-nians	(1 – Ukrainians, 2 – Poles)	other ethnicities	Poles	(1 – Poles, 2 – others)
Other official institutions chosen in private case scripts (0 – never, 4/5 – in all cases)	1.53 (1.33)	0.89 (1.09)	**t(156) = 2.69** **	1.57 (1.43)	1.36 (1.16)	t (130) = 0.89
Other official institutions chosen in public case scripts(0 – never, 3/4 – in all cases)	2.49 (1.53)	2.23 (1.51)	t(159) = 0.86	2.59 (1.51)	2.82 (1.58	t (134) = -0.87
Levels of significance: *** p<0.001, ** p<0.01, * p<0.05						

Listing all statistically significant differences in Górowo Iławeckie:

1. Poles less often than Ukrainians declared having a dispute in the last three years;
2. Poles more often chose court and Ukrainians mediation as the ideal dispute settlement pattern;
3. Poles also more often than Ukrainians chose another official agency to settle a dispute in general and in private disputes.

We also checked the significance of religious denomination findings with the help of the student's test in Górowo Ilaweckie (cf. Appendix B). Roman Catholics compared with Greek Catholics (Ukrainian church) less often reported any dispute in the last 3 years, more often chose court in general disputes and other official agencies in general and in private disputes, while Greek Catholics more often chose compromise in private disputes.

In Olesno the findings are quite different as there were no statistically significant differences between Poles not declaring any other ethnic identity and all other people (Silesians and/or Germans). Here, however, the minute community of Protestants differed significantly by choosing court and other official agencies in general and in public disputes more often than Roman Catholics and was more in favour of private pursuit of one's claims in public disputes.

Moving now to the results of the multilevel logistic regression analysis (Appendix A to this chapter) we see the differences and similarities of the minorities as compared with the Polish majority in both (Olesno and Górowo Iławeckie) local studies made in Poland. The results about the choice of the ideal dispute settlement pattern are in both cases statistically insignificant. The same was true of the outcome of the simple Multivariate Logistic Regression (MLR) analysis made with the indices of preference for court and for compromise in both localities. To sum up, except for the difference in means between Poles and Ukrainians in Górowo Ilaweckie we cannot support the theory of ethnic differentiation in dispute settlement patterns. But the above mentioned exception is important, as it shows that the underprivileged minority (Polish Ukrainians) is more reluctant to use courts.

We will now check the ethnic dimension theory in three multi-ethnic localities we studied abroad not far from Poland – Daugavpils in Latvia, Cluj-Napoca in Romania and Razgrad in Bulgaria. As comparative context we shall add the data from two Ukrainian cities – Drohobych, the middle sized town in Western Ukraine that before the World War 2 was part of Poland and Mariupol, a large industrial port in the East of Ukraine close to Russia and in the Donbass region torn by the civil war. Daugavpils under the name of Dueneburg (Dynaburg in Polish) had been the historical capital of Polish Livonia, part of the Polish-Lithuanian Commonwealth (Rzeczpospolita) until 1772 when it was annexed by Catherine the Great. Russia started to build up here the frontier bastion with Prussia and later in the mid-19th century the main railway hub. As part of independent Latvia since 1918 Daugavpils has remained its second largest city with 180,260 inhabitants of whom there are 58% Russian, 17% Latvian and 15% Polish. This is the site of the Educational University, judicial and administrative centre of the province without any important industry after the fall of Soviet economy. Daugavpils was annexed by the Soviet Union in 1940, then occupied by Germans and taken back after the WW 2 by the Soviet Union until 1990, when Latvia regained independence. The three main ethnic groups had the long history of changing position in the city that until World War II and the Holocaust had been mainly Jewish – local Poles (scf. Kurczewski and Fuszara 2009) may refer to days when the whole region was under Polish sovereignty, Russians remember they dominated politically from 1772 to 1918 and returned with Soviet occupation in 1940 that led to the wide re-Russification of the city, while Latvians came to the fore in the period between the wars. The local people are fierce however that the major ethnic/political conflict takes place on the Latvian national forum and in the capital Riga while Daugavpils remains a quiet place of co-habitation despite complaints made by Latvians who are numerically overwhelmed and by Slavs who are forced to learn and to use Latvian as the official national language (cf. Volkovs and Kurczewski 2013).

Cluj-Napoca until 1918 had been the judicial, administrative and cultural centre of Transylvania as part of the dual Austrian/Hungarian monarchy. After the Trianon Treaty it was taken by Romania though in the years of 1941–1944 the Hitler-Mussolini arbitration assigned it back to Hungary. It is a large city with

324,000 inhabitants in 2012 of whom 79% are Romanians and 19% Hungarians. Re-named as Cluj-Napoca during the large industrialization project by the Ceauseascu government it has, aside from its steel industry, the 2nd largest academic centre in Romania holding numerous university-level and cultural Romanian and Hungarian institutions, and Romanian and Hungarian operas and theatres. The historical conflict between two national groups did not end after 1989. Long standing Romanian nationalist city mayor Funar, busy with remodelling the public space, left Hungarian minority in disgust (Mica 2012). As Botea (2005) describes that Cluj-Napoca/Kolszvar is the city of ethnically distinct historical narrative and spatial arrangement as perceived by its residents but they co-habit in everyday life except for public festivals and social gatherings. As in Olesno the case with German language in Cluj-Napoca Hungarians also lost their right to use their own language in the official transactions as according to the Law of Public Administration No. 215/2001 the 20% threshold was introduced and between the two censuses the percentage of Hungarians fell below the requested level from 23% in 1992 to 19% in 2002 (Botea 2005).

Razgrad in 2014 had 33,568 inhabitants of whom 79% are Bulgarians and 19% Turks. The city is known for its pharmaceutical industry and the best Bulgarian football team – Ludogorets. The dramatic history of the relations between two national groups does not need to be retold here. Suffice to recall that while Razgrad was retaken by Bulgarians after Russian-Ottoman war of 1877–78, the process of Bulgarian repopulation ensured with the surrounding countryside remaining in majority Muslim and Turkish. The ethnic identity of the Muslim population is not totally unambiguous as apart from converts from the native inhabitants into Islam, the largely deserted area was repopulated by the semi-nomadic groups from Anatolia. The monumental structure of now unused mosque built by Ibrahim Pasha in 1530s witnessed the days when Razgrad was the vital centre of the Ottoman rule in Eastern Balkans. The Bulgarian re-settlers added quickly the Orthodox temples and modern municipal architecture as Razgrad became an important administrative outpost in the predominantly Muslim countryside from which part of the population resettled into the areas under Turkish rule. The situation continued until the 1980s when Bulgarian communist leader Todor Zhivkov launched the anti-Turkish campaign forcing the Bulgarian Turks to change names or to leave for Turkey. Turks were not allowed to attend Muslim religious ceremonies, speak Turkish in public places or wear traditional Turkish clothing. This led to the depopulation of the area with ca. 359,000 people suddenly leaving Bulgaria on tourist visa to Turkey, only a part (ca 150,000 people) of whom returned home after the fall of communist rule in 1990.

Before we start the description of our findings, a note of warning is necessary. A methodologically sound comparison is possible only within a given community where the construction of a sample and interviewing took place. The details are presented in the Appendix A at the end of the book. The research teams understood the task differently, we were not able to monitor in situ the process of interviewing, etc. After all, the legal, political and cultural context in each locality under study was different as well. But as for a given locality these factors are put under control, however, again, the context might have been different for different ethnic groups within a given community. Taking all this into account, we begin with the most risky part which is the comparison of the similarities and differences across the localities and countries. More conscientious readers would be advised to skip this part of the description and move immediately to the results of statistical analysis comparing Latvians, Russians and Poles in Daugavpils, Romanians and Hungarians in Cluj-Napoca and Bulgarians and Turks in Razgrad.

For those inclined to accept (as ourselves) the collected data as a kind of pilot reconnaissance to direct the more detailed and systematic research in the future we commence with the presentation of the selected indicators of what we label as "popular (folk) legal culture" in the region. These socio-legal indicators include reported experience with the use of courts, the respective assessment of court performance as well as some general beliefs about justice and law.

Table 2. Selected indicators of local legal culture in the region (in %)

	PL Cities	Ukraine		Daugavpils			Cluj - Napoca		Razgrad	
		D	M	Lv	Ru	Pl	Ro	Hu	Bg/R	T
Without court experience	48	74	77	90	80	82	73	82	46	41
Civil court experience	36	18	15	7	13	12	21	12	25	30
Criminal court experience	16	4	4	2	5	4	5	4	15	17
Other court experience	7	1	×	1	1	1	1	2	13	12
Verdict known from experience considered just	64	65	60	83	64	67	72	53	44	51
Approached the court on their own	65	19	18	9	20	14	21	16	44	37

	PL Cities	Ukraine		Daugavpils			Cluj - Napoca		Razgrad	
		D	M	Lv	Ru	Pl	Ro	Hu	Bg/R	T
Satisfaction with the effects of contact with court	55	36	43	69	68	50	67	60	39	43
Court in general unpleasant	69	60	62	86	71	73	52	71	48	42
Know an expert in law	8	17	16	16	21	14	10	27	54	33
Local people abide by law	50	36	42	61	69	63	50	45	41	47
Should one obey the law even if unjust	45	71	59	57	43	51	59	62	27	24
Total = N = 100%	480	361	270	222	200	180	300	200	300	200

Note: In the above and the following tables D means Drohobych, M – Mariupol, Lv - Latvians, Ru – Russians, Pl – Poles, Ro – Romanians, Hu – Hungarians, Bg – Bulgarians and T – Turks.

Urban Polish and Razgrad respondents are the most experienced in court proceedings, but this applies specifically to the criminal justice while urban Poles are the most experienced in civil justice taking into consideration all the groups interviewed, and Bulgarians and Turks from Razgrad in other types of justice (here we must rely on our respondents classification of their judicial experience). The lowest frequency of the court experience of all types is to be found amongst Latvians of Daugavpils. Poles are leading in terms of frequency of ever approaching the court for any reason (65%), the next closest groups being from Razgrad (44% of Bulgarians and 37% of Turks).

Interestingly, the assessment of the verdict that was pronounced in the case a respondent had personally experienced is rather similar across the groups interviewed. Latvians who had such experience the least often, would most often (83%) assess the judgment as just. They are followed by Romanians (72%) and Poles from Daugavpils (67%). The worst assessment was given by Razgrad respondents independent of ethnicity (42% of Bulgarian participants in a court case and 51% of Turks) and Hungarians in Cluj-Napoca (53%). In general, across the cities and ethnic groups a majority of localities gave the positive assessment of the justness of court's decisions. As for the satisfaction with the court as approached by the respondents for any reason (not necessarily to bring a suit) the respondents from Ukraine (36–43%) and from Razgrad (39–43%) in Bulgaria are markedly less often satisfied while Latvians (69%) and Russians (68%) from Daugavpils and Romanians (67%) from Cluj-Napoca gave the best notes. These two assessments differ in details but in general there is congruency as for good notes given to courts among Latvians and Romanians (more often positive) and among Razgrad respondents (more often negative).

Latvian respondents from Daugavpils (86%) most often perceived the court experience as unpleasant whereas Razgrad respondents (48–42%) were at the other end of the spectrum. This is a remarkably wide distance and calling for investigation even if the quality of the collected data is different in different localities where the study was made. The safest thing and the same time treating the said methodological problem respectfully is to compare the rank order of groups as to the proportion of those expressing their unpleasantness with rankings concerning other variables such as personal acquaintance with court proceedings. In this particular case the Spearman's rho rank correlation equals 0.918 and the two-tailed value of P is 0.00018, which is highly significant.

This arouses curiosity as to the other correlations within the above table and the total effect is presented in the table 2 below:

Table 3. Rank order (Spearmsn's Rho) correlations between variables related to court experience

General experience with courts	Approaching the courts	Justness of verdict	Satisfaction with court performance	Unpleasantness of courts
Experience	.912+++	-.549	-..628	-,.918 +++
Approaching		-.480	-.322	-.912+++
Justness			.560	.551
Satisfaction				.628

+++ *Rho significant at .001 level*

The paradox of a negative stereotype of court about which we shall write more in the concluding chapter appears here in form of a significant negative correlation between a feeling of unpleasantness associated with court and two different (but inter-correlated) measures of personal experience. The group that at the aggregate level is better acquainted with the work of court has also a better emotional association with it. The simple test could be done comparing the panel data on the clients of court, which is a project we leave for further students of the social psychology of justice and dispute settlement. This finding is of great importance when combined with the lack of significant correlation between two measures of evaluating court performance and court-related experience. Even though our samples differ as to the perceived unpleasantness of court experience, there is an overall majority agreement that courts are not a proper place to debate family matters

As for the perceived conformity to law at the local level the respondents from Ukrainian cities and Bulgarians from Razgrad in Bulgaria (36–41%) are of a worse opinion than people living in the other areas. But when asked about their own opinion related to law abidance no straight relationship emerges (rho = -.332, non-significant) – in Drohobych people think the worst about law abidance in practice but at the same time have the highest expectations as for the legalism, but the two variables are largely independent of each other.

In the following part of the chapter we will focus on the patterns of dispute settlement advocated in reaction to the eight case scripts of disputes described earlier in the book. The order of presentation of findings will be from the detailed description of the distribution of answers in all the ethnic samples studied in cities outside Poland using also the Polish data from a sub-sample of respondents being residents in cities with at least 20,000 inhabitants. Then we shall move to the more sophisticated statistical analysis on the aggregate indices of dispute settlement patterns also known already from the two preceding chapters.

Table 4. Ideal patterns of dispute settlement (in %)

Better:	**PL**	**U**		**LT**			**RO**		**BG**	
		D	**M**	**Lt**	**Ru**	**Pl**	**Ro**	**H**	**Bg**	**T**
A.1. Full satisfaction of one party's claims	12	31	30	33	30	37	21	27	42	26
A.2. Mutual agreement	86	69	69	66	69	62	79	74	58	73
A.3. DK	2	.	1	1	1	1	.	.	.	1
B.1. Strictly according to law	43	63	58	57	48	53	47	40	49	30
B.2. Compromise	50	36	39	42	51	47	53	60	51	70
B.3. DK	7	1	3	1	1	.	.	.	.	.
C.1. By court	55	72	68	57	59	56	64	67	57	49
C.2. By mediators	35	27	31	43	41	44	36	34	43	50
C.3. DK	10	.	1	1	.	.	.	.	.	.
Total = N = 100%	480	361	270	222	200	180	300	200	300	200

The Polish national urban sample is surprisingly low (12%) when it comes to full satisfaction of a legitimate party's claims in contrast to all other groups (including Poles from Daugavpils) amongst whom 21–42% support such zero-one approach. But in this large category the inter-ethnic differences are also marked: mutual agreement against the law but accommodating conflicting expectations as supported mostly by respondents from Cluj-Napoca independent of the ethnic affiliation (79–74%) and Turks from Razgrad (73%).

As for the next question that puts emphasis on the following scripture of the law, the positivist approach is the most popular in Drohobych (63%) and the least popular among Razgrad Turks (30%), the other groups being relatively close to each other (40–58%).

The inhabitants of Ukrainian cities (72–68%) and of Romanian Cluj-Napoca independent of ethnic affiliation (64–67%) are leading in terms of support for the authoritative dispute settlement. The respondents from Polish cities (55%) and from Daugavpils (56–59%) and Razgrad (49–57%) are more skeptical about the use of courts and other official authoritative bodies, with Turks at the bottom of the ranking (49%).

As those three questions are in the centre of our attention throughout the book we need to look at another possible way of arranging the findings. Until now the difference in the frequency of a hesitant lack of answer in different samples has been neglected but the fact of such a difference may be taken into consideration by counting the simple acceptance ratios where AR = % of answer 1 – % of answer 2/% of answer 1 + % of answer 2. Such re-counting of the variables would allow us to escape the difference in the technique of interviewing that might be responsible for differences in the lack of answers.

Table 5 below gives the figures for the re-calculated three variables measured by the questions about the ideal dispute settlement patterns:

Table 5. Acceptance ratios (AR) of ideal patterns of dispute settlement

Ideal patterns of dispute settlement	**PL**	**U**		**LT**			**RO**		**BG**	
		D	**M**	**Lt**	**Ru**	**Pl**	**Ro**	**H**	**Bg**	**T**
A. Full satisfaction of one party's claims/ Mutual agreement	-.75	-.38	-.39	-.33	-.39	-.35	-.58	-.53	-.16	-.53
B. Strictly according to law/ Compromise	-.07	.27	.20	.15	.00	.06	-.06	-.20	-.02	-.40
C. By court/by mediators	.20	.55	.37	.14	.18	.12	.28	.33	.14	.01
Total = N = 100%	480	361	270	222	200	180	300	200	300	200

After Don't Know answers have been put aside, the differences are more clear though the basic findings are in principle the same: Poles are extremely high when it comes to mutual agreement in opposition to Razgrad Bulgarians who are the least in favour of the negotiated mutual compromise; the settlements that strictly follow the letter of law are favoured least by Turks and court or another authoritative body that may impose a settlement are most often chosen by Ukrainians, especially from Drohobych in contrast to Razgrad Turks who mostly favour informal mediation.

We shall now move to the aggregate responses to the question about the preferred choice of finding a way out of the conflict as described in our eight hypothetical case scripts. The detailed tables of frequencies are in the Appendix C to this chapter, here we shall present a very simple aggregation of particular cases divided into three types: a) three (in Cluj-Napoca two) private disputes with neighbor or a friend as an opponent; b) two family disputes between two spouses and c) three "public disputes" by which we mean the disputes between a natural person and hospital, police or municipal authorities as an opponent. For each of these types the simple arithmetic means has been calculated as in the Tables 6–8 below.

Table 6. Means (%) for private disputes outside family

	PL	U		LT			RO		BG	
		D	M	Lt	Ru	Pl	Ro	H	Bg	T
Withdrawal	5	4	4	5	5	6	15	11	18	7
Compromise	58	55	28	48	47	40	58	47	29	24
Private pursuit	11	21	33	5	13	18	5	16	17	39
Court	12	11	28	22	24	19	16	22	12	7
Other public	8	3	3	13	10	16	5	2	24	21
DK	6	6	4	2	1	1	1	2	.	2
All public	20	14	31	35	34	35	21	24	36	28
Total = N = 100%	480	361	270	222	200	180	300	200	300	200

In Polish cities, Drohobych and Cluj-Napoca respondents are less prone to approaching public bodies in private disputes. Poles and Romanians are equally attached to the idea of compromise informally negotiated with an opponent. Compromise is the least popular in Razgrad and Mariupol. Turks are most prone to pursuing their claims privately on their own.

Table 7. Means (%) for family disputes

	PL	U		LT			RO		BG	
		D	M	Lt	Ru	Pl	Ro	H	Bg	T
Withdrawal	14	9	7	19	23	31	17	16	18	16
compromise	59	60	30	63	63	56	47	39	29	40
Private pursuit	3	9	30	8	8	9	5	15	17	13
Court	8	12	26	9	4	2	23	19	12	7
Other public	8	2	4	.	.	.	6	5	24	22
DK	8	8	3	1	2	2	2		.	2
All public	16	14	30	9	4	2	29	24	36	29
Total = N = 100%	480	361	270	222	200	180	300	200	300	200

As for family disputes public agencies are more likely to be approached in Mariupol, Razgrad and Cluj-Napoca while Poles, Ukrainians from Drohobych and Daugavpils inhabitants independent of ethnicity would prefer a direct compromise.

Table 8. Means (%) for disputes with a public opponent

	PL	U		LT			RO		BG	
		D	M	Lt	Ru	Pl	Ro	H	Bg	T
Withdrawal	2	3	5	6	4	5	1	7	6	11
Compromise	25	11	21	25	23	22	23	26	12	13
Private pursuit	4	7	26	9	8	10	7	3	11	9
Court	56	72	46	54	62	58	64	62	31	27
Other public	6	4	2	5	2	3	4	2	40	39
DK	7	3	.	1	3	2	1	.	.	1
All public	65	76	48	59	64	61	68	64	71	66
Total = N = 100%	480	361	270	222	200	180	300	200	300	200

In a dispute with a public body another public body should be most likely approached but there are differences as this is less likely in Mariupol. One cannot exclude the idea that this reflects the politicization of a local public life in the Ukraine that in Mariupol entered the stage of the civil war. In Razgrad court will be approached less often than other public bodies (municipality, police), in other localities court is almost a single instrument in making claims against other public agencies.

At the next stage we compare the means of the various socio-legal variables checking the statistical significance with Student's t test and all the means, values and significance are given in the Table 17 below:

Table 9. Student's and Fisher's test values for significance of differences between ethnic groups in Cluj-Napoca, Razgrad and Daugavpils

City	**Cluj - Napoca**			**Razgrad**			**Daugavpils**			
Ethnicity	**Ro-mani-ans**	**Hun-gari-ans**	**(1 - Hun-garians, 2 - Roma-nians)**	**Bulga-rians**	**Turks**	**(1 - Turks, 2 - Bul-garians)**	**Lat-vians**	**Russi-ans**	**Poles**	**(1 - Lat-vians, 2 - Rus-sians, 3 - Poles)**
Ideal dispute set-tlement (1 – court, 2 – mediation))	1.36 (0.48)	1.34 (0.47)	t (492) = 0.64	1.45 (0.50)	1.48 (0.50)	t (488) = -1.63	1.42 (0.49)	1.42 (0.49)	1.45 (0.50)	F (2,589) = 0.16
Dispute experi-ence in last 3 years (0 – none, 2 – at least once	2.36 (3.65)	0.00	**t (498) = 9.14** ***	9.10 (1.43)	9.22 (1.39)	**t (429) = -2.65** **	0.76 (2.35)	0.94 (2.57)	0.75 (2.31)	F (2,599) = 0.32
Lifelong court experience (0 – none, 1 – at least once)	0.28 (0.45)	0.17 (0.38)	**t(498) = 2.64** **	0.54 (0.50)	0.63 (0.48)	t (483) = -1.27	0.10 (0.30)	0.18 (0.39)	**0.18 (0.38)**	**F (2,589) = 3.55** *
Court experience in last 3 years (0 – none, 1 – at least once)	0.24 (0.37)	0.00	**(498) = 9.14** ***	1.48 (1.52)	1.24 (1.52)	**t (498) = 2.70** **	0.54 (3.13)	0.60 (3.34)	1.14 (4.43)	**F (2,599) = 3.50** *
Court chosen in case scripts (0 – never, 7/8 – in all cases)	1.85 (1.30)	2.02 (1.39)	t (498) = -1.34	1.08 (0.86)	0.91 (1.20)	**t (498) = 2.69** **	1.89 (1.27)	2.04 (1.28)	1.73 (1.22)	F (2,599) = 2.63
Compromise chosen in all script cases (0 – never, 7/8 – in all cases)	2.81 (1.31)	2.30 (1.66)	**t (498) = 3.88** ***	**2.19 (0.86)**	2.26 (0.83)	t (498) = -0.94	3.30 (1.55)	3.22 (1.56)	2.90 (1.63)	**F (2,599) = 3.79** *
Court chosen in private case scripts (0 – never, 3/4 – in all cases)	0.80 (0.89)	0.82 (0.94)	t (498) = -0.20	0.58 (0.86)	0.39 (0.70)	**t (498) = 3.39** ***	0.82 (0.99)	0.79 (0.94)	0.66 (0.85)	F (2,599) = 1.43

City	Cluj - Napoca			Razgrad			Daugavpils			
Ethnicity	**Ro-mani-ans**	**Hun-gari-ans**	**(1 - Hun-garians, 2 - Roma-nians)**	**Bulga-rians**	**Turks**	**(1 - Turks, 2 - Bul-garians)**	**Lat-vians**	**Russi-ans**	**Poles**	**(1 - Lat-vians, 2 - Rus-sians, 3 - Poles)**
Court chosen in public script cases (0 – never, 3/4 – in all cases)	1.85 (0.89)	1.93 (1.02)	t (498) = -0.82	0.91 (0.99)	0.86 (1.04)	t (498) = 1.44	1.64 (1.03)	1.86 (0.83)	1.69 (0.96)	F (2,599) = 2.79
Compromise chosen in private script cases (0 – never, 4/5 – in all cases)	2.12 (1.03)	1.73 (1.28)	**t (498) = 3.78** ***	1.48 (1.23)	1.56 (1.03)	t (498) = – 0.30	2.72 (1.27)	2.69 (1.29)	2.35 (1.33)	**F (2,599) = 5.07** **
Compromise chosen in public script cases (0 – never, 3/4 – in all cases)	0.78 (0.79)	0.68 (0.89)	t (498) = 1.37	0.34 (0.60)	0.38 (0.60)	t (498) = -0.92	0.77 (0.87)	0.71 (0.75)	0.68 (0.74)	F (2,599) = 0.55
Withdrawal chosen in all case scripts (0–0 – never, 7/8 – in all cases)	0.86 (0.98)	0.71 (0.83)	t (494) = 1.75	1.15 (1.38)	0.90 (0.98)	**t (480) = 2.22** *	0.73 (1.10)	0.76 (1.02)	0.96 (1.11)	F (2,594) = 2.48
Private pursuit chosen in all case scripts (0–0 – never, 7/8 – in all cases)	0.30 (0.74)	0.86 (1.11)	**t (494) = -6.73** ***	1.03 (1.27)	1.73 (1.38)	**t (480) = -5.76** ***	0.75 (0.96)	0.83 (1.13)	1.10 (1.35)	**F (2,592) = 4.97** **
Other official institutions chosen in all case scripts (0–0 – never, 7/8 – in all cases)	2.95 (1.46)	3.01 (1.71)	t (494) = -0.41	3.96 (1.71)	3.41 (1.69)	**t (480) = 3.50** ***	3.04 (1.58)	2.99 (1.40)	2.94 (1.51)	F (2,592) = 0.23
Withdrawal cho-sen in private case scripts (0 – never, 4/5 – in all cases)	0.63 (0.78)	0.65 (0.78)	t (496) = -0.25	0.97 (1.22)	0.54 (0.74)	**t (481) = 4.31** ***	0.55 (0.83)	0.63 (0.84)	0.79 (0.89)	**F (2,598) = 4.15** *
Withdrawal cho-sen in public case scripts (0 – never, 3/4 – in all cases)	0.22 (0.46)	0.06 (0.23)	**t (494) = 4.83** ***	0.19 (0.45)	0.35 (0.50)	**t (496) = – 3.87** ***	0.18 (0.47)	0.14 (0.37)	0.17 (0.43)	F (2,595) = 0.67

City	Cluj – Napoca			Razgrad			Daugavpils			
Ethnicity	**Ro-mani-ans**	**Hun-gari-ans**	**(1 – Hun-garians, 2 – Roma-nians)**	**Bulga-rians**	**Turks**	**(1 – Turks, 2 – Bul-garians)**	**Lat-vians**	**Russi-ans**	**Poles**	**(1 – Lat-vians, 2 – Rus-sians, 3 – Poles)**
Private pursuit chosen in private case scripts (0 – never, 4/5 – in all cases)	0.22 (0.57)	0.65 (0.83)	**t (496) = -6.66 *****	0.70 (0.99)	1.44 (1.19)	**t (496) = – 7.43 *****	0.48 (0.74)	0.59 (0.88)	0.75 (1.10)	**F (2,596) = 4.50 ****
Private pursuit chosen in public case scripts (0 – never, 3/4 – in all cases)	0.08 (0.31)	0.21 (0.53)	**t (494) = -3.50 *****	0.23 (0.66)	0.29 (0.55)	t (496) = 0.93	0.27 (0.54)	0.24 (0.48)	0.35 (0.62)	F (2,595) = 1.70
Other official institutions chosen in private case scripts (0 – never, 4/5 – in all cases)	1.04 (0.94)	0.96 (1.03)	t (496) = 0.83	1.82 (1.29)	1.46 (1.16)	**t (481) = 3.12 ****	1.24 (1.02)	1.08 (0.98)	1.12 (1.03)	F (2,596) = 1.16
Other official institutions chosen in public case scripts (0 – never, 3/4 – in all cases)	1.91 (0.86)	2.05 (0.99)	t (494) = -1.63	2.14 (0.89)	1.95 (0.84)	**t (496) = 1.99 ***	1.80 (1.00)	1.91 (0.82)	1.82 (0.94)	F (2,595) = 1.00
Levels of significance: *** p<0.001, ** p<0.01, * p<0.05										

As we see in Table 9 above there are a lot of the significant differences. There are, however, no significant inter-ethnic differences as to the general ideal pattern of dispute settlement.

Starting with Daugavpils the Latvians here are the least likely group to have had personal experience of court. They are also significantly more often in favour of seeking settlements in private disputes and in all disputes taken together, and the least interested in a private pursuit of their claims and withdrawal from private disputes. Poles, on the contrary, have most experience with the court, and they also have the lowest inclination to compromise in private disputes in contrast to Poles in Poland) and they most frequently support a private pursuit of claims.

In Cluj-Napoca Hungarians have significantly less dispute and court experience than Romanians. Hungarians also less frequently choose compromise in general and in private disputes, and less often choose to withdraw from public disputes and more often to make a of the claims.

In Razgrad Turks reported more disputes than Bulgarians and have had more court experience over their lifetime but less court experience in the last three years, which might be related to the turbulent history of this minority in the last decades of the 20th century. Turks choose court less often in private cases and other public agencies in all types of cases, they opt more frequently for a private pursuit of claims, and withdrawal in all types of cases.

This rather chaotic picture becomes more clear when the answers are dichotomized into two variables: (1) the choice of court versus all other advocated reactions and (b) the choice of compromise versus all other reactions. In Daugavpils Latvians were significantly less in favour of court settlement in the case of demolition of the house order (Phi = -.09, p = .0028) and more in the wife's battery case (Phi = .09, p = .030) while more respondents were for a compromise in the case of slapping someone in the face (Phi = .10, p = .017) and the house demolition order case (Phi = .08, p = ,048). Daugavpils Russians, in turn, are significantly more in favour of court in that last case (Phi = .12, p = .002) and in the wife's legacy case (Phi = .10, p = .017) and less for a compromise in the friends dispute over the debt case (Phi = -.10, p = .01) while Daugapils Poles are more in favour of court in the battered kids case (Phi = .16, p < .000) and less for a compromise in that case (Phi = -.14, p <.000).

In two of the eight case scripts the Hungarians were significantly more in favour of the choice of court than Romanians (pledge taken by a friend from the debtor Phi = .13, p = .003; house demolition ordered by authorities Phi = .10, p = .0025). A compromise was significantly more often chosen by Romanians in the pledge case (Phi = .14, p = .002), in the wife's legacy case (Phi = .17, p = .000) and in the case of the breach of confidentiality by hospital (Phi = .11, p = .019). In Razgrad Bulgarians were significantly more in favour of court in the pledge case (Phi = .12, p = .006) and in the wife's battery case (Phi = .14, p = .002) while less for a compromise in the house demolition order case (Phi = .01, p = .030) and wife's battery case (Phi = .15, p = .393) as compared to Turks

The details of these differences are of limited interest to us as we do not have a sufficient possibility to study the legal anthropology of these minorities. We leave this task to other researchers from these countries. This simple analysis shows clearly that in some circumstances ethnic differences matter. As sociologists we are inclined to explain these differences by making a reference to their minority status. If, however, the working theory behind our research holds that minorities in an underprivileged position refrain from the use of court and prefer informal ways of dealing with conflict situations, we cannot claim conclusive results. Certainly Turks keep themselves at a distance from the official Bulgarian state machinery of law and justice. The opposite has appeared to be true for the Hungarian minority in Romanian Cluj-Napoca. But in Daugavpils the official majority – Latvians – keep themselves out of court in some cases and in others they prefer court the most. This may be explained by the fact that they are a ruling minority in a city dominated by Russian-speaking Slavs of Russian, Polish and other origins.

The patterns of reaction to conflict with public bodies (hospital, police, municipality) are the most important indicator of the actual political status of the minority. It is edifying that nowhere in our research have we found significant differences between ethnic groups as to willingness to go to court for help in such a case. But what is of concern is the significant difference between the Bulgarians and Turks as to withdrawal from conflict situations. Here Turks declare a pattern which is typical of minorities that feel at risk when entering the world of power and authority. On the other hand, in Cluj-Napoca such a reaction is more frequent among the politically dominant Romanians and might be related to the difference in an average social status (education) of the two groups. Romanians are often newcomers from the rural areas, while Hungarians represent the old elite and the middle class of the Transylvanian society.

We finally move to the Multilevel or Hierarchical Logistic Regression analysis as made for us by Z. Karpiński (see Appendix E). The tables there show the estimates of parameters in a series of hierarchical logistic regression models. The first two columns show the results for the models with a "court dummy" as the dependent variable, and the two right-most columns — for the models with an "agreement dummy" as the dependent. The dummies represent subjects' responses to a series of the case scripts featuring a dispute, or conflict, between (*a*) two unrelated individuals (type I situation of "private dispute"), or (*b*) a citizen and an institution (type II situation of "public dispute"), or (*c*) two related individuals (spouses, to be more specific; these are type III situations of "family dispute"). For each case script, the subjects were asked to choose one of the following responses:

1. Don't react, do nothing
2. Arrive at an agreement and compromise with a friend
3. Use self-help to achieve in private what one considers due
4. Go to court
5. Go to some other institution

The court dummy was obtained by coding response 4 as 1 and all other responses as zero. Similarly, the agreement dummy assigns 1 to response 2 and 0 to all other responses.

The main reason for the use of the hierarchical or multilevel model in the present study is connected with the fact that each respondent responded to a series of case scripts. Because of this, a particular individual's responses are not stochastically independent since a response to the first case script is likely to affect the individual's responses to subsequent case scripts. In other words, the individual could respond to a case script in this way rather than another because he or she had responded in that way to a previous case script. The lack of stochastic independence of individual observations (e.g. case script–respondent combinations) violates a fundamental assumption of the "standard" logistic regression model, which makes it therefore unsuitable. The multilevel model solves the problem of the lack of independence by allowing for the individual responses to be "nested within" the respondents, so that the variability in the dependent variable has two sources: (*a*) differences between respondents and (*b*) different responses of a particular subject to different case scripts.

For each type of a dependent variable, two models were estimated — with the variable representing the subject's assessment of the justness of a court ruling, and without it. The questionnaire item asking the subject to assess the justness was asked only to those who declared they had participated in a trial as a witness or a party or in some other capacity. This is why the number of observations in the model including the assessment is much smaller than in a model without it, since the latter comprises all the participants in the study.

As regards the results presented in the tables in Appendix E, we will focus here only on the effects of a nationality. As we can see, the models include interactions between nationality and the type of situation (dispute). They were added to check the possibility whether a nationality affects responses differently depending on the type of a situation. Some of these interactions are significant at the ($p = 0.05$) level.

In Daugavpils, being Polish had a significant effect on choosing court in situations of type 1 (see Model 2) and on the informal compromise with an opponent in the private disputes (see Model 3), although the effects had different significance. This is to say that, relatives to Latvians (the reference category for the Daugavpils survey), Poles are more likely to indicate court as the preferred way of settling disputes in situations of type 1 and less likely to choose an agreement in these situations. It is important to keep in mind, however, that Model 2 is restricted to subjects who declared to have had some court experience in the sense of participating in a court trial in some capacity or another. In turn, Model 3 applies to all the survey participants.

As for situations of Type II and III, we see that their main effects are positive and significant in all the models with the court dummy as the dependent variable. This is to say that, in comparison with situations of Type I, Latvians are more likely to indicate court as the preferred way of settling disputes in situations of Type II and III. We also see that the type of situation interacts statistically significantly with the Polish dummy, which is to say that being Polish reduces the odds of selecting the court in these situations.

In Cluj-Napoca, Hungarians are significantly more likely to propose the use of the courts and less likely to opt for an agreement than Romanians. Interestingly, in the latter case the effect reverses if the analysis is restricted to subjects with court experience (see columns 2 and 4 in the Table for the agreement dummy). In other words, Hungarian subjects who said they had participated in a trial as witnesses, suspects, or in some other capacity, were more likely to opt for an agreement as compared with Romanians.

In Razgrad, after including both nationality and religion in the model, it turned out that not being Turkish, but being a Muslim is what matters. More specifically, the Turkish do not differ substantially from the Bulgarian when it comes to their preference for court as a way to settle disputes in situations of Type 1. On the other hand, Muslim respondents do differ from non-Muslim ones in this regards, but only when an analysis is restricted to those who declared they had some court experience (see Models 2 and 4). Further, both Turkish and Muslim respondents are significant in some models predicting an informal agreement. This opens the discussion of what the reality of minority is in different social contexts. Many Muslims in Bulgaria identify themselves as Bulgarians and not as the Turks, to be a Turk and a Christian as we have learnt is also an option. The religious and not the ethnic border seems thus a significant factor in the approach to state law and justice, not surprising result in view of what is widely known about different concept of the law of Islam.

Appendix A. Student's Test of Significance of Means for Denominational Groups in Multi-ethnic Polish Towns

RELIGION

	Górowo Iławeckie			Olesno		
Religion	**Roman Catholics**	**Greek Catholics**	**(1 – GC, 2 – RC)**	**Roman Catholics**	**Protestants**	**(1 – Protestants, 2 – Catholics)**
Ideal dispute settlement (1 – court, 2 – mediation))	1.56 (0.50)	1.69 (0.47)	t(166)= -1.12	1.57 (0.50)	1.25 (0.50)	t (138) = 1.29
Dispute experience in last 3 years (0 – none, 13 – all types	2.23 (3.81)	2.33 (0.78)	**t(168) = -2.18** *	0.96 (1.83)	0.25 (0.50)	t (141) = 1.03
Lifelong court experience (0 – none, 1 – at least once)	0.63 (0.49)	0.51 (0.50)	t(167) = 1.49	0.40 (0.49)	0.25 (0.50)	t (141) = 0.61
Court experience in last 3 years (0 – none, 1 – at least once)	0.01 (0.02)	0.01 (0.03)	t(168)= 0.22	0.12 (0.44)	0.00 (0.00)	t (141) = 0.55
Court chosen in case scripts (0 – never, 7/8 – in all cases)	2.17 (2.05)	1.65 (1.78)	**t(168) = 2.00** *	2.91 (2.11)	5.75 (1.89)	**t (141) = -2.67** **
Compromise chosen in all script cases (0 – never, 7/8 – in all cases)	4.83 (2.51)	5.71 (2.68)	t(168) = -1.75	6.07 (2.53)	4.00 (1.63)	t (141) = 1.63
Court chosen in private case scripts (0 – never, 3/4 – in all cases)	0.63 (1.01)	0.41 (0.80)	t(168) = 1.82	0.89 (1.07)	1.50 (1.00)	t (141) = -1.12
Court chosen in public script cases (0 – never, 3/4 – in all cases)	1.55 (1.36)	1.25 (1.10)	t(168) = 1.62	2.04 (1.41)	4.25 (2.06)	**t (141) = -3.05** **
Compromise chosen in private script cases (0 – never, 4/5 – in all cases) 0.50)	4.16 (1.55)	4.93 (1.25)	**t(168) = -2.05** *	4.86 (1.90)	3.75 (2.50)	t (141) = 1.15

	Górowo Iławeckie			Olesno		
Religion	**Roman Catholics**	**Greek Catholics**	(1 – GC, 2 – RC)	**Roman Catholics**	**Protestants**	**(1 – Protestants, 2 – Catholics)**
Compromise chosen in public script cases (0 – never, 3/4 – in all cases)	1.29 (4.16)	1.40 (4.93)	t(168) = -0.11	1.90 (1.36)	0.75 (0.96)	t (141) = 1.70
Withdrawal chosen in all case scripts (0–0 – never, 7/8 – in all cases)	2.69 (1.29)	2.72 (1.40)	t(156) = -0.19	2.17 (2.11)	1.25 (1.89)	t (114) = 0.86
Private pursuit chosen in all case scripts (0–0 – never, 7/8 – in all cases)	2.84 (2.69)	2.78 (2.72)	t(156) = 0.16	1.81 (1.86)	3.50 (1.73)	t (114) = -1.78
Other official institutions chosen in all case scripts (0–0 – never, 7/8 – in all cases)	4,02 (2.84)	3.18 (2.78)	**t(156) = 2.27** *	4.00 (2.29)	5.75 (1.89)	t (114) = -1.51
Withdrawal chosen in private case scripts (0 – never, 4/5 – in all cases)	1.52 (4.02)	1.32 (3.18)	t(159) = 0.75	1.32 (1.51)	0.50 (1.00)	t (121) = 1.07
Withdrawal chosen in public case scripts(0 – never, 3/4 – in all cases)	1.17 (1.52)	1.40 (1.32)	t(162) = -1.31	0.89 (0.93)	0.75 (0.96)	t (125) = 0.31
Private pursuit chosen in all case scripts (0 – never, 4/5 – in all cases)	1.76 (1.17)	1.78 (1.40)	t(159) = -0.01	0.58 (0.94)	0.25 (0.50)	t (125) = 0.71
Private pursuit chosen in public case scripts (0 – never, 3/4 – in all cases)	1.08 (1.76)	1.00 (1.78)	t(162) = 0.53	0.89 (1.34)	3.25 (2.06)	**t (121) = -2.93** **
Any official institutions chosen in private case scripts (0 – never, 4/5 – in all cases)	1.56 (1.08)	0.97 (1.00)	**t(159) = 2.52** **	0.58 (1.28)	1.50 (1.00)	t (121) = -0.10
Any official institutions chosen in public case scripts(0 – never, 3/4 – in all cases)	2.46 (1.56)	2.21 (0.98)	t(162) = 0.98	1.23 (1.49)	4.25 (2.06)	**t (125) = -2.18** **
Levels of significance: *** p<0.001, ** p<0.01, * p<0.05						

Appendix B. Multilevel Logistic Regression Analysis with Choice of Court and Choice of Compromise as Dependent Variables in Polish Multi-Ethnic Towns (Olesno and Górowo-Ilaweckie)

Multi-level logistic regression

Estimates and (Standard Error) values

	Dependent variable:	
	Court	**Agreement**
	(1)	(2)
Type of the dispute or conflict situation (reference: Type 1)		
Type II situation	4.460*** (0.808)	-2.160*** (0.244)
Type III situation	1.940** (0.821)	-0.108 (0.174)
Nationality (reference: Polish)		
Silesian	-0.309 (0.611)	0.287 (0.260)
Ukrainian	-1.170 (0.813)	0.321 (0.318)
Gender (reference: male)		
Female	-0.428** (0.201)	0.269** (0.133)
Age (reference: up to 34 years of age)		
Age 35–50	-0.454 (0.288)	0.347* (0.201)
Age 51–64	-0.910*** (0.297)	0.474** (0.202)
Age 65 and more	-0.983*** (0.326)	0.215 (0.223)
Degree of education (reference: primary)		
Vocational	-0.024 (0.360)	-0.369 (0.233)

	Dependent variable:	
	Court	**Agreement**
	(1)	**(2)**
Secondary	0.062 (0.325)	-0.280 (0.206)
Higher	0.294 (0.343)	-0.262 (0.223)
Religious denomination (reference: Roman – Catholic)		
Other or no religion	-0.482 (0.319)	0.057 (0.220)
Work situation (reference: working full time)		
Part time	0.154 (0.528)	0.368 (0.362)
Irregular	0.026 (0.478)	-0.357 (0.339)
No job	-0.075 (0.255)	0.186 (0.173)
Subjective assessment of socio-economic standing (reference: below average)		
Average or above average	0.050 (0.287)	-0.252 (0.183)
City (reference: Górowo Ilaweckie)		
Olesno	0.473* (0.283)	0.419** (0.190)
Responses to the item "Law should always be obeyed" (reference: Response 1)		
Response 2	0.088 (0.238)	-0.191 (0.160)
Response 3	0.022 (0.242)	-0.023 (0.158)
Response 4	0.231 (0.439)	-0.277 (0.300)
Responses to the item "Which is better?" (reference: Resolving the dispute by a court)		
Resolving a dispute by impartial individuals	0.034 (0.196)	-0.081 (0.130)

	Dependent variable:	
	Court	**Agreement**
	(1)	(2)
Have you ever taken part in a trial as a witness, suspect or in some other capacity? (reference: Never)		
At least once	-0.332 (0.207)	-0.097 (0.137)
Responses to the item: "How many people are there in your neighbourhood whose opinion you care about?" (reference: Many)		
Few people in the neighbourhood whose opinion I care about	0.522* (0.297)	-0.021 (0.191)
No people in the neighbourhood whose opinion I care about	0.252 (0.245)	-0.075 (0.157)
Interactions		
Silesian × Type II situation	0.157 (0.568)	-0.160 (0.337)
Silesian × Type III situation	0.118 (0.615)	-0.221 (0.291)
Ukrainian × Type II situation	0.034 (0.722)	0.050 (0.357)
Ukrainian × Type III situation	0.398 (0.805)	0.387 (0.307)
Constant	-3.550*** (0.919)	-0.143 (0.432)
Observations	2,192	2,192
Log Likelihood	-922.000	-1,233.000
Akaike Inf. Crit.	1,913.000	2,537.000
Bayesian Inf. Crit.	2,113.000	2,736.000
Note:	*Levels of significance: *** p<0.01, ** p<0.05, * p<0.1*	

Appendix C. The Eight Dispute Case Scripts Across the Cities and Ethnic Groups

Table 1. Somebody's children were beaten by a neighbour as he could not rest after work due to their noisy behaviour. In your opinion, what should the parents of the beaten children do? (in %)

	PL	U		LT			RO		BG	
	Cities	D	M	Lt	Ru	Pl	Ro	H	Bg	T
Withdrawal	2	3	1	2	3	1	X	X	15	4
Compromise	51	45	17	38	33	27	X	X	32	18
Private pursuit	7	17	28	6	10	15	X	X	17	41
Court	21	29	47	29	33	29	X	X	5	3
Other public	15	5	7	25	20	27	X	X	29	30
DK	4	1	.	.	1	1	X	X	2	4
All public	36	34	54	54	53	56	X	X	34	33
Total = N = 100%	480	361	270	222	200	180	300	200	300	200

Table2. An acquaintance of Mr K. was gossiping about him among their friends, so Mr K. slapped him in the presence of others. In your opinion, what should the acquaintance do? (in %)

	PL	U		LT			RO		BG	
	cities	D	M	Lt	Ru	Pl	Ro	H	Bg	T
Withdrawal	7	5	7	6	6	13	16	9	20	11
Compromise	61	52	36	51	57	43	55	47	22	23
Private pursuit	17	25	41	18	20	22	6	24	18	28
Court	4	16	14	11	12	11	16	16	16	11
Other public	2	1	1	10	4	11	7	3	24	27
DK	9	1	2	2	1	.	.	1	.	.
All public	6	17	15	21	16	22	23	19	40	38
Total = N = 100%	480	361	270	222	200	180	300	200	300	200

Table 3. A friend borrowed 250 euros and failed to repay the debt despite repeated demis. The lender came to the debtor's house and took something of the same value. In your opinion, what should the borrower (from whose house the item was taken) do? (in %)

	PL	U		LT			RO		BG	
	cities	**D**	**M**	**Lt**	**Ru**	**Pl**	**Ro**	**H**	**Bg**	**T**
Withdrawal	5	3	3	6	7	5	13	13	18	6
Compromise	63	67	42	55	51	50	61	47	34	32
Private pursuit	10	20	29	9	10	18	5	9	17	47
Court	12	7	24	25	26	17	17	29	14	6
Other public	6	2	.	5	5	10	4	2	18	8
DK	4	.	1		1					
All public	18	9	24	30	31	27	21	31	32	14
Total = N = 100%	480	361	270	222	200	180	300	200	300	200

Table 4. A husband battered a wife suspecting her of secretly meeting with another man. In your opinion, what should the woman do? (in %)

	PL	U		LT			RO		BG	
	cities	**D**	**M**	**Lt**	**Ru**	**Pl**	**Ro**	**H**	**Bg**	**T**
Withdrawal	5	5	7	22	22	34	5	4	17	15
Compromise	48	51	25	61	67	54	34	36	23	26
Private pursuit	6	17	19	10	8	10	8	19	3	6
Court	15	22	39	6	3	1	41	33	23	12
Other public	17	4	8	.	.	1	11	8	34	40
DK	9	1	2	1	.	.	1	.		1
All public	32	26	47	6	3	2	12	41	57	52
Total = N = 100%	480	361	270	222	200	180	300	200	300	200

Table 5. A dispute arose between the spouses when the wife inherited 10 000 euros and placed the funds on her own account, rather than contributing it to the family budget. In your opinion, what should her husband do? (in %)

	PL	U		LT			RO		BG	
	cities	**D**	**M**	**Lt**	**Ru**	**Pl**	**Ro**	**H**	**Bg**	**T**
Withdrawal	23	14	21	16	25	29	30	38	26	17
Compromise	70	70	58	66	60	59	61	43	39	54
Private pursuit	1	12	13	6	9	8	2	12	17	20
Court	2	3	7	12	6	3	6	5	2	3
Other public	.	.		.	.	.	1	1	16	6
DK	4	1	1	1	2	.	.	1	.	.
All public	2	3	7	12	6	3	7	6	18	9
Total = N = 100%	480	361	270	222	200	180	300	200	300	200

Table 6. An employer asked the hospital for information about the illness for which one of his employees was treated. The hospital provided the information which was then used against the patient. In your opinion, what should the patient do? (in %)

	PL	U		LT			RO		BG	
	cities	**D**	**M**	**Lt**	**Ru**	**Pl**	**Ro**	**H**	**Bg**	**T**
Withdrawal	2	1	7	5	3	7	5	1	2	1
Compromise	19	7	36	20	8	13	23	15	6	6
Private pursuit	6	11	41	11	8	12	2	7	16	18
Court	58	77	14	60	78	67	68	73	35	34
Other public	9	4	1	3	2	1	2	3	40	41
DK	6		1	1	1			1	1	
All public	67	81	15	63	80	68	70	76	75	75
Total = N = 100%	480	361	270	222	200	180	300	200	300	200

Table 7. Somebody built a house but due to a change in the local area development plan, the authorities ordered him to demolish it. In your opinion, what should the person who built the house do? (in %)

	PL	U		LT			RO		BG	
	cities	**D**	**M**	**Lt**	**Ru**	**Pl**	**Ro**	**H**	**Bg**	**T**
Withdrawal	1	2	2	4	3	1	15	1	15	32
Compromise	28	7	17	38	44	41	46	42	21	30
Private pursuit	2	3	14	6	5	10	2	7	5	3
Court	60	80	64	46	47	41	36	46	19	15
Other public	3	8	2	6	1	6	1	3	41	20
DK	6	.	1			1	.			.
All public	63	88	66	52	48	47	37	49	60	35
Total = N = 100%	480	361	270	222	200	180	300	200	300	200

Table 8. In the evening, a brawl started close to a restaurant. A police patrol was called in to calm the situation. Police officers used batons not only against the brawlers but against innocent bystanders as well. In your opinion, what should those bystanders do? (in %)

	PL	U		LT			RO		BG	
	cities	**D**	**M**	**Lt**	**Ru**	**Pl**	**Ro**	**H**	**Bg**	**T**
Withdrawal	4	3	6	9	7	6	2	2	1	1
Compromise	27	19	10	18	18	13	9	12	8	4
Private pursuit	4	8	22	11	10	9	4	7	13	6
Court	50	69	59	56	60	67	81	73	39	31
Other public	6	.	3	6	3	4	3	5	39	56
DK	8	1			2		1	1	.	2
All public	56	69	62	62	63	71	84	78	78	87
Total = N = 100%	480	361	270	222	200	180	300	200	300	200

Appendix D. Student's Test of Significance of Means for Denominational Groups in Multi-ethnic Cities Outside Poland

	Cluj-Napoca				Razgrad			Daugavpils					
Religion	**Orthodox**	**Protestants**	**Catholics**	**(1 -Orthodox, 2 – Protestants, 3 – Catholics)**	**Orthodox**	**Muslims**	**(1 – Muslims, 2 – Orthodox)**	**Protestants**	**Catholics**	**Orthodox**	**Old Believersy**	**IOher**	**(1 -Protestants, 2 -Catholics, 3 -Orthodox, 4 – Old Believers, 5 – others)**
Ideal dispute settlement (1 – court, 2 – mediation)	1.31 (0.46)	1.37 (0.48)	1.29 (0.46)	F (3,415) = 0.81	1.44 (0.50)	1.46 (0.50)	t(420) = -1.58	1.37 (0.49)	1.43 (0.50)	1.42 (0.50)	1.41 (0.50)	1.45 (0.52)	F (5,572) = 0.06
Dispute experience in last 3 years (0 – none, 2 – at least once)	2.46 (3.69)	0.15 (1.19)	0.35 (1.73)	**F (3,421) = 22.22** ***	9.01 (1.49)	9.42 (1.34)	**t(368) = -2.95** **	0.76 (2.44)	0.72 (2.23)	1.14 (2.90)	0.93 (2.62)	0.00	F (5,582) = 0.75
Lifelong court experience (0 – none, 1 – at least once)	0.28 (0.45)	0.13 (0.34)	0.31 (0.47)	**F (3,421) = 4.17** **	0.48 (0.50)	0.61 (0.49)	**t(414) = -2.06** *	0.11 (0.32)	0.15 (0.36)	0.19 (0.40)	0.09 (0.28)	0.18 (0.40)	F (5,572) = 0.98
Court experience in last 3 years (0 – none, 1 – at least once)	0.24 (0.37)	0.15 (0.12)	0.04 (0.17)	**F (3,421) = 22.22** ***	1.76 (1.65)	1.11 (1.36)	**t (428) = 5.19** ***	0.09 (0.42)	1.00 (4.36)	0.35 (2.11)	0.50 (2.15)	0.00	F (5,582) = 1.19
Court chosen in case scripts (0 – never, 7/8 – in all cases)	1.88 (1.33)	1.94 (1.29)	2.12 (1.46)	F (3,421) = 0.58	1.29 (1.35)	0.76 (1.04)	**t (428) = 5.18** ***	1.67 (1.36)	1.87 (1.25)	1.83 (1.06)	2.45 (1.39)	1.00 (1.26)	**F (5,582) = 3.64** **

	Cluj-Napoca				Razgrad			Daugavpils					
Religion	**Ortho-dox**	**Protes-tants**	**Catho-lics**	**(1 -Orthodox, 2 – Protestants, 3 – Catholics)**	**Ortho-dox**	**Mus-lims**	**(1 – Mus-lims, 2 – Or-thodox)**	**Protes-tants**	**Catho-lics**	**Ortho-dox**	**Old Belie-versy**	**IOher**	**(1 -Protestants, 2 -Catholics, 3 -Orthodox, 4 – Old Belie-vers, 5 – others)**
Compromise chosen in all script cases (0 – never, 7/8 – in all cases)	2.81 (1.36)	2.36 (1.43)	2.22 (1.75)	**F (3,421)** = **5.23** ***	2.21 (0.93)	2.19 (0.78)	t (428) = 1.22	2.96 (1.70)	3.12 (1.59)	3.39 (1.50)	2.83 (1.55)	4.00 (1.79)	F (5,582) = 1.87
Court chosen in private case scripts (0 – never, 3/4 – in all cases)	0.82 (0.90)	0.78 (0.91)	0.90 (0.96)	F (3,421) = 0.39	0.65 (0.90)	0.35 (0.66)	**t (428)** = **4.41** ***	0.74 (0.94)	0.78 (0.93)	0.58 (0.76)	1.10 (1.10)	0.27 (0.65)	**F (5,582)** = **3.50** **
Court chosen in public script cases (0 – never, 3/4 – in all cases)	1.86 (0.93)	1.94 (0.92)	1.97 (1.05)	F (3,421) = 0.56	1.11 (1.08)	0.75 (0.94)	**t (428)** = **4.33** ***	1.59 (1.08)	1.67 (0.98)	1.83 (0.80)	1.97 (0.90)	1.45 (1.04)	F (5,582) = 1.58
Compromise chosen in private script cases (0 – never, 4/5 – in all cases)	2.12 (1.06)	1.76 (1.20)	1.73 (1.27)	**F (3,421)** = **4.41** **	1.51 (1.33)	1.48 (1.04)	t (428) = 0.86	2.33 (1.44)	2.54 (1.28)	2.90 (1.23)	2.34 (1.33)	3.27 (1.35)	**F (5,582)** = **2.93** **
Compromise chosen in public script cases (0 – never, 3/4 – in all cases)	0.79 (0.83)	0.68 (0.77)	0.60 (0.95)	F (3,421) = 1.44	0.38 (0.68)	0.31 (0.53)	t (428) = 1.45	0.78 (0.93)	0.74 (0.79)	0.67 (0.73)	0.69 (0.84)	0.81 (0.87)	F (5,582) = 0.17

	Cluj-Napoca				Razgrad			Daugavpils					
Religion	**Ortho-dox**	**Protes-tants**	**Catho-lics**	**(1 -Orthodox, 2 – Protestants, 3 – Catholics)**	**Ortho-dox**	**Mus-lims**	**(1 – Mus-lims, 2 – Or-thodox)**	**Protes-tants**	**Catho-lics**	**Ortho-dox**	**Old Belie-versy**	**IOher**	**(1 -Protestants, 2 -Catholics, 3 -Orthodox, 4 – Old Belie-vers, 5 – others)**
Withdrawal chosen in all case scripts (**0–0** – never, 7/8 – in all cases)	0.85 (1.02)	0.75 (0.88)	0.69 (0.74)	F (3,417) = 1.03	1.05 (1.36)	1.11 (1.22)	t (416) = -0.53	1.14 (1.65)	0.82 (1.05)	0.71 (0.96)	0.78 (1.18)	0.72 (1.19)	F (5,590) = 0.69
Private pursuit chosen in all case scripts (**0–0** – never, 7/8 – in all cases)	0.27 (0.70)	0.86 (1.10)	0.78 (1.12)	**F (3,417) = 13.48** ***	0.95 (1.25)	1.47 (1.40)	**t(416) = -3.82** ***	0.86 (1.04)	0.89 (1.14)	0.91 (1.23)	0.80 (1.22)	1.18 (0.98)	F (5,588) = 0.32
Other official institutions chosen in all case scripts (**0–0** – never, 7/8 – in all cases)	2.97 (1.54)	2.92 (1.52)	3.19 (1.87)	F (3,417) = 0.45	4.02 (1.80)	3.61 (1.63)	**t (416) = 2.37** *	2.89 (1.69)	3.02 (1.52)	2.79 (1.25)	3.42 (1.50)	2.00 (1.67)	**F (5,588) = 2.15** *
Withdrawal chosen in private case scripts (0 – never, 4/5 – in all cases)	0.63 (0.80)	0.68 (0.84)	0.57 (0.63)	F (3,419) = 1.10	0.91 (1.14)	0.77 (1.08)	t (417) = 1.25	0.93 (1.18)	0.64 (0.83)	0.59 (0.78)	0.60 (0.98)	0.59 (0.93)	F (5,594) = 0.89
Withdrawal chosen in public case scripts(0 – never, 3/4 – in all cases)	0.22 (0.45)	0.06 (0.24)	0.12 (0.41)	**F (1,417) = 5.02** **	0.14 (0.43)	0.34 (0.51)	**t (427) = -4.33** ***	0.21 (0.63)	0.18 (0.44)	0.12 (0.35)	0.18 (0.39)	0.18 (0.60)	F (5,591) = 0.75

	Cluj-Napoca				Razgrad			Daugavpils					
Religion	**Ortho-dox**	**Protes-tants**	**Catho-lics**	**(1 -Orthodox, 2 – Protestants, 3 – Catholics)**	**Ortho-dox**	**Mus-lims**	**(1 – Mus-lims, 2 – Or-thodox)**	**Protes-tants**	**Catho-lics**	**Ortho-dox**	**Old Belie-versy**	**IOher**	**(1 -Protestants, 2 -Catholics, 3 -Orthodox, 4 – Old Belie-vers, 5 – others)**
Private pursuit cho-sen in all case scripts (0 – never, 4/5 – in all cases)	0.20 (0.54)	0.65 (0.88)	0.59 (0.87)	**F (3,419) = 13.46 *****	0.55 (0.85)	1.20 (1.19)	**t (417) = -5.96 *****	0.50 (0.79)	0.60 (0.90)	0.63 (0.96)	0.68 (1.05)	0.64 (0.81)	F (5,592) = 0.41
chosen in all case scripts (0 – never, 3/4 – in all cases)	0.08 (0.30)	0.21 (0.51)	0.19 (0.55)	**F (1,417) = 3.18 ****	0.41 (0.71)	0.27 (0.59)	**t (427) = 2.31 ***	0.36 (0.68)	0.29 (0.55)	0.29 (0.53)	0.12 (0.37)	0.55 (0.69)	F (5,591) = 1.61
Other official insti-tutions chosen in private case scripts (0 – never, 4/5 – in all cases)	1.06 (0.94)	0.88 (0.97)	1.10 (1.09)	F (3,419) = 1.25	1.54 (1.33)	1.41 (1.16)	**t (417) = 3.26 *****	0.36 (0.84)	1.21 (0.99)	1.21 (1.01)	0.88 (0.88)	1.38 (1.06)	**F (5,592) = 3.15 ****
Other official institutions chosen in public case scripts(0 – never, 3/4 – in all cases)	1.91 (0.91)	2.04 (0.88)	2.09 (1.06)	F (3,417) = 1.12	2.06 (0.93)	2.06 (0.85)	t (427) = -0.34	1.68 (1.06)	1.81 (0.94)	0.92 (0.80)	2.03 (0.92)	1.45 (1.04)	F (5,591) = 1.32
Significance levels: ***p<0.001, **p,0.01, *p<0.05													

Appendix E. Results of Multilevel Logistic Regression on Choice of Court and Choice of Compromise as Dependent Variables In Cities Outside Poland

1. Results for Daugavpils

	Dependent variable:			
	Court		**Agreement**	
	(1)	**(2)**	**(3)**	**(4)**
The type of dispute or conflict situation (reference category: Type 1 situation)				
Type II situation	0.856*** (0.190)	2.400** (1.010)	0.028 (0.137)	0.045 (0.468)
Type III situation	0.735*** (0.203)	1.980* (1.060)	0.389** (0.152)	-0.004 (0.514)
Nationality (reference category: Latvian)				
Russian	0.269 (0.225)	1.610 (0.985)	0.044 (0.189)	0.510 (0.517)
Polish	0.282 (0.217)	2.310** (0.990)	-0.520*** (0.182)	-0.637 (0.522)
Gender (reference category: male)				
Female	0.075 (0.083)	-0.248 (0.259)	0.236*** (0.086)	0.353* (0.213)
Age (reference category: up to 34 years old)				
Age 35–50	-0.128 (0.108)	-0.610* (0.336)	0.021 (0.111)	0.678** (0.285)
Age 51–64	-0.040 (0.117)	-0.275 (0.446)	-0.057 (0.122)	0.387 (0.379)
Age 65 or more	0.017 (0.141)	-0.468 (0.597)	-0.026 (0.149)	0.688 (0.526)
Degree of education (reference category: primary)				
Vocational	-0.283 (0.238)	0.966 (0.725)	0.239 (0.246)	-0.830 (0.627)
Secondary	-0.210 (0.172)	0.785 (0.673)	0.190 (0.180)	-0.680 (0.520)

	Dependent variable:			
	Court		**Agreement**	
	(1)	**(2)**	**(3)**	**(4)**
Higher	-0.075 (0.169)	0.501 (0.656)	0.185 (0.177)	-0.227 (0.499)
Religious denomination (reference category: Lutheran)				
Roman – Catholic	0.254 (0.206)	-0.079 (0.939)	0.222 (0.208)	0.191 (0.704)
Orthodox	0.102 (0.237)	0.162 (0.965)	0.361 (0.240)	0.088 (0.737)
Old believers	0.451^{*} (0.246)	0.632 (1.170)	0.002 (0.254)	-0.276 (0.928)
Other or no religion	-0.007 (0.294)	-1.800 (1.530)	0.620^{**} (0.292)	1.030 (0.956)
Work situation (reference category: working full time)				
Part time	-0.231 (0.174)	-0.532 (0.567)	-0.152 (0.174)	-0.291 (0.431)
Irregular	0.402^{*} (0.218)	0.758 (0.749)	-0.746^{***} (0.242)	-1.910^{**} (0.786)
No job	0.068 (0.123)	0.250 (0.544)	-0.193 (0.129)	-0.578 (0.474)
Subjective assessment of one's socio-economic standing (reference category: below average)				
Average or above average	0.116 (0.102)	-0.075 (0.307)	-0.015 (0.104)	0.279 (0.256)
Response to the item: "Law should always be obeyed" (reference: Response 1)				
Response 2	0.008 (0.087)	-0.535^{*} (0.314)	-0.113 (0.090)	0.018 (0.259)
Response 3	-0.371^{*} (0.190)	-1.120^{**} (0.566)	0.185 (0.183)	0.633 (0.441)
Response 4	-0.206 (0.202)	-1.260 (0.809)	0.032 (0.202)	0.720 (0.600)

	Dependent variable:			
	Court		**Agreement**	
	(1)	(2)	(3)	(4)
Responses to the questionnaire item: "Which is better?" (reference: Resolving a dispute by a court or other institution.)				
Resolving a dispute by impartial individuals	-0.149* (0.084)	-0.242 (0.287)	-0.071 (0.086)	0.269 (0.235)
Responses to the item "How many people are there in your neighbourhood whose opinion you care about?" (reference: Many).				
Few people in the neighbourhood whose opinion I care about	-0.042 (0.113)	0.408 (0.439)	0.099 (0.118)	0.090 (0.363)
No people in the neighbourhood whose opinion I care about	-0.132 (0.120)	0.067 (0.393)	-0.034 (0.124)	-0.103 (0.344)
Trust in others (reference: You should trust no one)				
You can only trust those you know well	0.020 (0.100)	0.064 (0.343)	-0.018 (0.102)	0.126 (0.279)
You should trust everyone unless they take advantage of you	0.171 (0.123)	0.503 (0.354)	-0.089 (0.128)	-0.496* (0.298)
Have you ever taken part in a court trial as a witness, suspect, or in some other capacity? (reference: Never)				
At least once	-0.152 (0.118)		0.061 (0.119)	
Court experience in the past 3 years	0.203 (0.152)	0.296 (0.384)	-0.197 (0.163)	-0.543 (0.338)
How fair do you think the court's ruling in this case was (reference: unfair)				
Fair		0.379 (0.436)		0.407 (0.351)
Fair in some respects, unfair in others		-0.014 (0.535)		0.419 (0.437)
Interactions				
Russian × Type II situation	-0.011 (0.236)	-1.320 (1.020)	-0.194 (0.198)	-0.246 (0.566)

	Dependent variable:			
	Court		**Agreement**	
	(1)	**(2)**	**(3)**	**(4)**
Russian × Type II situation	-0.376 (0.259)	-1.720 (1.100)	-0.092 (0.219)	0.569 (0.628)
Polish × Type II situation	-0.425* (0.244)	-2.290** (1.050)	0.345* (0.209)	0.624 (0.615)
Polish × Type II situation	-0.595** (0.269)	-2.280** (1.130)	0.399* (0.229)	0.962 (0.670)
Constant	-1.760*** (0.340)	-3.670** (1.620)	-0.625* (0.324)	-1.320 (1.090)
Observations	3,946	567	3,946	567
Log Likelihood	-2,252.000	-282.000	-2,639.000	-357.000
Akaike Inf. Crit.	4,585.000	647.000	5,357.000	796.000
Bayesian Inf. Crit.	4,836.000	825.000	5,608.000	974.000
	*Levels of significance: * p<0.1, ** p<0.05, *** p<0.01*			

2. *Results for Cluj-Napoca*

	Dependent variable:			
	Court			
	(1)	(2)	(3)	(4)
Type of situation (reference: Type 1 situations)				
Type 2 Situations	3.520*** (0.369)	6.320*** (1.980)	3.550*** (0.373)	6.300*** (1.990)
Type 3 Situations	1.700*** (0.378)	4.330** (1.980)	1.730*** (0.381)	4.300** (2.000)
Nationality (reference: Romanian)				
Hungarian	0.829** (0.400)	-0.377 (1.420)	0.892** (0.405)	-0.304 (1.430)
Gender (reference: male)				
Female	0.027 (0.121)	-0.300 (0.246)	0.032 (0.121)	-0.262 (0.249)

	Dependent variable:			
	Court			
	(1)	**(2)**	**(3)**	**(4)**
Age (reference: up to 34 years of age)				
Age 35–50	-0.104	0.293	-0.111	0.297
	(0.156)	(0.335)	(0.155)	(0.334)
Age 51–64	-0.278	-0.038	-0.299*	-0.071
	(0.179)	(0.331)	(0.179)	(0.332)
Age 65 or more	-0.228	0.481	-0.230	0.485
	(0.211)	(0.397)	(0.211)	(0.394)
Degree of education (reference: primary)				
Vocational	0.139	-0.058	0.122	0.012
	(0.233)	(0.430)	(0.233)	(0.439)
Secondary	0.514**	1.010**	0.504**	0.992**
	(0.225)	(0.399)	(0.225)	(0.397)
Higher	0.246	1.220***	0.237	1.200***
	(0.237)	(0.419)	(0.237)	(0.415)
Religious denomination (reference: Orthodox)				
Evangelical Reformed	-0.082	0.902*	-0.053	0.870*
	(0.237)	(0.475)	(0.237)	(0.474)
Roman-Catholic	0.018	0.426	0.034	0.407
	(0.259)	(0.468)	(0.258)	(0.466)
Other	-0.214	-0.632	-0.169	-0.631
	(0.217)	(0.474)	(0.217)	(0.473)
None	0.187	0.449	0.182	0.474
	(0.251)	(0.555)	(0.250)	(0.554)
Work situation (reference: working full time)				
Part time	0.334	0.895*	0.321	0.867*
	(0.258)	(0.496)	(0.257)	(0.494)
Irregular	-0.035	0.599	-0.097	0.597
	(0.255)	(1.170)	(0.257)	(1.170)

	Dependent variable:			
	Court			
	(1)	**(2)**	**(3)**	**(4)**
No job	-0.165 (0.146)	-0.005 (0.270)	-0.183 (0.146)	-0.031 (0.271)
Subjective assessment of one's socio-economic standing (reference category: below average)				
Average or above	0.079 (0.146)	-0.682** (0.301)	0.080 (0.145)	-0.667** (0.297)
Response to the item: "Law should always be obeyed" (reference: Response 1)				
Response 2	-0.459*** (0.162)	-0.760** (0.321)	-0.438*** (0.162)	-0.765** (0.318)
Response 3	0.109 (0.180)	-0.040 (0.373)	0.112 (0.179)	-0.027 (0.371)
Response 4	0.042 (0.242)	0.949** (0.396)	0.057 (0.241)	0.917** (0.394)
Responses to the questionnaire item: "Which is better?" (reference: Resolving a dispute by a court or another institution.)				
Dispute settled by impartial observers	-0.253** (0.127)	-0.454* (0.267)	-0.272** (0.127)	-0.447* (0.266)
Responses to the item "How many people are there in your neighbourhood whose opinion you care about?" (reference: Many).				
Only a few such people in my neighbourhood	0.393** (0.195)	-0.028 (0.407)	0.403** (0.195)	-0.0002 (0.407)
No such people in my neighbourhood	0.412** (0.190)	-0.014 (0.406)	0.408** (0.190)	0.009 (0.406)
Trust in others (reference: You should trust no one)				
Trust only those you know	0.187 (0.150)	-0.160 (0.299)	0.181 (0.150)	-0.163 (0.298)

	Dependent variable:			
	Court			
	(1)	**(2)**	**(3)**	**(4)**
Trust everyone unless they betray your trust	0.289*	-0.285	0.269	-0.288
	(0.167)	(0.330)	(0.167)	(0.328)
Have you ever taken part in a court trial as a witness, suspect, or in some other capacity? (reference: Never)				
At least once	-0.059		-0.040	
	(0.144)		(0.144)	
How fair do you think the court's ruling in this case was (reference: unfair)				
The ruling was unfair		0.223		0.190
		(0.313)		(0.315)
The ruling was unfair in some respects, and fair in others		-0.142		-0.125
		(0.414)		(0.413)
Court experience past three years			0.347*	0.310
			(0.198)	(0.401)
Interactions				
Type 2 situations × Hungarian	-0.474	-0.198	-0.479	-0.198
	(0.340)	(1.370)	(0.343)	(1.370)
Type 3 situations × Hungarian	-0.965***	-1.520	-0.965***	-1.500
	(0.370)	(1.460)	(0.373)	(1.460)
Constant	-3.570***	-5.890***	-3.660***	-5.930***
	(0.490)	(2.090)	(0.495)	(2.110)
Observations	3,225	762	3,225	762
Log Likelihood	-1,743.000	-383.000	-1,742.000	-382.000
Akaike Inf. Crit.	3,558.000	839.000	3,557.000	841.000
Bayesian Inf. Crit.	3,777.000	1,011.000	3,782.000	1,017.000
Note:	*Levels of significance: * p<0.1, ** p<0.05, *** p<0.01*			

	Dependent variable:			
	Agreement			
	(1)	**(2)**	**(3)**	**(4)**
The type of dispute or conflict situation (reference category: Type 1 situation)				
Type 2 Situations	-1.570***	-0.981***	-1.560***	-1.330***
	(0.130)	(0.293)	(0.130)	(0.002)
Type 3 Situations	-0.533***	0.307	-0.532***	-0.080***
	(0.133)	(0.308)	(0.133)	(0.002)
Nationality (reference category: Romanian)				
Hungarian	-0.584**	1.740**	-0.565**	1.150***
	(0.263)	(0.747)	(0.265)	(0.002)
Gender (reference category: male)				
Female	-0.189*	0.184	-0.188*	0.167***
	(0.111)	(0.273)	(0.111)	(0.002)
Age (reference category: up to 34 years old)				
Age 35–50	-0.024	0.459	-0.026	0.075***
	(0.144)	(0.368)	(0.144)	(0.002)
Age 51–64	0.114	0.212	0.108	-0.195***
	(0.163)	(0.372)	(0.163)	(0.002)
Age 65 or more	0.101	0.314	0.102	0.005***
	(0.190)	(0.435)	(0.190)	(0.002)
Degree of education (reference category: primary)				
Vocational	0.133	0.446	0.129	0.396***
	(0.209)	(0.471)	(0.209)	(0.002)
Secondary	-0.112	0.215	-0.115	-0.227***
	(0.204)	(0.432)	(0.204)	(0.002)
Higher	-0.099	-0.081	-0.102	-0.505***
	(0.215)	(0.450)	(0.215)	(0.002)
Religious denomination (reference category: Lutheran)				
Evangelical Reformed	-0.011	-0.623	-0.003	-0.975***
	(0.216)	(0.532)	(0.216)	(0.002)

	Dependent variable:			
	Agreement			
	(1)	**(2)**	**(3)**	**(4)**
Roman-Catholic	-0.187 (0.238)	0.099 (0.527)	-0.181 (0.238)	-0.415*** (0.002)
Other	0.138 (0.195)	0.747 (0.486)	0.152 (0.197)	0.513*** (0.002)
None	-0.302 (0.236)	0.373 (0.628)	-0.303 (0.236)	-0.018*** (0.002)
Work situation (reference category: working full time)				
Part time	-0.084 (0.238)	-0.202 (0.543)	-0.088 (0.238)	-0.483*** (0.002)
Irregular	-0.295 (0.236)	0.685 (1.300)	-0.313 (0.238)	0.997*** (0.002)
No job	0.041 (0.133)	0.287 (0.298)	0.035 (0.134)	0.099*** (0.002)
Subjective assessment of one's socio-economic standing (reference category: below average)				
Average or above	0.100 (0.133)	0.828** (0.336)	0.100 (0.133)	0.792*** (0.002)
Response to the item: "Law should always be obeyed" (reference: Response 1)				
Response 2	0.289** (0.145)	0.374 (0.345)	0.294** (0.145)	0.283*** (0.002)
Response 3	-0.029 (0.166)	-0.914** (0.439)	-0.029 (0.166)	-0.504*** (0.002)
Response 4	-0.126 (0.224)	-1.320*** (0.448)	-0.122 (0.224)	-1.240*** (0.002)
Responses to the questionnaire item: "Which is better?" (reference: Resolving a dispute by a court or another institution.)				
Dispute settled by impartial observers	0.157 (0.116)	0.217 (0.290)	0.151 (0.116)	0.234*** (0.002)

	Dependent variable:			
	Agreement			
	(1)	**(2)**	**(3)**	**(4)**
Responses to the item "How many people are there in your neighbourhood whose opinion you care about?" (reference: Many).				
Only a few such people in my neighbourhood	-0.208 (0.175)	0.324 (0.467)	-0.204 (0.175)	0.502*** (0.002)
No such people in my neighbourhood	-0.256 (0.171)	0.486 (0.471)	-0.257 (0.171)	0.507*** (0.002)
Trust in others (reference: You should trust no one)				
Trust only those you know	-0.003 (0.137)	-0.130 (0.327)	-0.006 (0.137)	-0.014*** (0.002)
Trust everyone unless they betray your trust	-0.054 (0.152)	-0.034 (0.362)	-0.061 (0.152)	0.129*** (0.002)
Have you ever taken part in a court trial as a witness, suspect, or in some other capacity? (reference: Never)				
At least once	0.070 (0.131)		0.076 (0.131)	
How fair do you think the court's ruling in this case was (reference: unfair)				
The ruling was unfair		-0.475 (0.342)		-0.520*** (0.002)
The ruling was unfair in some respects, and fair in others		0.148 (0.446)		0.092*** (0.002)
Court experience past three years			0.109 (0.181)	0.882*** (0.002)
Interactions				
Type 2 situations × Hungarian	0.244 (0.220)	-1.300** (0.637)	0.244 (0.220)	-0.120*** (0.002)
Type 3 situations × Hungarian	0.233 (0.227)	-1.470** (0.663)	0.232 (0.227)	-0.242*** (0.002)
Constant	0.615** (0.312)	-1.440* (0.822)	0.596* (0.313)	-0.594*** (0.002)

	Dependent variable:			
	Agreement			
	(1)	**(2)**	**(3)**	**(4)**
Observations	3,225	762	3,225	762
Log Likelihood	-1,975.000	-463.000	-1,975.000	-454.000
Akaike Inf. Crit.	4,023.000	1,000.000	4,024.000	984.000
Bayesian Inf. Crit.	4,242.000	1,171.000	4,249.000	1,160.000
Note:	*Levels of significance:* * *p<0.1,* ** *p<0.05,* *** *p<0.01*			

3. Results for Razgrad

	Dependent variable:			
	Court			
	(1)	**(2)**	**(3)**	**(4)**
Type 2 Situations	2.040***	1.300***	2.250***	1.500***
	(0.233)	(0.212)	(0.301)	(0.277)
Type 3 Situations	0.293	-0.055	0.454	0.265
	(0.263)	(0.256)	(0.391)	(0.344)
Turkish	-0.287	-0.319	-0.144	-0.103
	(0.303)	(0.244)	(0.426)	(0.354)
Female	-0.080	0.347**	-0.009	0.350
	(0.131)	(0.162)	(0.200)	(0.247)
Age 35–50	0.043	0.332	0.140	0.425
	(0.169)	(0.212)	(0.302)	(0.360)
Age 51–64	0.109	0.357	0.170	0.220
	(0.193)	(0.246)	(0.340)	(0.403)
Age 65 or more	0.023	0.357	0.204	0.880
	(0.255)	(0.319)	(0.480)	(0.557)
Vocational	-0.138	0.379	-0.174	0.737
	(0.243)	(0.298)	(0.401)	(0.479)
Secondary	-0.059	0.595**	-0.044	0.670*
	(0.197)	(0.241)	(0.359)	(0.407)

	Dependent variable:			
	Court			
	(1)	**(2)**	**(3)**	**(4)**
Higher	0.034	0.790***	0.031	0.947**
	(0.233)	(0.289)	(0.416)	(0.480)
Muslim	0.049	-0.522***	-0.0001	-0.449*
	(0.149)	(0.182)	(0.226)	(0.273)
Other	0.103	0.400	-0.166	-0.575
	(0.454)	(0.552)	(0.889)	(1.090)
Atheist	-0.164	0.069	-0.208	0.398
	(0.235)	(0.284)	(0.310)	(0.368)
Part time	-0.107	-0.012	-0.004	-0.650*
	(0.211)	(0.254)	(0.331)	(0.384)
Irregular	0.114	-0.011	-0.002	0.118
	(0.268)	(0.333)	(0.416)	(0.500)
No job	0.049	0.077	-0.019	-0.408
	(0.202)	(0.253)	(0.348)	(0.403)
Average or above	0.078	0.283	0.021	0.047
	(0.175)	(0.212)	(0.288)	(0.329)
Response 2	0.180	-0.315	0.244	0.038
	(0.200)	(0.249)	(0.305)	(0.374)
Response 3	0.055	-0.595***	0.091	-0.520
	(0.172)	(0.212)	(0.279)	(0.329)
Response 4	-0.010	-0.914***	0.148	-0.610*
	(0.193)	(0.239)	(0.284)	(0.344)
Dispute settled by impartial observers	-0.201	-1.250***	-0.326	-1.490***
	(0.160)	(0.192)	(0.281)	(0.313)
At least once	-0.041	-0.386**		
	(0.139)	(0.169)		

	Dependent variable:			
	Court			
	(1)	**(2)**	**(3)**	**(4)**
Only few such people in my neighbourhood	-0.017 (0.179)	0.410* (0.221)	-0.150 (0.273)	0.302 (0.322)
No such people in my neighbourhood	-0.065 (0.178)	0.300 (0.223)	-0.132 (0.296)	0.239 (0.352)
Trust only those you know	-0.014 (0.153)	-0.690*** (0.188)	-0.032 (0.234)	-0.594** (0.280)
Trust everyone unless they betray your trust	-0.200 (0.186)	-0.719*** (0.227)	-0.297 (0.312)	-0.832** (0.368)
Court experience past three years	1.070*** (0.060)		1.110*** (0.080)	
The ruling was unfair			-0.086 (0.350)	0.601 (0.398)
The ruling was unfair in some respects, and fair in others			0.146 (0.339)	0.907** (0.397)
Type 2 situations X Turkish	0.484 (0.357)	0.380 (0.289)	0.386 (0.481)	0.303 (0.411)
Type 3 situations by Turkish	-0.051 (0.447)	-0.022 (0.356)	-0.541 (0.678)	-0.284 (0.498)
Constant	-4.760*** (0.428)	-1.960*** (0.428)	-4.980*** (0.684)	-3.140*** (0.767)
Observations	3,231	3,231	1,650	1,650
Log Likelihood	-959.000	-1,218.000	-451.000	-573.000
Akaike Inf. Crit.	1,990.000	2,507.000	976.000	1,217.000
Bayesian Inf. Crit.	2,209.000	2,720.000	1,176.000	1,412.000
Note:	*Levels of significance: * p<0.1, ** p<0.05, *** p<0.01*			

	Dependent variable:			
	Agreement			
	(1)	**(2)**	**(3)**	**(4)**
Type 2 Situations	-1.340^{***} (0.225)	-1.400^{***} (0.225)	-1.500^{***} (0.001)	-1.620^{***} (0.397)
Type 3 Situations	0.247 (0.163)	0.233 (0.162)	0.254^{***} (0.001)	0.358 (0.244)
Turkish	-0.316^{*} (0.182)	-0.304^{*} (0.179)	-0.495^{***} (0.001)	-0.527^{*} (0.276)
Female	-0.223^{*} (0.122)	-0.244^{**} (0.122)	-0.567^{***} (0.001)	-0.604^{***} (0.187)
Age 35–50	0.076 (0.156)	0.042 (0.156)	-0.290^{***} (0.001)	-0.304 (0.262)
Age 51–64	0.228 (0.172)	0.195 (0.172)	-0.020^{***} (0.001)	-0.023 (0.279)
Age 65 or more	0.243 (0.228)	0.204 (0.228)	0.019^{***} (0.001)	-0.011 (0.387)
Vocational	0.173 (0.194)	0.132 (0.194)	-0.359^{***} (0.001)	-0.382 (0.319)
Secondary	0.165 (0.165)	0.120 (0.164)	-0.014^{***} (0.001)	-0.010 (0.274)
Higher	0.162 (0.205)	0.108 (0.204)	0.006^{***} (0.001)	-0.002 (0.332)
Muslim	-0.014 (0.141)	0.037 (0.140)	-0.107^{***} (0.001)	-0.073 (0.220)
Other	0.593 (0.369)	0.569 (0.371)	1.980^{***} (0.001)	2.080^{***} (0.715)
Atheist	0.170 (0.218)	0.171 (0.219)	0.110^{***} (0.001)	0.114 (0.298)
Part time	-0.466^{***} (0.180)	-0.472^{***} (0.181)	-0.148^{***} (0.001)	-0.169 (0.273)

	Dependent variable:			
	Agreement			
	(1)	**(2)**	**(3)**	**(4)**
Irregular	-0.222 (0.224)	-0.237 (0.225)	0.598*** (0.001)	0.640* (0.352)
No job	-0.178 (0.180)	-0.173 (0.180)	0.146*** (0.001)	0.187 (0.283)
Average or above	-0.256* (0.150)	-0.283* (0.150)	-0.137*** (0.001)	-0.148 (0.228)
Response 2	-0.188 (0.189)	-0.154 (0.189)	-0.344*** (0.001)	-0.388 (0.306)
Response 3	-0.410** (0.165)	-0.359** (0.163)	-0.781*** (0.001)	-0.827*** (0.261)
Response 4	-0.591*** (0.182)	-0.529*** (0.180)	-0.846*** (0.001)	-0.910*** (0.278)
Dispute settled by impartial observers	-0.003 (0.141)	0.077 (0.136)	0.055*** (0.001)	0.075 (0.238)
At least once	-0.322*** (0.124)	-0.289** (0.123)		
Only few such people in my neighbourhood	-0.068 (0.149)	-0.089 (0.149)	-0.391*** (0.001)	-0.417* (0.225)
No such people in my neighbourhood	-0.098 (0.153)	-0.110 (0.154)	-0.437*** (0.001)	-0.455* (0.250)
Trust only those you know	0.145 (0.140)	0.189 (0.139)	0.111*** (0.001)	0.137 (0.215)
Trust everyone unless they betray your trust	0.017 (0.165)	0.066 (0.164)	-0.229*** (0.001)	-0.227 (0.269)
Court experience past three years	-0.092** (0.045)		-0.030*** (0.001)	
The ruling was unfair			0.378*** (0.001)	0.411 (0.285)

	Dependent variable:			
	Agreement			
	(1)	**(2)**	**(3)**	**(4)**
The ruling was unfair in some respects, and fair in others			0.530*** (0.001)	0.573** (0.279)
Type 2 situations X Turkish	0.366 (0.266)	0.366 (0.267)	0.573*** (0.001)	0.623 (0.408)
Type 3 situations by Turkish	0.752*** (0.240)	0.750*** (0.238)	0.566*** (0.001)	0.608* (0.348)
Constant	-0.338 (0.324)	-0.509 (0.313)	-0.158*** (0.001)	-0.247 (0.532)
Observations	3,231	3,231	1,650	1,650
Log Likelihood	-1,594.000	-1,596.000	-741.000	-741.000
Akaike Inf. Crit.	3,259.000	3,261.000	1,556.000	1,554.000
Bayesian Inf. Crit.	3,478.000	3,474.000	1,757.000	1,748.000
Note:	*Levels of significance: * p<0.1, ** p<0.05, *** p<0.01*			

Part IV. Conclusions

Jacek Kurczewski, Małgorzata Fuszara

1. Our initial assumption is that the legal sociology is just a specific way of looking at the same social facts that are dealt with differently by other sociological approaches. Far from tending to avoid the conceptual and disciplinary disputes, and wishing to make it clear that the legal sociology starts not with the law as understood in an official way, but with the legal facts, that is, the social facts that are <<interpreted in terms of rights and duties and the derivative categories>>. Only after the domain of thus interpreted social facts is created, is the proper study in sociology of law, or more adequately, in legal sociology possible. Whether this initial reconstruction of social reality seems to be a distortion of the latter or not, it is a step that is a necessary condition for any scientific inquiry, be it the physics or psychology. The second point is that, if we agree that rights and duties are materially rooted in the events of the psychic life, then the proper way of building the scientific theories of the legal life is to assume the psychological reference of our basic concepts and not to seek the primordial elements in the codes, written texts, utterances of the officials, institutional behaviour or metaphysical facts as it happens in the common assumptions of the sociology of law or the theory of law in general. Thirdly, the lesson that is thought by a continuous debate between the humanistic and objectivistic currents in sociology, together, with a rather compromising failure of the Third Positivism, includes the contention that social events cannot be fully understood without taking some peculiarities of human mind into consideration, and even if our existence is limited by the environment and by our organic apparatus and its needs, we still do create and keep alive the specific cultural realities that on their side affect our conduct even if the reality is totally dependent upon our and others' intellectual and other activities, that is to say, that it exists conditionally. The recent „new" sociologies and meta-sociologies seem to play precisely that melody, although in different keys. With these three basic premises, that the legal sociology is a study of social facts through the concepts of rights and duties, that these latter are to be interpreted as the psycho-cultural facts and that this interpretation needs to take into account both what exists in the common, socio-cultural reality and in the individual mind – and the list of the basic premises of any legal cosmology still seems far from being exhausted and precise – we must attempt to reconcile this humanistic approach with the already too familiar

ideal of the systematic theoretical thinking and investigation that is called a scientific approach.

2. The Polish sociology of law, which exploded after the liberalization of communist rule in 1956, remained the only cradle of the empirical socio-legal studies in the whole communist bloc for decades. As the freedom of information was limited, the sociological surveys made by academicians, not as in the West by commercial polling agencies, were rare opportunities – also for the ruling Party – to learn what people think. The preoccupation with the empirical study of the legal consciousness was soon the distinctive characteristic of the sociology of law in Poland which could in this way escape the administratively monitored duty to expose the official Marxist-Leninist doctrine that was supposed to be faultless and serve as the only true theory of everything social (and not only). The study of disputes was started by Jacek Kurczewski in the mid-1970s and the research presented in this volume is in fact the continuation of the empirical studies of dispute and dispute settlement behavior from those years.

3. There are some basic continuities in our findings. Summing up the findings from 1970s J. Kurczewski (1982:76) stressed that of the basic socio-demographic variables – gender, age, social habitat of residence, socio-occupational status and education – checked systematically in the research conducted in several localities of an urban and countryside character, only age was related to the choice of court in a significant way, and as for the authoritative way of dispute settlement generally younger people were more inclined to choose the court and the elderly to choose the informal mediatory procedures. The social habitat was the second important factor as in the metropolitan area the choice of court was much more frequent than in the countryside. There is not much surprise therefore that the same factors continue their importance in the early 2010s despite the fact that Poland is in terms of its legal, political, economic and social arrangements a different country from what it was when our study of disputes and disputing behavior patterns started.

4. Our research on private prosecution cases led to a differentiation between many types of them. Finally it let us present a typology of conflicts submitted to the courts.

A. A simple unilateral conflict

As noted earlier (Fuszara 1989), this denotes a simple conflict which is described in the charge sheet in its entirety and in which the roles are clearly defined: the rights of only one party had been violated, and in consequence, this party took the matter to court. The model of the conflict and the dispute is quite simple:

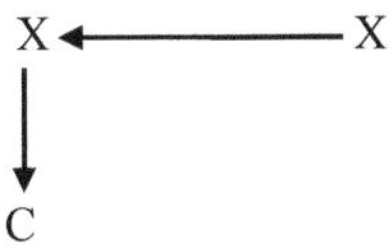

Here is an example: two men work together. One admonishes the other for doing his work poorly. In response, he gets punched. This becomes the basis for charges filed in the private prosecution mode. Court fees in this specific case were not paid and thus the matter was not heard by the court. In general, simple conflicts are the easiest to solve, whether in a court or privately by the parties.

B. A simple bilateral conflict, a unilateral court dispute

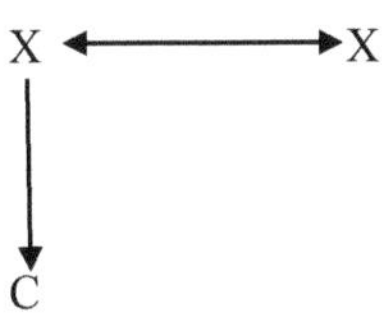

Here is an example: at a party, a fight breaks out between the revelers. Both parties infringe each other's rights, but only one party takes the matter to court. Typically, this is the party who suffered greater damage. However, earlier research indicates that it is not always the case: some respondents were resolutely opposed to going to court when involved in any conflict whatsoever, even when they themselves were the victims. These persons preferred to solve the conflicts on their own, resorting to "self-help" and generally operating outside the law. When a case of this type is heard, the fact that violations were mutual is revealed, which either prompts the parties to settle or, in the absence of a settlement, helps the defendant to get acquitted.

C. A simple bilateral conflict, a bilateral court dispute

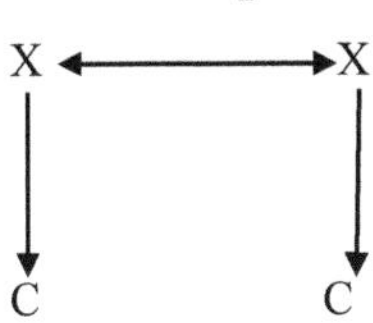

The conflict again is usually simple, and a description of the conflict in its entirety fits into the charge sheet. Both parties mutually violate each other's rights and both parties press charges by private prosecution. A fight among party-goers can serve as an example here too, with the difference that both participants take the matter to court. Usually, the second case is brought in response to the first victim pressing charges. Under such circumstances, the two cases are heard jointly. Reaching a settlement or mutual withdrawal from the charges tends to be quite easy in these conflicts.

D. A concentric conflict

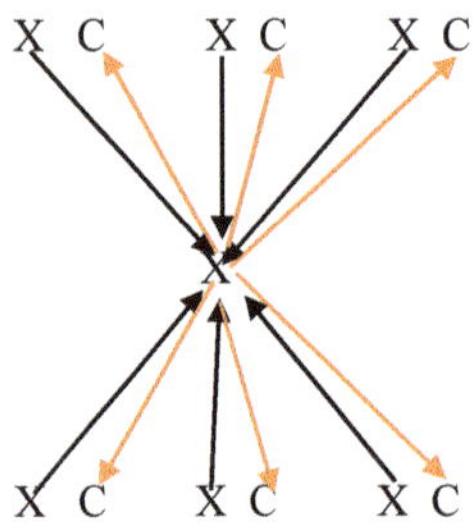

A dispute here is between one private prosecutor and numerous persons who, in the prosecutor's opinion, have infringed his or her rights. An example: during a previously held trial, numerous witnesses spoke about the conduct of a specific person as possibly violating certain norms (there were suspicions of pedophilia). This person brought charges against all the witnesses, alleging defamation. For the court, this is a relatively easy case, because witnesses who testify in good faith are protected against such accusations. While the court arrives at a formal resolution quite easily, the conflicts between the parties are not actually easily resolved, and may continue past the final court hearing.

The cases which are more difficult to handle result from a different type of concentric conflicts. For instance, someone spreads defamatory information online. The person who feels defamed brings charges against everyone who has disseminated the information both online and in more direct ways, e.g. by repeating it in face-to-face conversations. The spread of the allegedly defamatory information and the sheer number of persons involved in the matter makes it very difficult to find a solution, in particular an amicable one.

E. A complex conflict with multiple components

The most complex conflicts resemble a chain with many links, with multi-layered connections between the links. Numerous persons take legal action against one another. Here is a diagram of a conflict in which, in the studied period, at least 8 cases were brought to court and further 2 cases were connected:

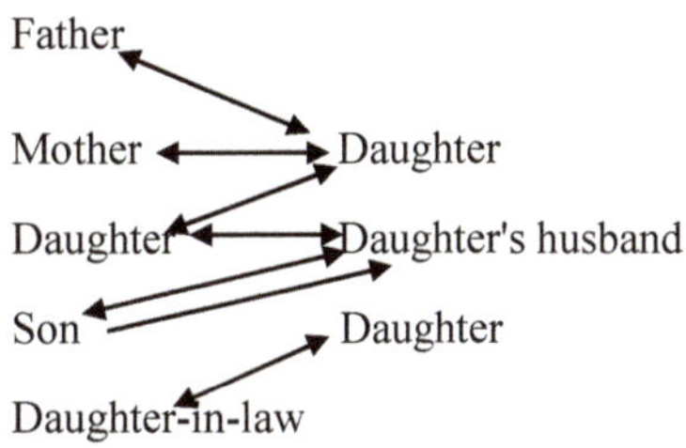

The rights of the participants have been violated in many ways: there are infringements of the right to good name (reputation) by means of allegations of extramarital affairs and cheating; insults; violations of physical integrity; actual assaults. This is accompanied by property disputes and other types of disputes often occurring between neighbours, e.g. boundary disputes. Cases involving these persons repeatedly return to the courtroom. If charges are withdrawn, or even if a settlement is reached, the conflict dies down and is temporarily suspended, but not completely extinguished. All that the courts can do is to mitigate the outward manifestations of the conflict and to curb the attacks of the parties against one another.

F. Inherited disputes among neighbours

The most long-lasting conflicts among neighbours and family members are "inherited", and passed down from one generation to another. Here is a diagram presenting such a conflict. For the sake of clarity, we only marked the generations and not the specific persons involved.

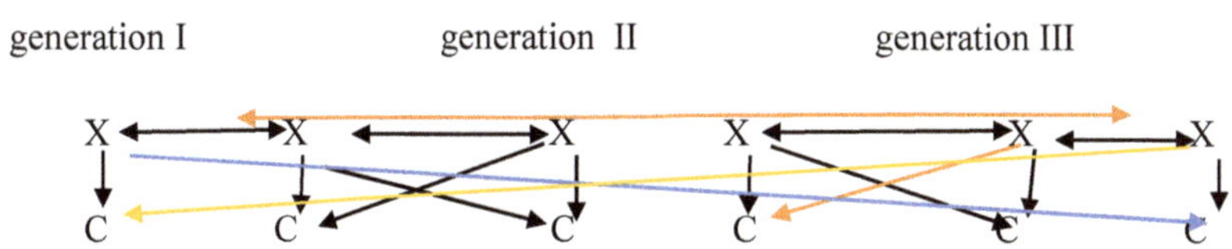

There is a strong similarity here to a complex conflict with multiple components. The complexity and longevity of the conflict are immense, and it is practically unsolvable for the court. Research demonstrates that conflicts like this shift and transform, constantly absorbing new components. Years later, nobody can remember how the dispute actually started, what allegations were once made, and how many court cases arose from the matter. Respondents explain that they witnessed the dispute when it was propelled forward by their parents, and now not only are they involved but also their children. Efforts are made to teach the youngest generation (the grandchildren) about the importance of living in peace, but the effectiveness of these assurances is undermined by the fact that grandchildren also witness the dispute as it progresses. However, the multiple courtroom sessions generated by the conflict do have an effect: the dispute becomes more "civilized". "We've been to court many times, and to the court of appeal too [...]. The last time was a good few years back, maybe even more than ten. For one thing [...], we learned to keep our mouths shut and not respond to their taunts, and for another thing [...] now they don't yell insults, they don't hit any more, they just act meanly out of malice" (Fuszara 2004, p. 55). As a result, while the conflict continues, it no longer involves actual crimes and thus no longer generates court cases.

5. A fundamental question prompted by the comparison of private prosecutions over the years (in particular in defence of the private prosecutor's honour) is why the number of these cases has seen such a dramatic decline. There are no reasons to believe that insults and defamation attempts occur less frequently now than they used to. Research demonstrates that this is the most typical conflict in which Poles in a representative nationwide sample are involved. So why such a sharp drop in court case numbers? Sociological studies give no support to the hypothesis that this is due to diminishing trust in the court system. While the levels of this trust fluctuate, they were quite high during the period under study (contrary to a popular belief). We must therefore search for the answers that are more empirically reliable. The first option is to consider the costs. Fees and other associated costs are on the rise, and the courts are more reluctant to waive them for private prosecutors, and thus the number of cases filed with the courts is decreasing. This simple explanation is likely to be relevant for a good number of scenarios, which points to a highly worrying fact that the pursuit of justice is contingent on one's financial situation. This would mean that the rich(er) go to court and the poor(er) avoid it. However, this is not a fully satisfactory explanation. In the research, we considered the earliest stages of court cases, before the court rules on whether or not to waive the fees. Persons who are poorer are probably more likely not to pay the required fees, but this does not mean that they will never file cases with courts.
   Another similar reason is the relative increase in the costs of pursuing matters in the court system after the political transformation in Poland. In the early 2000s our respondents, who still had a fresh memory of how things used to be before the transformation, emphasized the fact that the introduction of the free market economy meant that people became less willing to spend money on court cases. Other options of spending money became more important than

going to court, even in defence of one's honour. "Honour is less important now than time and money", said a president of a court back then (Fuszara 2004, p. 66). The respondents today appear to have a similar attitude. As shown by the nationwide poll, they go through a clear calculation of profit and loss. "It is a waste of time and money" is a common answer to the question why, despite the insults or defamation, no legal steps have been taken.

Another possible interpretation hinges on the trust towards expressed opinions, including opinions that are defamatory to certain persons. Taking a matter to court is a defence against admitting that the defamatory allegations are true. Today, there is a lot of awareness that information distributed online may be just "hating on someone" (whether with hidden interest or without), a lie, or misinformation. One could argue that defence against defamation has lost significance in the era of post-truth, defined by the Oxford Dictionary as "relating to or denoting circumstances in which objective facts are less influential in shaping public opinion than appeals to emotion and personal belief". From this perspective it is pointless to attempt to defend one's reputation by proving what is and what is not true.

While this approach to publicly disseminated information is likely to generate an increased number of defamatory claims and false accusations, it also diminishes their power at the same time. R. Keyes, the author of what is probably the first book on post-truth (2004), argues that the boundaries between the truth and lies are becoming fluid. This in turn means that being truthful is no longer a condition *sine qua non* of being an honourable person. "A regard for honesty or disdain for lying has not disappeared altogether (…). The problem is that a commitment to honesty in principle too often goes hand in glove with routine lying in practice" (Keyes 2004, p. 6). The research conducted on a sample of thousands students (in secondary schools and universities) has revealed that they are generally content with their own character and ethics, yet "nearly three-quarters admit to being >compulsive liars<." No comparable studies have been carried out in Poland. Yet if we agree that this attitude is widespread nowadays and can be considered universal in the post-truth era, then lying is no longer considered shameful (whether a person is lying or others are lying about that person), because it is generally understood that public speech has little value and requires no defence against its content. However, this interpretation would require further research to demonstrate whether in Poland too the boundary between the truth and lies has become muddy and fluid, and whether the awareness of this fact has resulted in a loss of trust in the speech of others.

Yet another interpretation suggests that defamation today is much less stigmatizing than it used to be. There is an important concept in contemporary criminology: shaming, which is also present in the discourse of restorative justice. Braithwaite notes in *Crime, Shame and Reintegration* (1989), a fundamental volume on the topic, that shaming is effective when two conditions are met, namely those of interdependency and communitarianism. This suggests that the number of cases taken to court in defence of good name and reputation has been on the decline in Poland and other post-communist countries because after the political transformation, interdependency has been replaced by individualism, independence, and a lesser role of a community. Thus, the potential of shaming has also declined. In the society that is more atomized and less integrated, allegations that infringe on the right to reputation and honour have a much lesser power to cause shame and embarrassment. Hence, there is a decrease in honour-invoking court cases in general, and also the decline in cases e.g. brought by women against whom allegations are made regarding violations of acceptable sexual codes of conduct. In the past, women often filed defamation cases when facing such allegations. Nowadays, they do so much less often, because they are much less dependent on others. Moreover, individualism and weaker community ties mean that many people understand when they are being insulted or offended, but feel that it is irrelevant and unimportant. On the other hand, in the cases where the defamation attempt is considered relevant and important, the court is used to "transfer the shame" from the person who was insulted upon the person who did the insulting. The formal apology (and its acceptance) serves to place the shame on the perpetrator and clear the insulted person of it. This helps to put an end to a dispute and restore social order.

6. For a sociologist of law, it is fascinating to consider the overlap between the categories used by lawyers and those developed by sociologists and supported by the theoretical framework of sociology which is designed to provide explanations and interpretation of what actually happens in conflicts and disputes, including those that are taken all the way to the courtroom. Let me begin with the fundamental categories. They are very general and leave much room for interpretation. In each specific case a message must be identified, and specifically, it must be indicated whether it is information or defamation. These general categories reflected in the legal regulation are quite similar to Blumer's „sensitizing concepts": „(…) the concepts of our discipline are fundamentally sensitizing instruments. Hence, we call them "sensitizing concepts" and put them in contrast with definitive concepts (…). A definitive concept refers precisely to what is common to a class of objects,

by the aid of a clear definition in terms of attributes or fixed bench marks. This definition, or the bench marks, serve as a means of clearly identifying the individual instance of the class and the make-up of that instance that is covered by the concept. A sensitizing concept lacks such specification of attributes or bench marks and consequently it does not enable the user to move directly to the instance and its relevant content. Instead, it gives the user a general sense of reference and guidance in approaching empirical instances. Whereas definitive concepts provide prescriptions of what to see, sensitizing concepts merely suggest directions along which to look. The hundreds of our concepts—like culture, institutions, social structure, mores, and personality—are not definitive concepts but are sensitizing in nature. They lack precise reference and have no bench marks which allow a clean-cut identification of a specific instance and of its content. Instead, they rest on a general sense of what is relevant". (H. Blumer, (1954), p. 7). It is no accident that Blumer lists "mores" among the "sensitizing concepts", and "defamation" is similar. It is a crime and thus punishable, but what defames whom and in what context is determined by court on a case-by-case basis. This changes over time, and differences in social status ("average Joe" vs. a public person) also mean that the same words may be considered defamation in one context but admissible criticism in another. In contrast to crimes such as theft or bodily harm, which are much more precisely defined and qualify as "definite concepts", defamation and insult require the court to undertake the effort on each occasion anew to bring a "sensitizing concept" closer to a "definite concept." As opposed to sociologists, judges must attempt to do so in every case.

7. The sociological categories are applicable to all actors involved in the criminal cases by private prosecution: the parties, the court, the lawyers, etc. They also provide a framework for interpretation of what has happened, and for a decision what outcomes are possible. The symbolic interaction perspective is particularly useful here. It addresses the interpretation and meaning assigned to objects, words, gestures, and behaviours. Blumer, who presents and develops the ideas of George Herbert Mead, argues that a society consists of individuals, each of whom has a self and i.a. the ability to indicate to oneself. When an individual acts, the purpose is not just to trigger a reaction. Instead, the action is a construct enabled by the fact that an individual perceives and interprets elements of the situation in which these actions take place. Collective action comes into being when individual actions are collated, which occurs when others perceive and interpret the actions of an individual (Blumer 1969). The crucial categories are the self and the ability to create meaning: „First, to indicate something is to extricate it from its

setting, to hold it apart, to give it a meaning or, in Mead's language, to make it into an object „(Blumer 1962). This is how an object is created: „anything that an individual indicates to himself is different from a stimulus; instead of having an intrinsic character which acts on the individual and which can be identified apart from the individual, its character or meaning is conferred on it by the individual" (*ibidem*). Crucially, the interactionist perspective distinguishes between the object itself (an utterance, a set of written words, a gesture, a behaviour) and the meaning that actors attach to it. The meaning may be different for at least three of those actors: the person who makes the gesture or says the words; the other person(s) involved in the situation; and finally, the observer (Schutz 1962). This gives rise to the notion of subjective interpretation of meaning, and i.a. an interpretation in which we attempt to understand the meaning of other people's actions. In the context of cases brought to court in defence of the right to reputation and honour, this consists in an attempt to find the meaning of words, gestures, behaviour, etc. which they have not for three, but for four groups of persons: those who speak the words, those whom they concern, others who hear them, and the court. The procedure prescribed by the law in private prosecution criminal cases suggests that the subjective meaning is crucial: it is the decision of a person who feels offended by an utterance, a gesture, behaviour, etc. whether to take the case to court. A person who feels offended may (but not necessarily does) decode the meaning which the words had for the person who spoke them. Sometimes the private prosecutor knows that the intention was to offend. Sometimes, it is just that the words are offensive in their own interpretation. Also the interpretation that other people give to a given event (the environmental perception and the reflected appraisal) is important, according to a person who feels slighted. Spurred by Alfred Schutz's „in-order-to motive", victims takes the case to court because they believe the offensive event could damage their reputation, lead to gossip that would harm them, or damage their relations with others. This is in stark contrast to the attitude of those respondents in the public opinion poll who declared that they had been insulted or offended in public, but the matter was petty, unworthy of attention and response. While these respondents realized that the actions had been intended to offend, they attached no importance to them, and had no interpretation that would cause them to actually feel offended. „This person is unable to offend me" was a typical response that reveals the process whereby the recipient of the words understands the meaning that the author intended to give them but chooses to reject that meaning.

8. Another sociological category with explanatory power in this context is the „generalized other". Subjective interpretations cannot be ignored in cases regarding honour and reputation, but the Polish Supreme Court has ruled[74] that „whether an utterance was insulting cannot be evaluated in accordance with the individual sensitivity of the person who feels slighted but rather must be assessed according to objective criteria that take into account the reactions of an average reasonable person". The „average reasonable person" is a standard often invoked by judges. It is precisely the „generalized other", as conceptualized by the adjudicating panels. This standard is used in place of the subjective meanings, which used to be taken into account more often in the past. An interesting case where the subjective interpretation was contested took place in the Lesko region in the 1970s. The private prosecutor took offence at being called „an organist". The court made a genuine effort to explain that the term had no offensive meaning. The defendant was of course not punished (which would be the case today too). But interestingly, the court did not stop at explaining that the term would not be considered offensive by an „average reasonable person". Instead, it painstakingly tried to reach a situation where that particular private prosecutor would accept the inoffensiveness of the term. As an aside, it is worth noting that invoking the „standard reasonable person" the court disregards the meaning attached to the words by the person who speaks them. As a result, the possibility that the author may actually have had a different, offensive intention when uttering the words (which the court may not have recognized) goes unnoticed. The interpretation assigned to the „generalized other" is given priority over the subjective interpretations of the actors involved in the interaction.
9. As to the surveys into the living law or popular legal culture described in part II of the book the very old "sensitizing concepts" of power and authority need to be invoked. Polish socio-legal theory starting with Leon Petrażycki neglected the issue, understandably as Petrażycki was opposed to the concept of the State power as the legitimization of the monopoly of law and justice. The communist era censured the deliberation on the nature of relations between the law and the State as in the Leninist political theory and practice there was no alternative to the unitarian State power vested in hands of the ruling communist vanguard (the Central Committee of the Party). Only in

74 Judgement of the Polish Supreme Court dated 18 June 2009, file number II CSK 58/09. In the statement of grounds, the Supreme Court invoked similar earlier judgements of the same court in cases regarding the defence of honour, including a judgement entered in 1971.

exile did Podgórecki raise the topic of legitimization of legal order as one of the top issue of the sociological theory of law. The concept of unofficial law introduced by Petrażycki remained nevertheless in contrast to the usual official (professional as Petrażycki commented) concept of law and public order (Kurczewski 1976).

Once in the world of living law that is outside the professional legal culture we may resume the issue not from the conceptual point of view but from the alternative between "informal", that is unofficial ways of dispute treatment and the "official" authoritative one. This has been the core of our surveys.

Let us repeat the apology for the mixed strength of the data used. The national representative survey discussed in Chapter VI is the strong one as made by the professional polling centre with decades-long record of national and international research. The field research made by our students and by Latvian, Ukrainian, Romanian and Bulgarian students constituted the best attempts to make sound sampling possible under the time and budget restraints. There were other restraints as well, especially in Mariupol on the frontline of the civil war. The reader may ask why to use such feeble data and the answer is that whatever the data we first calculate the numbers in order to escape from unfounded verbal generalizations and next, we need to escape the trap of paying too much attention to the numbers as such. Our aim is to make verbal generalization based upon the figures. And this is the aim of the following remarks.

One of the recurrent motifs in the statistical analysis of the parameters of choice between authoritative dispute settlement and the unofficial (informal) ones is the social position of the respondents. Whenever the index of social position is in the statistically significant relationship with socio-legal variables it is in the direction we have predicted in the initial set of hypotheses presented in the Introduction, that is the higher the position the more likely it is that the court or authoritative settlement will be chosen as proper in a dispute. This is not independent of the type of dispute involved, but if there is a difference then the better off will more likely choose court and not the unofficial alternative. This is a crucial point to understand the relationship between the "official legal culture" and the "unofficial one". The world of power is simply the world close to those who have power, even if in life there are shades of power and of influence. The seemingly trivial correlation between age and the choice of dispute settlement pattern reflects the same general social fact. The elderly are less confident in their social position and more afraid of the power the authorities have. The further one lives from the societal centre, that is in the countryside, the more one is removed from the centre of official power. This makes people of lower social position feel vulnerable to loss in confrontation with their opponents.

The same reasoning applies to the ethnic dimension scrutinized in the Chapter VIII. The lack of difference between ethnic samples and the existence of differences may be generally explained in terms of the relative power of people as members of the imagined cultural communities whether construed in ethnic or in denominational categories. Muslim Turks in Bulgaria are in the weaker position and consequently tend to use the authorities for settling their disputes to a lesser extent. In Daugavpils the mutual balance between three main nationalities which may think of themselves as the real "owners" of the public space leads to lack of clear cleavage in the dispute settlement patterns. The same holds for Olesno and Górowo Iławeckie in Poland. In the first case, "native" Silesians and "Polish newcomers" after 1989 were able to show the ability to win their cases at the local political level. In Górowo Ilaweckie as Herman (2014) points the Ukrainians after 1989 were able to achieve the positions in the local and national politics as well. The more complex situation seems to prevail in Cluj-Napoca where Hungarians continue their cultural power in defiance to the Romanian influx from the surrounding countryside that has already outnumbered them. In our sample of Hungarians the share of free profession exceeds significantly the one among the Romanians. Even if it not true about the social groups in general, this may suffice to explain the difference between our two ethnic samples. This cultural capital gives Hungarians self-assertiveness necessary to approach the court. So the power we are talking about is not necessary the political only but also economic and cultural one to use Bourdieu's way of thinking. In this context, however, it is equally important that we have rather rarely noticed the significant tendency of better educated to be more likely to enter the official world of law and justice.

10. Now we need to enter the more imaginative image of social reality. Even if power is closer to authority, still this is not the only way the choice between the "unofficial" and "official" is likely to be determined. In our reconnaissance we entered into the relationship between the religiosity and the choice suggesting that at least in Poland, the only case where the religious factor was introduced for some people who are strongly religious, the very idea of the lay official justice seems unfounded. There are two kinds of religiosity, the traditional ritualistic one correlated with lower social position and the ideological religiosity independent of social position. We should advise here the further inquiry into the ways of popular (in contrast to professional) legal thinking to check if the idea of the Heavenly Justice and the Last Judgment does not

intervene directly here and if the fallible judicial professional judgment is not marginalized in favour of the direct human compromise and reconciliation. The choice between "formal" and "informal", "unofficial" and "official" seems thus to be multi-dimensional. This has been manifested, as it seems to us, in the manifold segmentation presented in Chapter VIII. Even if the statistical strength of the otherwise significant coefficients is very low (and this permeates our whole statistical analysis) the outcome is clear, the same patterns of dispute treatment might be chosen in different constellations of characteristics of individuals and groups. To give one example, both groups termed as SELECTIVE and INFORMAL tend to choose informal settlement in private disputes but the context of their choices is different as INFORMAL tend to do it always, even in public disputes. The next step would be to isolate those contexts and present them in greater detail but it cannot be done in this publication.

There is also the third line of division that results from the last line. From time to time the significance of the type of a dispute reappears in our analysis of the surveys' data. The crude difference between "private", "family" and "public" types has most often a visible effect in our analysis. In other words, the institutionalized "official" world imposes upon people the technical need to communicate. One may easily withdraw from contacts with a nasty neighbor but it is difficult to do so in relation with the police or municipal government. "Public disputes" necessitate "public settlement". Moreover, the entrance into the "official world" is technically necessary for many private matters. This has not been sufficiently researched in our publication. The most of the caseload involving individuals in courts are the so-called non-litigious matters. In Poland where private farming continued for decades despite Communist rule (differently than in all other former Communist countries) land transactions were often made unofficially, that is without written records. But even then the inheritance had to be legalized through the court. The triumphant comeback of the capitalist economy meant a radical rise in the use of courts not for litigation but for the legalization (in the "official" sense of the term "law") of private transactions. So one is forced (power again!) to use courts even if one distrusts courts and feels at high risk of uncertainty when appearing before the judge.

References

Abel, Richard (1973), „A Comparative Theory of Dispute Institution in Society", Law and Society Review 8: p. 217–347

Aubert, Vilhelm (1983), In Search of Law. Sociological Approaches to Law, Oxford, Martin Robertson

Banaszak, Lee Ann, Karen Beckwith & Dieter Rucht(2003), Women's Movements Facing the Reconfigured State, Cambridge University Press

Bartkowski, Jerzy (2003), Tradycja i polityka: wpływ tradycji kulturowych polskich regionów na współczesne zachowania społeczne i polityczne, Żak, Warszawa

Borucka-Arctowa Maria and Krzysztof Pałecki (Eds.) (2003). Sądy w opinii społeczeństwa polskiego. Kraków: Ratio.

Bilewicz,Michał; Marchlewska, Marta; Soral, Wiktor; Winiewski, Mikołaj (2014), Mowa nienawiści. Raport z badań. Fundacja im. Stefana Batorego, Warszawa

Black, Donald, (1976), The Behavior of Law. Emerald Group Publishing

Blankenburg, Erhard (1991), Dutch Legal Culture, Kluwer, Amsterdam.

Blumer, Herbert (1954), "What is Wrong with Social Theory," American Sociological Review 18: 3–10

Blumer, Herbert (1962), Society as Symbolic Interaction, in: A. M. Rose (ed): Human Behaviour and Social Processes, Houghton Miffin Co

Blumer, Herbert (1969), Symbolic Interactionism. Perspective and Method. Prentice-Hall Inc. Englewood Cliffs, New Jersey

Botea Bianca, *La Transylvanie : entre coexistence et négociation socjale* Une approche anthropologique de la construction du territoire (2005), Thèse de doctorat en cotutelle, Université Lumière – Lyon 2 / Université Babes – Bolyai de Cluj-Napoca, Faculté d'anthropologie et de sociologie / Facultatea de sociologie si asistenţa social http://www.google.pl/url?sa=t&rct=j&q=&esrc=s&source=web&cd=3&ved=0ahUKEwikst-kjtbSAhVBaxQKHR81DEgQFggsMAI&url=http%3A%2F%2Ftheses.univ-lyon2.fr%2Fdocuments%2Fgetpart.php%3Fid%3D788%26action%3Dpdf&usg=AFQjCNF6Bfz1Hyv7RG71YtLCU1Pvn-Glsw&bvm=bv.149397726,d.d24 (accessed 13.03.2017).

Braithwaite, John (1989), Crime, Shame and Reintegration. Cambridge University Press, Cambridge

Braithwaite, John (2002), Restorative Justice and Responsive Regulation, Oxford University press, Oxford

Brugger, Winfried (2003), "The Treatment of Hate Speech in German Constitutional Law": German Law Journal No 1 p 1–44

Christie, Nils (1977), "Conflict as a property" in: The British Journal of Criminology, No 17 (1) , p 1–15

Cicourel, Aaron (1973), Cognitive Sociology, Penguin Books, Harmondsworth

Czykwin, Elżbieta (2000), Białoruska mniejszość narodowa jako grupa stygmatyzowana, Trans Humana, Białystok

Dmowski, Stanisław, Rudnicki Stanisław (2011), Komentarz do Kodeksu cywilnego. Księga pierwsza. Część ogólna [A Commentary to the Civil Code. Book One. General Section], Warsaw

Domingo, Pilar & Tam O'Neil (2014): *The politics of legal empowerment. Legal mobilisation strategies and implications for development*, June 2014, https://www.odi.org/sites/odi.org.uk/files/odi-assets/publications-opinion-files/9008.pdf

Eckhoff, Torstein (1966), „The Mediator, The Judge and the Administrator in Conflict Resolution": Acts Sociologica, No. 10. p. 148–172

Felstiner, William (1975), „Avoidance as Dispute Processing; An Elaboration" Law and Society Review No. 9 p 695–706.

Fuszara, Małgorzata (1989), Codzienne konflikty i odświętna sprawiedliwość. Zakład Socjologii Obyczajów and Prawa IPSiR Univeristy of Warsaw, Warsaw

Fuszara, Małgorzata (2004), "Sprawy sądowe z oskarżenia prywatnego", In: J. Kurczewski, M. Fuszara (ed) Spory and sądy, ISNS University of Warsaw, Warsaw

Genn, Hazel, (1993), "Tribunals and Informal Justice" In: The Modern Law Review, May: 393–411

Grzybowski, Stefan (1957), Ochrona dóbr osobistych według przepisów ogólnych prawa cywilnego[Protection of Personality Rights based on General Provisions of the Civil Law]. Warsaw

Herman, Aleksandra (2014), "Ukraińscy grekokatolicy i Polacy mariawici wśród Polakow rzymskich katolików. Lokalne zróznicowanie społeczne i mechanizmy jego utrzymywania w perspektywie porównawczej": Studia Humanistyczne AGH 13/2: 41—62

Kawashima, Takeoshi (1963), "Dispute Resolution in Contemporary Japan," in A. von Mehren (ed.), *Law in Japan.* Cambridge, MA: Harvard University Press p 41–72

Keyes, Ralph (2004), The Post-Truth Era: Dishonesty and Deception in Contemporary Life. St. Martin's Press, New York

Kojder, Andrzej (1996), "The Prestige of Law 30 Years Later" in: The Polish Sociological Bulletin, No.4.

Kurczewski, Jacek (1973), Prawo prymitywne: zjawiska prawne w społeczeństwach przedpaństwowych, Wiedza Powszechna" Warszawa

Kurczewski, Jacek (1976), „Due dimension del diritto: diorite positive o intuitive e dirroto ufficiale o non ufficiale" [Positive or Intuitive Law and Official or Unofficial Law], Sociologia del Dirrito, No.1.

Kurczewski, Jacek; Frieske Kazimierz (1978), "The Social Conciliatory Commissions in Poland: A Case Study of Non- Authoritative and Conciliatory Dispute Resolution as an Approach to Access to Justice", in: Access to Justice, Mauro Cappelletti and Join Weisner (eds.) vol. 2: Promising Institutions, book 1, Giuffre/Sijthoff and Noordhoff.

Kurczewski, Jacek (1979), "A sequential model of disputes", The Polish Sociological Bulletin 2: 83–96.

Kurczewski, Jacek (1982), Spór i sądy, Pracownia Socjologii Prawa, IPSiR Univeristy of Warsaw, Warsaw

Kurczewski, Jacek (1993), The Resurrection of Rights in Poland, OUP Oxford

Kurczewski, Jacek (2004), „Spory i sądy dwadzieścia pięć lat później"; „Polskie spory i sądy – podsumowanie" in: Kurczewski and Fuszara, Eds., Polskie spory i sądy, OBS ISNS UW, Warszawa: 9–41; 245–258.

Kurczewski, Jacek and Małgorzata Fuszara (2004), Eds. Polskie spory i sądy, OBS ISNS UW, Warszawa.

Kurczewski, Jacek (2007), "Antagonizm "polsko-niemiecki" w małym miescie na Śląsku Opolskim" in: J. Kurczewski (Ed.), Lokalne wzory kultury politycznej, Trio, Warszawa: 427–472.

Kurczewski, Jacek and Małgorzata Fuszara (2009), Eds. Polacy nad Dźwiną, Wyd. Uniwersytetu Warszawskiego, Warszawa.

Kurczewski, Jacek (2014), Ed., Reconciliation in Bloodlands, Peter Lang, Franfurt aM.

Kurczewski, Jacek (2014a), "Compelled to be Neighbors: a Small Polish Town in Former Germany" in: Kurczewski (2014) Ed.: 313–335.

Kurczewski, Jacek and Aleksandra Herman (2013), Eds., Antagonizm i pojednanie w środowiskach wielokulturowych, Słowo/obraz terytorium, Gdańsk.

Making hate crime visible in the European Union: Acknowledging victims' rights. FRA 2012

Mica, Adriana (2013), "Pojednanie przez kozla ofiarnego – przestrzeń publiczna i piłka nozna w Kluż-Napoka w Rumunii" in: Kurczewski and Herman (2013):271–312.

Marshall, Tony F (1999), Restorative justice. On overview. A Report by the Home Office, Research Development and Statistics Directorate, London

Murayama, Masayuki (2011) „Is There a Japanese Way of Dispute Resolution": Societas/Communitas (2) 12, 137–154.

Murayama, Masayuki (2016), "What Counts in Navigating Behavior. Do General Attitudes Matter?", Societas/Communitas (2) 17: 235–252.

Nazaruk, Piotr (2014), "Komentarz do atr 23 Kc" in: J. Ciszewski, K. Jędrej, G. Karaszewski, J. Knabe, P. Nazaruk, B. Ruszkowska, G. Sikorski, A. Stępień-Sporek: Kodeks cywilny. Komentarz. Wyd. Lexis Nexis Warszawa 2014

Ossowska, Maria (1970): Normy moralne. Państwowe Wydawnictwo Naukowe, Warszawa

Ossowska, Maria (1983), "O pojęciu godności" in: M, Ossowska: O człowieku, moralności and nauce miscellanea. Państwowe Wydawnictwo Naukowe, Warszawa

Parekh. Bhikhu (2012), "Hate Speech", in: M. Herz, P. Molnar (ed): The Content and Contex of Hate Speech, Cambridge University Press, New York

Podgórecki, Adam (1966), Prestiż prawa, Ksiązka i Wiedza, Warsaw.

Podgórecki, Adam (1991), Sociological Theory of Law, Giuffre, Milno

Resenfeld Michel (2012), "Hate Speech in Constitutional Jurisprudence: A comparative Analysis" in: M. Herz, P. Molnar (ed): The Content and Contex of Hate Speech, Cambridge University Press, New York

Skąpska, Grażyna and Grzegorz Bryda (2013), "Apolityczność czy sprawiedliwość proceduralna? Zaufanie do sądowego wymiaru sprawiedliwości na tle innych instytucji publicznych w Polsce" in: Studia Socjologiczne 2013 | 1(208) pp. 77–94

Schutz, Alfred (1962), "Common-Sense and Scientific Interpretation of Human Action", in: Collected Papers, vol. I p. 3-47

Wojakowski, Dariusz (2014), "Past, Conflict and Seeking of Reconciliation on the Polish-Ukrainian Borderland" in: Kurczewski (2014): 271–300.

Volkovs, Vladislavs and Jacek Kurczewski (2013), The Latvians, Russians and Poles of Present-Day Daugavpils: Integration, Acculturation and Historical Reconciliation, Zinatne, Riga.

Paweł Orzechowski

Appendix A.

Brief Note on Sampling

The all-Polish survey of 1059 people was carried out during the period from 22.04 to 4.05.2014 by the professional part-time staff of the Centre for Research of Social Opinion (CBOS) being the only public polling agency in Poland functioning as the public foundation. The survey was funded by the NCN research grant No. **DEC-2012/07/B/HS6/02496**: „Dispute and dispute settlement patterns as element of popular legal culture" and the questionnaire (see Appendix B) was prepared by J. Kurczewski and M. Fuszara. The standard method used by the CBOS was the CAPI supported individual face-to-face interview with respondents randomly taken from the all- Polish address base.

Samples in Polish localities **(Lesko, Olesno, Węgrów, Warszawa – Ursynów):**

GENDER

GENDER [%]	Lesko		Olesno		Węgrów		Warszawa - Ursynów	
	collected	corrected	collected	corrected	collected	corrected	collected	corrected
Male	49.8%	49.7%	45.5%	50.0%	46.6%	50.0%	50.5%	50.0%
Female	50.2%	50.3%	54.5%	50.0%	53.4%	50.0%	49.5%	50.0%
Total N=100%	200	175	189	152	178	162	210	192

AGE

AGE [%]	Lesko		Olesno		Węgrów		Warszawa - Ursynów	
	collected	corrected	collected	corrected	collected	corrected	collected	corrected
Until 34 yrs	20.4%	23.4%	25.4%	30.3%	39.9%	38.3%	37.1%	32.3%
35–50	25.4%	27.4%	24.3%	30.3%	27.5%	25.9%	19.0%	20.8%
51–64	27.9%	29.7%	23.3%	22.4%	21.3%	23.5%	21.0%	22.9%
65 +	26.4%	19.4%	27.0%	17.1%	11.2%	12.3%	22.9%	24.0%
Total N=100%	200	175	189	252	178	162	210	192

EDUCATION

EDUCATION [%]	Lesko		Olesno		Węgrów		Warszawa – Ursynów	
	collected	corrected	collected	corrected	collected	corrected	collected	corrected
Elementary	21.5%	20.7%	11.6%	11.8%	15.7%	17.3%	1.9%	1.0%
Secondary certified	41.0%	39.7%	41.3%	39.5%	52.2%	52.5%	23.8%	25.0%
Post-secondary	11.5%	11.5%	24.3%	22.4%	10.7%	9.3%	28.1%	27.1%
University level	26.0%	28.2%	22.8%	26.3%	21.3%	21.0%	46.2%	46.9%
Total N=100%	200	175	189	152	178	162	210	192

The local surveys sponsored by the NCN research grant No. **DEC-2012/07/B/HS6/02496**: „Dispute and dispute settlement patterns as element of popular legal culture" were conducted in Lesko (23–30.06.2014), Olesno (20–28.09.2014), Warszawa – Ursynów (1.07–21.12.2015) and Węgrów (13–15.05.2016) with the students of the Institute of Applied Social Sciences University of Warsaw as interviewers. Each of the survey was made as part of the week-long field research workshop. The interviewers were obliged to write down the original answers of the interviewed persons on the paper or as a computer questionnaire and to make notes during home visits.

In each of the towns the assumption was to interview 200 people and this was almost fulfilled as in Lesko 200 interviews were made, in Olesno – 189, in Węgrów – 178 and in Warsaw – Ursynów – 210 interviews (see N collected). Before statistical data analysis in the SPSS program, the size of the sample had to be corrected in order to fit the socio-demographic characteristics of each of the towns. Due to that the final number of interviews subject to the further statistical analysis was lowered in Lesko to 175 people, in Olesno to 152, in Węgrów to 162 and in Warsaw – Ursynów to 192 people (see N corrected). The correction brought back the distribution of three variables – gender, age and education – in the samples to the actual one as in the official statistical data available.

As the interviewing had to be completed within one week of the IASS University of Warsaw students field practice workshop under our direction, the mixed scheme of sampling had to be applied. The one route was using the random address lists (Lesko – 138, Olesno -94, Węgrów – 108. Warsaw – Ursynów – 110) while in the second the supplementary per quota sampling had to be used.

Sampling in **Górowo Iławeckie** was made in the specific way as this township with bi-ethnic composition of population was meant to be the testing site for the influence of ethnicity upon the dispute settlement patterns. Respondents were collected in 2 ways: random address list (130 people), and snowball quota sampling of Ukrainians in town (40) and in four adjacent Ukrainian villages (38). Interviews were made by the students of the University of Warsaw (IASS) under our supervision within the period from 30.06 to 8.07 2013.

GENDER

GENDER [%]	Górowo Iławeckie	
	collected	corrected
Male	46.6%	49.4%
Female	53.4%	50.6%
Total N=100%	208	174

AGE

AGE [%]	Górowo Iławeckie	
	collected	corrected
Until 34 yrs	25.0%	21.3%
35–50 yrs	19.2%	23.0%
51–64 yrs	32.2%	27.6%
65 yrs and above	23.6%	28.2%
Total N=100%	208	174

EDUCATION

EDUCATION [%]	Górowo Iławeckie	
	collected	corrected
Elementary	17.5%	17.9%
Secondary certified	48.5%	49.7%
Post-secondary	16.5%	16.2%
University level	17.5%	16.2%
Total N=100%	208	174

The need to substitute respondents emerged when in the field a large number of addresses were found wrong or the persons from the list were missing. Another factor was the need to have the sample consisting of possibly the largest representation of the Ukrainian minority. As nationality was not given on the list, the collection of the Ukrainian respondents was due to be made on another basis. As a result, the following religious and ethnic minority distribution in the sample was achieved: 54.8% of Roman Catholics and 43.2% of Greek Catholics and 2% of other religious affiliation; 58.7% respondents of Polish identity, 36.5% Ukrainians, 4.3% respondents of mixed or another identity.

Survey samples in cities outside Poland:

GENDER

	Mariupol	Daugavpils	Drohobycz	Razgrad	Cluj- Napoca
Male	45.9%	42.4%	55.5%	49.6%	45.8%
Female	54.1%	57.6%	44.5%	50.4%	54.2%
Total N=100%	270	602	361	500	500

AGE

	Mariupol	Daugavpils	Drohobycz	Razgrad	Cluj Napoca (collected)
- 34	27.4%	30.9%	45.0%	23.7%	36.6%
35–50	33.0%	29.3%	35.4%	41.4%	25.8%
51–64 l	28.1%	22.0%	14.9%	22.2%	20.2%
65 +	11.5%	17.8%	4.7%	12.7%	17.4%
Total N=100%	270	602	361	500	500

EDUCATION

EDUCATION [%]	Mariupol	Daugavpils	Drohobycz	Razgrad	Cluj Napoca (collected)
Elementary	0.7%	5.8%	1.4%	20.5%	11.0%
Secondary	8.5%	15.6%	6.9%	15.0%	20.8%
Post-secondary	72.2%	63.7%	77.1%	58.0%	57.0%
University level	18.5%	14.9%	14.6%	6.4%	11.2%
Total N=100%	270	602	361	500	500

The individual face-to-face interviews were made in Mariupol (Ukraine, 3.11.2015–4.01.2016), Daugavpils (Latvia, 1.06.2014–15.09.2015), Drohobycz (Ukraine, 8.03–15.12.2014), Razgrad (Bulgaria, 28.09.2015–4.01.2016) and Cluj Napoca (Romania, 15.06–15.08.2016).

Survey in **Mariupol** was directed by prof. Svitlana Schudlo, head of Law, Sociology and Political Sciences Department at Ivan Franko State Educational University in Drohobych and prof. Bohdan Sluschchinski, Chair of Sociology, Philosophy and Educational Sciences at State University in Mariupol. 270 interviews were made from 3.11.2015 to 04.01.2016 with inhabitants of Mariupol and (Greek Minority) localities of: Sartana, Stariy Krim, Talakivka, Hnutovo and Lomakyno. Here the difficulty of completing the random address sampling under the civil war conditions were extreme so the snowball method combined with purposive quota scheme had to be used promptly. It is obvious that with a response rate about 50%, the effective sample is politically biased as it includes mostly people of non-separatist orientation.

In **Daugavpils** during the period from 1.06.2014to 15.09.2015 602 interviews were made by prof. V. Volkovs from State Latvian University (Riga) and his students on three quota samples of 200 people representing three main ethnic groups – Latvians, Russians and Poles – living in the city.

In **Drohobych** the 361 interviews were collected from 8.03 to 15.12.2014 by the students association „Alter" under the guidance of Professor Svitlana Schudlo (I. Franko State Educational University in Drohobych) and Andrij Yurkevych. 140 interviews were made on random address sample supplemented then by 221 interviews using the quota representative scheme.

In **Razgrad** interviews were made during the period from 28.09.2015 to04.01.2016 by a team of students directed by Professor Stefka Naoumova (Institute for Legal Studies, Bulgarian Academy of Sciences). 300 ethnic Bulgarians were interviewed using random address list in Razgrad and purposive quota sample of 300 people of Turkish ethnicity (200 in Razgrad and 100 in Turkish village Samuil).

In **Cluj Napoca** the survey was conducted by dr Cristina Rat, dr Cristina Pop and Andrada Tobias from Centre for Study of Inter-ethnic Relations at Babes-Bolyai University in Cluj-Napoca from 15.06 to 15.08.2014 using professionally skilled students who collected 300 interviews with respondents declaring Romanian nationality and 200 interviews with Hungarians.

In all the local samples listed above the questionnaire prepared by J. Kurczewski and M. Fuszara was administered together with questions of the local interest. In Daugavpils the whole questionnaire was co-authored by Professor Vladislavs

Volkovs. Questionnaires were translated into Latvian, Russian, Polish in Daugapils, into Ukrainian in Drohobych and Mariupol, into Romanian and Hungarian in Cluj-Napoca and into Bulgarian and Turkish in Razgrad. Respondents were offered a choice of the version to be used during the interview. Respondents were informed about anonymity of the interview but in Mariupol the lack of confidence on part of the many approached for the interview was evident. The data base was then sent to us at the IASS (Institute of Applied Social Science), University of Warsaw to be coded and put under statistical analysis in the SPSS program.

Appendix B. Questionnaire used in the Polish representative national survey 2014 (CBOS)

How Disputes are settled. Law, Courts, and Justice.

Hello! My name is ..... I work for the Centre for Public Opinion Research (Centrum Badania Opinii Społecznej). We carry out various questionnaire-based surveys. We draw the persons we interview from the national PESEL database.

The purpose of this survey is to assess how helpful the law is in settling various disputes that arise between people. We would like to ask you about your opinions with regard to dispute settlement and about your experiences in this area. We are asking you to be honest and specific in your answers. We guarantee that our conversation will remain completely confidential and will only provide material for an aggregated report generated at the University. There are no right and wrong answers. We are simply interested in what people really think and how they solve their problems in practice.

If you have any problems answering any of the questions, for example: it is hard to choose from the answers provided, or you don't know how to answer, or for whatever reason you'd rather not answer, please just tell me about it.

We would like to start the conversation from some popular opinions about the **law**. Please choose the answer that is the closest to your personal view. Before we begin, we would like to find out:
1. In your opinion, generally, the law in our country: 1) requires major changes 2) is generally OK but is not applied properly 3) is generally OK, both the law and its application 7) It is hard to say. 8) Refusal to answer.
2. In your opinion, what purpose **should** the law serve first of all? 1) The law should help our society change and develop. 2) The law should help people solve disputes and conflicts between them. 3) The law should safeguard order and discipline in the country. 4) The law should help people fulfil their needs and interests. 7) It is hard to say. 8) Refusal to answer.

3. Which opinion about respecting the law do you like best? 1) We should always abide by the law, even if we think it is unfair. 2) If we encounter laws that we believe are unfair, we should only superficially abide by them but in practice try to circumvent them. 3) We should not abide by the laws we find unfair. 4) AND have a different opinion (what is it? ....) 7) It is hard to say. 8) Refusal to answer.
4. What do you think is better when solving disputes between people? Is it better when... 1) the justified demands of one party are met even if the other party is unsatisfied or 2) a consensus is reached where each party gives up a part of their demands? 7) It is hard to say. 8) Refusal to answer.
5. What do you think is better: 1) solving a dispute by applying the law in a very strict way, even if not every party is satisfied or 2) finding a solution that satisfies all parties, even if it is not strictly in line with the law? 7) It is hard to say. 8) Refusal to answer.
6. What do you think is better: 1) when an official institution (e.g. a court), which has the power to enforce its decision, solves a dispute or 2) when uninvolved persons (third parties), who can only offer advice, solve the dispute? 7) It is hard to say. 8) Refusal to answer.
7. Have you ever appeared in court as a witness, a party or a stakeholder? 1) No, never **[move on to question 9A]** 2) Yes 7) It is hard to say. **[move on to question 9A]** 8) Refusal to answer. **[move on to question 9A]**
8A_1. Have you ever appeared in court **IN A CIVIL MATTER?** 1) No **[move on to question 8B_1]** 2) Yes 7) It is hard to say. **[move on to question 8B_1]** 8) Refusal to answer. **[move on to question 8B_1]**

8A_2. How many years ago? **[INTERVIEWER: If there were several court cases, ask about the last one. If the case was heard less than a year ago or is still pending, write "1" (1 year).]** …………………… 97) It is hard to say. 98) Refusal to answer.
8A_3. What was your role, who were you? **[INTERVIEWER: If there were several court cases, ask about the last one.]** 1) a witness 2) a party 3) a stakeholder 7) It is hard to say. 8) Refusal to answer.
8A_4. In your opinion, was the decision entered in this case fair? Was the decision **[INTERVIEWER: If there were several court cases, ask about the last one.]** 1) fair 2) unfair 3) in some ways fair and in other ways unfair 4) AND can't say yet – the decision has not yet been entered 7) It is hard to say. 8) Refusal to answer.
8B_1. Have you ever appeared in court **IN A CRIMINAL MATTER?** 1) No. **[move on to question 8C_1]** 2) Yes. 7) It is hard to say. **[move on to question 8C_1]** 8) Refusal to answer. **[move on to question 8C_1]**
8B_2. How many years ago? **[INTERVIEWER: If there were several court cases, ask about the last one. If the case was heard less than a year ago or is still pending, write "1" (1 year).]** …………………… 7) It is hard to say. 8) Refusal to answer.
8B_3. What was your role, who were you? **[INTERVIEWER: If there were several court cases, ask about the last one.]** 4) a witness 5) a party 6) a stakeholder 7) It is hard to say. 8) Refusal to answer.

8B_4. In your opinion, was the decision entered in this case fair? Was the decision **[INTERVIEWER: If there were several court cases, ask about the last one.**]

5) fair
6) unfair
7) in some ways fair and in other ways unfair
8) AND can't say yet – the decision has not yet been entered
   7) It is hard to say.
   8) Refusal to answer.

8C_1. Have you ever appeared in court **IN A MATTER THAT WAS NEITHER CIVIL NOR CRIMINAL?**

1) No [**move on to question 9).**
2) Yes. ……… (What kind of case was it? Please, describe it.)
   7) It is hard to say. [**move on to question 9**]
   8) Refusal to answer. [**move on to question 9**]

8C_2. How many years ago? [**INTERVIEWER: If there were several court cases, ask about the last one. If the case was heard less than a year ago or is still pending, write "1" (1 year).**]

………………………

97) It is hard to say.
98) Refusal to answer.

8C_3. What was your role, who were you? [**INTERVIEWER: If there were several court cases, ask about the last one.**]

7) a witness
8) a party
9) a stakeholder
   7) It is hard to say.
   8) Refusal to answer.

8C_4. In your opinion, was the decision entered in this case fair? Was the decision [**INTERVIEWER: If there were several court cases, ask about the last one.**]

3) fair
4) unfair
5) in some ways fair and in other ways unfair
6) AND can't say yet – the decision has not yet been entered
   7) It is hard to say.
   8) Refusal to answer.

9A. **(This is a question for everybody REGARDLESS of their response to questions 7 and 8)** Are you aware of any case in which, after 1989, an unfair court judgement was entered?

1) No [**move on to question 10**]
2) Yes.
   7) It is hard to say. [**move on to question 10**]
   8) Refusal to answer. [**move on to question 10**]

9B. In what way was it unfair?
[PLEASE NOTE: this question pertains to Polish courts after 1989]:

....

Scripter: rotate items.

10. In your opinion, which factors have an impact on winning a case in court? AND read out several factors that could potentially have an impact. Please tell me, with regard to each one of them, whether this factor is of primary importance, secondary importance, or without impact. Is/ Are .... [**INTERVIEWER: read out the items in the question in sequence**] of primary importance, secondary importance, or without impact on winning a case?

It depends.		primary importance 1	secondary importance 2	no impact 3
1	being right			
2	the person of the judge			
3	the legal counsels			
4	witnesses			
5	who you know and how well you are positioned			
6	bribes			
7	luck			
8	other elements (what?) ....)			

7) It is hard to say.
8) Refusal to answer.

11A. Have you ever involved a court in a matter:
(It is OK to select 2, 3 and 4 at the same time.)

1. Never [**move on to question 12A**]
2. yes, before 1989
3. yes, after 1989, but more than 3 years ago
4. yes, in the last 3 years

7) It is hard to say.
8) Refusal to answer.

11B. Were you satisfied with what the court did? [**INTERVIEWER: If there were several court cases, ask about the last one.**]

1. Yes.
2. No.

Yes and no, it depends.

7) It is hard to say.
8) Refusal to answer.

12A. Some people say that taking **one's own matter** to court is always unpleasant, even if you are completely in the right. Do you agree with this opinion?

1. Yes, involving a court in a matter is always unpleasant.
2. No, involving a court in a matter does not always have to be unpleasant.
3. No, involving a court in a matter is not unpleasant at all.

    7) It is hard to say.
    8) Refusal to answer.

12B. Why do you think so?

....

AN INVENTORY OF DISPUTES

At the beginning we have told you that we are interested in various ways in which people settle disputes. Now we would like to ask about your personal experience in this area.

[INTERVIEWER: What is a dispute? If the respondent doesn't know how to use the word, let's say that a dispute is a conflict which is <u>overt</u>, words have been said, there has been a discussion or an argument – generally, this is a clash of claims, e.g. the parties disagree whether one of them is behaving appropriately in a matter, or both parties disagree about what is due to whom. When conducting this survey, it is impossible to use sharply-defined criteria and therefore we have to use a broad interpretation of what a dispute is. It is important to gather information about all conflict situations in which people find themselves, but also to be clear as to whether the types of disputes listed in the survey actually take place.

13A. In the **last three years**, have you had a conflict or dispute <u>related to an infringement of the right to a good name (reputation)</u>, e.g. somebody was gossiping maliciously about you and more and more people knew this gossip, or somebody you know shouted insults at you in the street?

1) No **[move on to 13J]**
2) Yes

    7) It is hard to say.
    8) Refusal to answer.

13B. When did this conflict / dispute take place? Did it take place:

1) Within the last year
2) More than a year but less than two years ago
3) More than two years but less than three years ago

    7) It is hard to say.
    8) Refusal to answer.

[INTERVIEWER: If there were several conflicts, ask about the last one]

13C. Please describe this conflict / dispute. What was the subject matter? What did you disagree about? What did you want to achieve and what did the other part want? ....
13D. Who was the other party? Please describe your opponent in this dispute (e.g. was it an acquaintance, a family member, an unknown person, an official? We are of course not asking about names.) ....
13E. How do you feel **today** about your opponent in this dispute? Select three emotions. 1) Dislike 2) Fear 3) Shame, guilt 4) Friendliness 5) Indifference 6) A different emotion (What? ....) 97) It is hard to say. 98) Refusal to answer.
13F. How did this conflict / dispute end? Did the matter end up in court? 1) No. 2) Yes. **[move on to 13H]**
13G. Why <u>didn't</u> you take the matter to court? ....
13H. What would you do today? Would you take the matter to court? 1) No **[move on to 14A]** 2) Yes **[move on to 14A]** 3) It depends. (What does it depend on? Please specify. ....) **[move on to 14A]** 7) It is hard to say. **[move on to 14A]** 8) Refusal to answer. **[move on to 14A]**
13J. If something like this happened, would you take the matter to court? 1) No. 2) Yes 3) It depends. (What does it depend on? Please specify. ....) 7) It is hard to say. 8) Refusal to answer.

SCRIPTER, TAKE NOTICE! **Questions 13A through 13J are repeated in relation to all the subsequent disputes.**
14. In the last three years, have you had a conflict or dispute related to infringement of the right to personal inviolability, e.g. a drunk passer-by assaulted you, or somebody slapped you at a party, in the street, or in another public place?
15. In the last three years, have you had a conflict or dispute with your neighbours, e.g. neighbours regularly make a lot of noise at night and you can't sleep well, or they argue with you about how to use the cellar, or where a boundary between the plots of land is located?
16. In the last three years, have you had a conflict or dispute related to a loan or another issue involving money, e.g. somebody borrowed money from you and refused to pay it back, or the owner of the flat in which you live wants you to move out and you don't want to?
17. In the last three years, have you had a conflict or dispute with a company that sells goods or offers services, e.g. your TV was past its guarantee and a repair shop took money to repair it but couldn't actually do it, or a shop refused to accept a return of a faulty item?
18. In the last three years, have you had a conflict or dispute with an authority or a unit of public administration, e.g. a tax office demanded more money in taxes than it was due, or the city hall refused to issue a permit for renovation or construction [**all disputes with official bodies fall here**]
19. In the last three years, have you had a conflict or dispute related to work or payment for work, e.g. somebody hired you and refused to pay on time or paid less than it was previously agreed, or a superior at work refused to promote you or pay you for overtime?
20. In the last three years, have you had a conflict or dispute related to the healthcare system, e.g. treatment that was done poorly, malpractice, or were you or a person close to you refused admission to a hospital?
21. In the last three years, have you had a conflict or dispute related to a traffic incident, or an accident in road traffic, e.g. about the amount of compensation?
22. In the last three years, have you had a conflict or dispute at home, within your household?

We are now going to present to you a few situations that could happen in real life. Please think about them for a moment and tell us: in your opinion, what is the best way to proceed for the person who feels they are a victim in this situation?
23. Somebody's children were beaten by a neighbour as he could not rest after work due to their noisy behaviour. In your opinion, what should the parents of the beaten children do? 1) Don't react, do nothing 2) Reach an agreement and compromise with the neighbour 3) Use their own resources to get the due outcome 4) Go to court 5) Go to another agency (which?) ....) 7) It is hard to say. 8) Refusal to answer.

24. An acquaintance of Mr K. was gossiping about him among their friends, so Mr K. slapped him in the presence of others. In your opinion, what should the acquaintance do? 1) Don't react, do nothing 2) Reach an agreement and compromise with Mr K. 3) Use his own resources to get the due outcome 4) Go to court 5) Go to another agency (which?) ....) 7) It is hard to say. 8) Refusal to answer.
25. A friend of Mr M.'s borrowed EUR 250 (PLN 1000) and failed to repay the debt despite repeated demands. Mr M. went to the debtor's house and took something of the same value. In your opinion, what should Mr M.'s friend (from whose house the item had been taken) do? 1) Don't react, do nothing 2) Reach an agreement and compromise with Mr M. 3) Use his or her own resources to get the due outcome 4) Go to court 5) Go to another agency (which?) ....) 7) It is hard to say. 8) Refusal to answer.
26. An employer asked the hospital for information about the illness for which one of his employees was treated. The hospital provided the information which was then used against the patient. In your opinion, what should the patient do? 1) Don't react, do nothing 2) Reach an agreement and compromise with the hospital 3) Use his or her own resources to get the due outcome 4) Go to court 5) Go to another agency (which?) ....) 7) It is hard to say. 8) Refusal to answer.
27. In the evening, a brawl started close to a restaurant. A police patrol was called in to calm the situation. Police officers used batons not only against the brawlers but against innocent bystanders as well. In your opinion, what should those bystanders do? 1) Don't react, do nothing 2) Reach an agreement and compromise with the police 3) Use their own resources to get the due outcome 4) Go to court 5) Go to another agency (which?) ....) 7) It is hard to say. 8) Refusal to answer.

28. Somebody built a house but due to a change in the local area development plan, the authorities ordered him to demolish it. In your opinion, what should the person who built the house do? 1) Don't react, do nothing 2) Reach an agreement and compromise with the authorities 3) Use their own resources to get the due outcome 4) Go to court 5) Go to another agency (which?) ....) 7) It is hard to say. 8) Refusal to answer.
29. A dispute arose between spouses when the wife inherited PLN 20 000 (EUR 4 000) and placed the funds on her own account, rather than contributing it to the family budget. In your opinion, what should her husband do? 1) Don't react, do nothing 2) Reach an agreement and compromise with the wife 3) Use his own resources to get the due outcome 4) Go to court 5) Go to another agency (which?) ....) 7) It is hard to say. 8) Refusal to answer.
30A. A husband battered a wife suspecting her of secretly meeting with another man. In your opinion, what should the woman do? 1) Don't react, do nothing 2) Reach an agreement and compromise with the husband 3) Use her own resources to get the due outcome 4) Go to court **[move on to 30B]** 5) Go to another agency (which?) ....) 7) It is hard to say. 8) Refusal to answer.
30B. You said that the wife should go to court. In your opinion, should she go to court: 1) with charges against her husband for battery 2) with a divorce petition 3) both with battery charges and a divorce petition 7) It is hard to say. 8) Refusal to answer.

31. Do you agree or disagree with the opinion that in the case of a dispute, there are different approaches for people we are close to and different approaches for other people? Please tell us which of the opinions is closes to how you feel. **[INTERVIEWER: show the screen to the respondent.]** 1. If a dispute takes place within a family, you can never take it to an institution, but if the opponent is not a family member, it is OK to go to an institution, e.g. a court. 2. It does not matter whether a dispute is within a family or not. If your interests are at risk, you have to go to an institution (e.g. a court), even if the other person is a family member. 3. Generally when there is a dispute in a family, you shouldn't go to court or another institution, but sometimes if a dispute is about something very important (e.g. assault, reputation, major assets) you have to go to court or another appropriate institution. 7) It is hard to say. 8) Refusal to answer.
32A. In your city, town etc., do you know a person to whom people go when they are arguing and want somebody to help them reconcile, and they don't want to go to court? 1. Yes 2. No [**move on to 33**] 7) It is hard to say. [**move on to 33**] 8) Refusal to answer. [**move on to 33**]
32B. In relation to you, who is this person? Is it: 1) a member of your close or extended family 2) a friend 3) a person whom you don't know well or somebody you have only heard of 7) It is hard to say. 8) Refusal to answer.
32C. What is this person's job, or what job did this person use to do in the past? ....
33. In your opinion, in the city, town, etc. where you live, do people in general abide by the law, even the Traffic Code? definitely yes mostly yes mostly no definitely no 7) It is hard to say. 8) Refusal to answer.

34. Please imagine the following situations and then think about the moral aspect: is it morally OK to do this?
Scripter: rotate items.

1) Yes, a person has / people have the right to do this
2) No, a person doesn't have / people don't have the right to do this
7) It is hard to say.
8) Refusal to answer.

A. Amarried couple with children decides to split up, with both spouses agreeing to it. Can the couple do this?

B. A woman terminated her pregnancy simply because she didn't want to havea child. Can the woman do this?

C. Unsatisfied with their earnings, workers go on strike even though the management didn't agree to it. Can the workers do this?

D. Police and similar forces use violence to break up an illegal anti-government demonstration on the street. Can the police do this?

E. The authorities forbid the existence of a political party because the party wants to abolish democracy and return to non-democratic forms of government. Can the authorities do this?

F. The authorities decide to build an nuclear power plant without asking the residents of the area about their opinion. Can the authorities do this?

G. The management of a school decided to teach students in high school about the use of contraceptives to avoid unwanted pregnancy. Can the management do this?

H. Adult nudists organize a fenced-off beach where people can sunbathe naked if they want to. Can the nudists do this?

AND. A newspaper publishes caricatures making fun of church dignitaries. Can the newspaper do this?

46. In your neighbourhood, do people usually know well what is going on in the houses of their closest neighbours?

1) Definitely yes
2) Mostly yes
3) Mostly no
4) Definitely no
7) It is hard to say.
8) Refusal to answer.

47. In your opinion, who is best suited to solving the dispute in the following situations:

INTERVIEWER: Show the screen to the respondent.

Local authorities agree to the construction of a nuclear power plant or to shale gas extraction without asking the local residents about their opinion, and the local residents are opposed to the plan.

1. the matter should be settled by a court
2. it is necessary to bring the parties together to have negotiations and find a compromise
3. it is necessary to wait for new elections when the authorities can change
4. the matter should be settled by the parliament in a vote
5. the matter should be settled by the local council in a vote
6. the matter should be settled by all citizens in a referendum
7. the matter should be settled by the local residents in a referendum

97) It is hard to say.
98) Refusal to answer.

48. Some members of the local council want to commemorate a politician they respect by naming a bridge after him, and others are against it.

1. the matter should be settled by a court
2. it is necessary to bring the parties together to have negotiations and find a compromise
3. it is necessary to wait for new elections when the authorities can change
4. the matter should be settled by the parliament in a vote
5. the matter should be settled by the local council in a vote
6. the matter should be settled by all citizens in a referendum
7. the matter should be settled by the local residents in a referendum

97) It is hard to say.
98) Refusal to answer.

49. The residents in one part of town don't want a new ring road to cut through their neighbourhood, but the ring road will make life easier for residents of other parts of the town.

1. the matter should be settled by a court
2. it is necessary to bring the parties together to have negotiations and find a compromise
3. it is necessary to wait for new elections when the authorities can change
4. the matter should be settled by the parliament in a vote
5. the matter should be settled by the local council in a vote
6. the matter should be settled by all citizens in a referendum
7. the matter should be settled by the local residents in a referendum

97) It is hard to say.
98) Refusal to answer.

50. Some residents of a region want the language they speak in their everyday life to become an official language in that region in addition to Polish, and others are against it. 1. the matter should be settled by the Supreme Court, the Supreme Administrative Court or the Constitutional Court 2. it is necessary to bring the parties together to have negotiations and find a compromise 3. it is necessary to wait for new elections when the authorities can change 4. the matter should be settled by the Sejm in a vote 5. the matter should be settled by the local elected body (*sejmik*) in a vote 6. the matter should be settled by all citizens of that region in a referendum 7. the matter should be settled by all citizens in a national referendum another solution (what is it?) .... 97) It is hard to say. 98) Refusal to answer.
51. In your opinion, nowadays: 1) Yes 2) No. 7) It is hard to say. 8) Refusal to answer. A. Men feel offended when somebody says about them that they "behave inappropriately", they have sexual relations with women other than their wife, have a child out of wedlock. B. Women feel offended when somebody says about them that they "behave inappropriately", they have sexual relations with men other than their husband, have a child out of wedlock. C. People feel offended when somebody says about them that theyhave given a bribe to get something sorted. D. People feel offended when somebody says about them that they hava taken a bribe for getting something sorted.
52. Do you think that: 1. people involved in disputes are generally troublemakers, like to argue, are litigious. 2. people involved in disputes believe that you have to stand up for yourself and your interests, your rights, even if you don't like arguing and going to court. 7) It is hard to say. 8) Refusal to answer.
53A. Do you agree with the following opinion: in case of minor disputes between people, willing neighbours or other persons should be available to offer help and advice to the parties in dispute, free of charge, and to help them reach a compromise (similar to the community reconciliation committees, *społeczne komisje pojednawcze*, in communist Poland)? 1. Yes 2. No. 7) It is hard to say. 8) Refusal to answer.

53B. Why do you think so? ....
54. What is your opinion about trusting people? 1. you shouldn't trust people – you can only trust yourself 2. you can only trust the people you know well 3. you should trust everybody until that person betrays your trust 7) It is hard to say. 8) Refusal to answer.
55A. Now we would like to ask you about trust between nations. Because historically, disputes typically occurred between neighbours, we are asking about the relations of Poles with all the nations that Poland is neighbouring now or used to neighbour in the past. How would you describe the relations between Poles and: .... [INTERVIEWER: read out the subsequent elements of the question] **INTERVIEWER: Show the screen to the respondent.** a. Russians b. Lithuanians c. Belarussians d. Ukrainians e. Slovaks f. Czechs g. Germans h. Jews 1) There was never a dispute so there is no need to reconcile. 2) There were some disputes but we have reconciled and now we only need to continue developing good mutual relations. 3) There were some disputes and they were not completely clarified, reconciliation is only possible if certain conditions are met (What conditions? ....) 4) The disputes were so major that during the lifetime of this generation there will be no reconciliation. During the lifetime of the next generation, maybe. 5) The disputes were so major that there will never be reconciliation. 7) It is hard to say. 8) Refusal to answer.

55B. What are your feelings towards Poland's neighbouring nations? Please choose three most important feelings. With regard to ……, [INTERVIEWER: read out subsequent elements of the question] do you feel: **INTERVIEWER: Show the screen to the respondent.** a. Russians b. Lithuanians c. Belarussians d. Ukrainians e. Slovaks f. Czechs g. Germans h. Jews 1) Dislike 2) Fear 3) Shame, guilt 4) Friendliness 5) Indifference 6) Another emotion (What? …………………) 97) It is hard to say. 98) Refusal to answer.
56. What are the crucial elements in bringing nations to reconcile? Please choose the three most important elements. **INTERVIEWER: Show the screen to the respondent.** *Scripter: rotate.* 1. the work of national leaders, presidents and other politicians 2. the work of religious leaders such as the pope, bishops, and leaders of faith communities 3. the work of the media 4. the work of outstanding scholars and artists 5. the work of non-governmental organizations (NGOs) 6. commercial interests and business 7. the will of the common people 8. an international tribunal 97) It is hard to say. 98) Refusal to answer.

57. In the last year:

	Yes 1	No. 2	It's hard to say. 7	Refusal to answer 8
A) Did you speak in public, e.g. at a meeting?	1	2	7	8
B) Did you write a letter or make a phone call to the press, radio or TV?	1	2	7	8
C) Did you take part in a strike or were you part of an organized effort to be ready to go on strike?	1	2	7	8
D) Did you take part in a demonstration, protest, etc.?	1	2	7	8
E) Did you run for an office in local government, an NGO, etc.?	1	2	7	8
F) Have you EVER held any office in a local government, an NGO, etc., or have you EVER run for such an office?	1	2	7	8

VERSION OF THE CBOS QUESTIONS

58A. These five pictures represent various types of societies. Please read the descriptions of these types of societies and have a look at the pictures.
What type of society is Poland today? Which of the pictures on the screen represents it best?

1. Type A – A small elite at the top, very few people in the middle, most people at the bottom
2. Type B – A society that resembles a pyramid, a small elite at the top, more people in the middle, most people at the bottom.
3. Type C – A pyramid but with fewer people at the bottom.
4. Type D – A society where most people fit in the middle.
5. Type E – Most people at the top and only few at the bottom.

7) It is hard to say.
8) Refusal to answer.

58B. Please look at the picture that is the best representation of Poland today . Where in this picture would you put yourself and your family: at the top, in the middle, or more towards the bottom?

Scale 1 (top) to 7 (bottom)

Scripter: the respondent should be looking at the picture selected in the previous question.

59. Below you will find 12 opinions about the functioning of democracy. Please tell us which ones you agree with and which ones you disagree with.

1) I agree
2) I disagree

7) It is hard to say.
8) Refusal to answer.

Scripter: rotate items.

1. The interest of a broader community, region or nation is more important that the interest of a local community.

2. It is not important how matters are handled as long as they get handled in a way consistent with the social interest.

3. All the important decisions of the authorities should be consulted with the residents in a referendum.

4. You should always abide by the law, even if you believe it is wrong.

5. There must be a strong leader who is capable of mobilizing a majority.

6. To get good results, sometimes you have to form a coalition even with the devil himself.

7. In politics, the best solution is a compromise between differing views.

8. Democracy has its problems, but overall it is better than the Soviet times.

9. Most people who have power in the country are trying to exploit us.

10. It is best if a member of the local council is not linked to any political party because then this person does a better job looking after the interests of the constituents.

11. A member of the local council should be looking further ahead than the constituents and be able to decide what is best for the community even if the constituents disagree.

12. A member of the local council should only monitor the work of the mayor and not stick his or her nose into everything the board is doing.

DEMOGRAPHICS

We would also like to ask you a few questions about yourself and your life. This will conclude the interview.
Place of residence?

M1 Sex

1) Male
2) Female

☐

M2 Age [INTERVIEWER: enter the number of complete years]

………………….. years ☐☐

M3 Education [INTERVIEWER: enter the educational attainment (e.g. primary) and how many grades of school or years at university completed (e.g. 3 grades)]

01) incomplete primary
02) primary
03) lower secondary
04) secondary vocational, no high school graduation exam
05) incomplete secondary
06) secondary, high school graduation exam
07) secondary vocational, high school graduation exam
08) post-secondary
09) incomplete university
10) bachelor's degree or equivalent vocational degree
11) master's degree

☐☐

M4. Are you currently working for money on a full-time basis (as an employee, at your own business, at an agricultural enterprise) or do you take short-term jobs, regardless of whether this is your primary source of income?

1) Yes, full time.

☐

2) Yes, part time.
3) Yes, occasionally.
4) No … **[move on to question M7]**

INTERVIEWER: If YES, hand Card B to the respondent

☐

INTERVIEWER: hand Card Z to the respondent
M6. In your current situation, which of the groups listed here do you think you belong to? ☐ **[INTERVIEWER: If the response to M6 was 01–09, move on to M8. If the response to M6 was 10–15, move on to M7.]**
INTERVIEWER: hand Card N to the respondent
M7. And when you last worked, which of the groups listed here do you think you belonged to? ☐
Religiosity
M11. General assessment of living conditions: In your opinion, are the living conditions of yourself and your family members who live in the same household as you: **[INTERVIEWER: note the answer together with a comment, if the respondent provides one (e.g. if the respondent explains, or tells you with whom he/she is comparing him- or herself)]**
1) Much better than average in M 2) Somewhat better than in M 3) Average for M 4) Somewhat worse than average in M 5) Much worse than average in M ☐
M12. Community activism: at present, are you a member of any organization or initiative, whether community-based or political or religious (a political party, an NGO, a trade union, the volunteer corps of fire-fighters, a church-based group, etc.)?
1) Yes, religious 2) Yes, community-based 3) Yes, political 4) No, none ☐
M14. Do you hold any official position in any of them? 1) Yes 2) No. ☐

To conclude, we would like to thank you very much for assisting us in the survey and to apologize for taking up your time. Have a good day!

Polish Studies in Culture, Nations and Politics

Edited by Joanna Kurczewska and Yasuko Shibata

Vol. 1 Adriana Mica / Arkadiusz Peisert / Jan Winczorek (eds.): Sociology and the Unintended. Robert Merton Revisited. 2011.

Vol. 2 Adriana Mica: Scandals and Party Moots. Mass Protests during the Ceauşescu Regime in Romania. 2012.

Vol. 3 Jacek Kurczewski (ed.): Reconciliation in Bloodlands. Assessing Actions and Outcomes in Contemporary Central-Eastern Europe. 2014.

Vol. 4 Yasuko Shibata: Discrimination for the Sake of the Nation. The Discourse of the League of Polish Families against "Others" 2001-2007. 2013.

Vol. 5 Vasil Navumau: The Belarusian Maidan in 2006. A New Social Movement Approach to the Tent Camp Protest in Minsk. 2016.

Vol. 6 Jacek Kurczewski / Małgorzata Fuszara: How People Use the Courts. The Disputes and Courts in Poland. 2017.

www.peterlang.com

www.ingramcontent.com/pod-product-compliance
Ingram Content Group UK Ltd.
Pitfield, Milton Keynes, MK11 3LW, UK
UKHW021008120926
8556IPUK00029B/241

9 783631 723715